STATE EXECUTIONS

Patterson Smith Series in
Criminology, Law Enforcement & Social Problems
Publication No. 170

STATE EXECUTIONS

VIEWED HISTORICALLY AND SOCIOLOGICALLY

THE HANGMEN OF ENGLAND
Reprinted from the 1929 work of
HORACE BLEACKLEY
Historian

&

THE DRAMATURGY OF
STATE EXECUTIONS
an Original Commentary by
JOHN LOFLAND
Sociologist

PATTERSON SMITH
Montclair, New Jersey
1977

The Hangmen of England by Horace Bleackley was originally published 1929 by Chapman and Hall, Ltd.

This book is printed on permanent/durable paper

Library of Congress Cataloging in Publication Data

Main entry under title:

State executions, viewed historically and sociologically.

(Patterson Smith series in criminology, law enforcement, and social problems: publication no. 170)

Bibliography: p.

Includes index.

CONTENTS: Bleackley, H. The hangmen of England, reprinted from the 1929 work.—Lofland, J. The dramaturgy of state executions, an original commentary.

1. Executions and executioners—England—History. I. Bleackley, Horace William, 1868—1931. The hangmen of England. 1977. II. Lofland, John. The dramaturgy of state executions. 1977.

HV8699.G8S78 364.6'6'0942 77-2187 ISBN 0-87585-170-3

CONTENTS

I. THE HANGMEN OF ENGLAND

By Horace Bleackley

THE HANGMEN OF ENGLAND

By Horace Bleackley

THE TRIPLE TREE AT TYBURN

[*Frontispiece.*

THE HANGMEN OF ENGLAND

How they hanged and Whom they hanged. The life story of " Jack Ketch " through two centuries. . . .

by

HORACE BLEACKLEY
F.S.A.

CHAPMAN AND HALL Ld.
LONDON: MCMXXIX

[*facsimile of original title page*]

"Ye hangmen of Old England,
How sturdily you stood,
A-smoking pipes by Tyburn Tree,
A-swigging pots in the Old Bailee,
And strung up all you could."

Old Ballad.

LIST OF ILLUSTRATIONS

IN GRATITUDE

I wish to express my thanks to the following gentlemen for the help that they have given me:

Mr. A. H. Thomas, F.S.A., Guildhall Record Office.

Mr. Henry D. Roberts, M.B.E., Public Library, Brighton.

Mr. Sidney Phipson, Inner Temple.

Mr. William Roughead, Edinburgh.

Sir Kingsmill Key, Bart.

Mr. Vere L. Oliver, Greenhill House, Weymouth.

Mr. F. C. Lingard, Barbers Hall, Monkwell Street.

Mr. Sydney Perks, F.S.A., City Surveyor.

Rev. A. W. Oxford.

And I am grateful also to the Corporation of the City of London for permission to reproduce the plan of Newgate Prison.

WHY AND HOW

DURING the spring of 1928, when a friend put in my hands a copy of a book called "A Hangman's Diary, being the Journal of the Public Executioner of Nuremberg," I had all the feelings of resentment experienced by the famous poet while being compelled to listen to a gentleman named "hoarse Fitzgerald," who was accustomed to "bawl his creaking couplets in a tavern hall." Why on earth, thought I, should a mere undistinguished Hun hangman have a whole volume devoted to his commonplace performances when the manifold accomplishments of the hangmen of England, with all their infinite variety, remained unhonoured and unsung? All vestiges of the "Locarno spirit" vanished from my breast, and I prepared for retaliation.

For years I had been on terms of some intimacy with many of our own hangmen of bygone days, for the simple reason that I have rarely come across a reference to one of them while engaged upon research work, which had a different object in view, without making a note of it. Upon assembling these notes my resolve was confirmed to make them public property. It appeared to me that I knew as much about the hangmen of England as the hangman of Nuremberg knew about himself. If I did not sing of our fellows it seemed likely that no one else would celebrate them, with the result that German supremacy must remain unchallenged.

Not that the diary of the hangman of Nuremberg is an unworthy book by any means. It appears to have had many admirers. But the chronicles of one small man in one small town over a small number of years are scarcely comparable with those of fifteen stalwarts, which concerned the whole of Great Britain during a period of two centuries. Nor did the functionary of Nuremberg move in the exalted criminal circles with which our own executioners were associated. There is nothing to convince us that any of his victims had a personality or a proud record in sin. None seems to have left footprints on the sands of crime like scores of English malefactors. Moreover, the grave responsibilities of the Englishman did not rest upon the shoulders of the German. Sheltered in a house abutting upon his gallows, surrounded by a bodyguard of janissaries, he was never called upon to face the peril of the march to Tyburn nor the hostility of an Old Bailey mob. In whatever way we make the comparison between the hangman of Nuremberg and the hangman of London, the former will appear in contrast to be a mere creature of toyland. Such, one may be assured, would be the pronouncement if the question were submitted to the literary committee of the League of Nations.

Any one of the team of fifteen hangmen whom I have collected together is a much more interesting character, to the best of my belief, than the fellow from Bavaria. Both as a man and as a craftsman, the Englishman in every case will be found to hold by far the more remarkable record. There is nothing humdrum or conventional about the incidents of his career. As variable in his actions as a woman, he is never the same on two occasions—hanging, drawing, quartering, beheading, whipping at the cart's tail and exhibiting in the pillory; equally at home at Tyburn or Kennington Common or in the Old Bailey; his victims being all sorts and conditions of men and women, young and old, high-born and beautiful, some cut-purses, some footpads, some forgers, some highwaymen, some house-breakers, and a certain number of more or less atrocious murderers. Besides which, on occasions, he does a murder on his own. No hangman from toy-town can show traditions like these.

However, the context will prove the truth of what I say.

> "Prepare for crime—I'll publish right or wrong;
> Hanging 's my theme, let hangmen be my song."

INTRODUCTION

THE late Alfred Marks, in his annals of "Tyburn Tree"—an encyclopædic work that is not as well known as its merits deserve—makes the complaint that the British public has always under-valued the services of its public executioners.

"Selected by the State to carry out its decrees, it would seem that he should have been invested with a dignity but little inferior to that of the judges who pronounced the sentence carried out by him in co-partnership. Without the practical assistance of the executioner, the solemn sentence of the robed, ermined, full-bottom-wigged judge would be of no effect. Nevertheless, this officer of the State, practically inculcating on the scaffold the great truths of morality impressed on the public from the bench, this great public officer has never received the homage due to him. . . . Nor have posthumous honours in the smallest degree compensated for want of respect during life. The statues of London are, with few exceptions, and these recent, almost wholly devoted to royal personages, to soldiers, to ground landlords. Among them we seek in vain monuments to the executive officer, without whose aid law and order would have been mere empty names." [1]

In emphasising this ingratitude towards the hangman, the author of "Tyburn Tree" might have gone further,

[1] "Tyburn Tree, its History and Annals," Alfred Marks, p. 44.

pointing out that the necessity to perform unpleasant duties in other walks of life does not involve a social stigma. The occupations of the dentist and the dustman, the butcher, the sanitary inspector and the man-midwife are frequently of an unsavoury description, and yet we do not ostracise these persons in consequence. The surgeon kills many more people every year than "Jack Ketch," but the reason that we refrain from placing him beyond the pale is not because, unlike the hangman's work, it is not done on purpose. He happens to belong to a trade that is not taboo, whereas "Jack Ketch" does not.

It has become a convention that the public executioner cannot be received into the smart set, as a Lord Chief Justice, for instance, may be; and, until the Socialists come into power and there are equal opportunities for everyone, it is improbable that hangmen will be allowed to put on Court dress and attend a ministerial banquet. Meanwhile, something may be done to remove their social disabilities. Now that their biographies have been compiled, they have a right to literary recognition, and historians of crime no longer should conceal their names when giving a description of their deeds and actions. Since also it is known where many of them lived and moved and had their being, the London County Council would be well employed to place discs of identification upon the walls of their respective habitations. These, besides adding to the historical knowledge of the man in the street, would serve as a warning to the rising generation.

It is unnecessary to say anything in introduction of

my hangmen, even though it is a spate of hangmen such as was never seen before. As far as it has lain in my power, I have told the truth about them. In none of my stories is there a word of invention. I am content that their careers should speak for themselves.

In conclusion let me point out that my volume might be found to serve a useful purpose as a gift-book. The donor, when slipping it into the hands of his *bête-noire*—perhaps a writer of plays, or a novelist of alien origin, or a member of parliament—would have the opportunity of plagiarizing the words of Mr. Edgar Wallace in one of his most effective " curtains " :—

" Let me present the Hangmen of England. . . . Some day you'll meet one of them again."

SOME EARLY HANGMEN

SOME EARLY HANGMEN

NOT a great deal is known about the executioners of the sixteenth and seventeenth centuries—the little information which we possess about them being fragmentary. The first to appear on the pages of history is a person named BULL, who held the position in the year 1593, in the days of Queen Elizabeth, but neither the length of his tenure of office nor the date of his death has been recorded.

Bull was succeeded by the much more famous DERRICK, the executioner of the unfortunate Earl of Essex in 1601. Oddly enough, Essex had been the man's benefactor, having saved his life, it is said, some years previously when he had been condemned to death for a rape at Calais. There are innumerable references to Derrick in contemporary tracts during the early days of the reign of James I, and he is mentioned by Sir Walter Scott in "The Fortunes of Nigel." It is believed that the Derrick crane was called by his name because of its likeness to his gallows.

GREGORY BRANDON, the next in order, was Derrick's assistant for several years. Evidently he was officiating in 1616, since Garter King of Arms of that day granted him a coat of arms by mistake, being the victim of a practical joke played upon him by York Herald. By this means Brandon became a gentleman, and was spoken of in jest as "Esquire," a title by which he was known for the rest of his life and which was transmitted to each of his successors. He died about the year 1640.

RICHARD BRANDON, his son, succeeded his father, having qualified for the post as a young boy by beheading cats and dogs. He was executioner during the latter part of the reign of Charles I, cutting off the head of the Earl of Strafford. Rumour persisted for a long time that he decapitated the King himself, but evidence now seems to point in another direction. The question is discussed in Mr. G. J. Muddiman's "Trial of Charles I," one of the most admirable volumes in the *Notable British Trials Series*. Richard Brandon died on the 20th of June, 1649, and was buried next day in Whitechapel churchyard.

One LOWEN, an obscure person, seems to have followed the younger Brandon, since he carried out an execution not long after Brandon's death. His reign, however, must have been a short one.

EDWARD DUN, who apparently was dubbed "Esquire" more often even than the Brandons, was the successor of Lowen. Besides being immortalized by Samuel Butler in "Hudibras," he is the subject of a tract all to himself. In all probability Dun was the executioner who hanged the exhumed bodies of Cromwell, Ireton, and Bradshaw in 1661. He "dyed Naturally in his Bed" on the 11th of September, 1663.

JACK KETCH, most famous of all the executioners, came next in succession, holding office from 1663 until 1686. The merry days of Charles II brought busy times for the hangman, who did all the beheading as well, which accounts for much of Ketch's celebrity. Judging from the manner in which he bungled the executions of Lord Russell in 1683 and the Duke of Monmouth in 1685, he must have been a brutal fellow, and he became more hated by the populace than any previous hangman. In January, 1686, he was turned out of his office for insulting the Sheriff, one Pasha Rose, a butcher, being installed in his stead; but in the May of the same year Rose had to be hanged, and so Ketch was reinstated. It is believed that he died in the November following, and, ever since, his name has been used as a synonym for all hangmen.[1]

[1] "Dictionary of National Biography," under "Richard Brandon" and "Jack Ketch"; Mr. Edward F. Rimbault in *Notes and Queries*, 2nd Series, XI., pp. 445–8; "Tyburn Tree," Alfred Marks," pp. 45–6; "London Past and Present," Wheatley and Cunningham, III., pp. 417–18.

JOHN PRICE
(1714-1715)

I

JOHN PRICE
(1714–1715)

I

" THE hangman who was hanged and gibbeted afterwards." Such is the distinction that has been earned by John Price, and his record is exceptional among the public executioners. A coarse and brutal creature, with the worst vices of the lower orders of his epoch, he suffered a just fate for a vile crime.

John Price was born in the year 1677 in Old Soho, in the parish of St. Martin-in-the-Fields, now the parish of St. Ann's, Westminster. His father, a soldier in the ranks, was killed in an explosion while engaged in blowing up the fortifications of Tangiers when the place was evacuated by the English in 1684, and his mother was left penniless. Under these circumstances the boy could have no schooling, being obliged to earn his living immediately. The sorriest of occupations was chosen for him—in the yard of a dealer in rags, to whom he was bound apprentice when he was eight years old.[1]

Evidently his servitude was irksome or his taskmasters were unkind, for when his master died at the end of two years he ran away from his mistress and found work elsewhere. Having no knowledge of a craft, he was forced to become a casual labourer, and being a sturdy, well-grown lad, he got regular employment in loading

[1] " Newgate Calendar," Knapp and Baldwin, I. 114.

wagons. In this state of life he seems to have spent most of his boyhood. Then, at last, he grew anxious for a change. Going in search of another occupation, he fell into the hands of a press-gang or enlisted voluntarily, since he had become a seaman in the Royal Navy before the year 1695. During the next eighteen years he served before the mast in H.M.S. *Russell*, *Grafton*, and *Devonshire*, until at the Peace of Utrecht in 1713 he was paid off and discharged.

It is believed that he behaved well in the navy. At all events his character could not have been besmirched by habits of drunkenness or insubordination, because he was appointed almost at once to a place of trust. Recently death had claimed the public hangman, who in theory was supposed to be a sober, honest, and industrious citizen, and when John Price sent in his application for the post to the Worshipful Court of Aldermen at Guildhall, his credentials were good enough to obtain the situation for him. Thus he became "Finisher of the Law" for the City of London and the County of Middlesex, a functionary now known to everybody as "Jack Ketch."

In those days the office of hangman was not an unprofitable one. Although the salary was small, there was payment by piece-work, and the money earned therefore was constant and regular. The dress of the innumerable malefactors, often gentlemen of property, belonged to the executioner, whose fees were augmented by gratuities from the Company of the Barber-Surgeons in return for the corpses which he delivered to them for dissection. And soon, although John Price could not foresee the event, both Tyburn and Tower Hill were to witness the execution of a number of illustrious Jacobites, from whom " Jack Ketch " would receive purses of gold. According to a newspaper paragraph, the post of metropolitan hangman was worth about £40 a year, and, at the risk of causing the present holder of the office to go on strike, I may mention that this sum is equivalent to £400 in the present day.

According to the standard of the times, he performed his duties efficiently. A sailor's knowledge of knots was invaluable to him in his new calling, for in those days it was the custom to fashion the halter from a length of rope after arrival at the gallows. Accustomed to the iron discipline of the navy, he served the Sheriffs of London as submissively as he had obeyed the bosun or master's mate of a man-of-war. During the space of twelve months he treated scores of clients without hearing a word of complaint. Then, after a year of prosperity, his share of good fortune came to an end.

Unfortunately, as he confessed at a later date, he was never able to live within his means, besides which habits of intemperance began to grow upon him. When off duty he had always a wench on his knee or a bottle at his elbow, in sailor fashion, and his extravagance soon embarrassed him with a burden of debt. For awhile he was able to dodge his creditors by changing his lodgings, until at last one pertinacious tradesman set the bailiffs upon him while he was returning from an execution at Tyburn. " Jack Ketch " had the ignominy of being arrested publicly in Holborn, and for the trifling sum of seven shillings and sixpence !

Price happened to be able to raise the money on the spot, and was released from custody, but the publicity caused by the incident prompted others to whom he was in debt to make an effort to obtain payment likewise. Before long " other actions," so he complained subsequently, " were clapt upon him." Not being able to meet these demands, he was arrested once more and thrown into the Marshalsea, the gaol for debtors in High Street, Southwark, adjoining the King's Bench prison.

As luck would have it, he was unable to obtain his discharge before the next Sessions at the Old Bailey, when several criminals were capitally convicted, for whom a hangman had to be provided. Since Price was not available, the Sheriffs were obliged to find a substitute, and one William Marvell, a blacksmith by trade, was given the place. The weeks elapsed and still the prisoner in the Marshalsea remained in captivity. Release was impossible now, since his only source of income, the hangman's wages, had come to an end. So William Marvell continued to reign in his stead. It was a heavy misfortune, for the Jacobite rebellion of 1715 had taken place, and soon the hangman's salary was more than doubled by rich presents from distinguished victims of the scaffold. There is little doubt that Price became soured by misfortune. Henceforth he was a turbulent and brutal fellow.

For a couple of years or more he continued to live in the Marshalsea. Eventually he was allowed to go outside the prison, according to custom, as long as he kept " within the rules," and thus was able to wander into the adjacent streets, picking up odd jobs during the day as a labourer for the bricklayers or masons, but always obliged to return to the Marshalsea at night. Probably the meagre wages that he earned were all squandered on drink—now his habitual vice—since he was unable to save money to pay his debts and become a free man. Or perhaps he deemed it absurd to purchase his liberty when he could obtain it without spending a penny. For he did obtain it eventually. Breaking through a wall of the prison one dark night in the early months of 1718, he and a comrade managed to make their escape.

II

John Price, already, had acquired the greatest odium among the mass of the population as "Finisher of the Law." The hangman, naturally, was detested by the lower orders, since none could be sure that he would not be the next to pass through his hands. But the evil repute was increased a thousandfold soon after the flight from the Marshalsea, about the middle of April, when it was rumoured that the former "Jack Ketch" had committed a most cowardly murder.

The report was true, and it happened thus. An old woman, named Elizabeth White—the wife of William White, a watchman—kept a stall in Upper Moorfields, near the Bunhill Fields burying-ground, where she sold nuts, apples and gingerbread. Here one Sunday night, on the 13th of April, she was doing business until long after sunset, for the fine spring weather had tempted the people out of doors, and the holiday crowds were returning from the countryside beyond Kingsland and

Dalston. About ten o'clock, when most folks had passed on their way, John Price came reeling by, fresh from a tavern, and mad drunk, as he usually was at such an hour. An evil chance caused him to stop at the beldame's stall; and, as soon as he understood that she was alone and defenceless, he flung her to the ground and attempted to ravish her. The night was pitch dark, so there was no reason for him to be fastidious.

Poor Betty put up a stout resistance, terrified by his violence, not beguiled in the least by his tipsy endearments, which were provoked obviously by strong drink and not by her personal attractions. And when she continued to shout and struggle, giving no heed to his bestial entreaties, the cruel scoundrel began to cudgel her savagely. Attracted by her screams, several wayfarers came running up to the spot and dragged the ruffian away. Some held him, while others went for the constables, who took him in custody to the roundhouse.

The old woman was in a dreadful plight. One of her arms had been broken and an eye knocked out, while her head was bruised and battered all over. Bleeding and unconscious, she was put to bed in a neighbouring house, whither a surgeon and a nurse were brought to attend her. From the first her case was hopeless. After lingering for four days she died on the 17th of April.

Retribution pursued her infamous assailant speedily. In the following week the Proceedings on the King's Commission of Peace of Oyer and Terminer and Gaol Delivery of Newgate commenced at the Old Bailey, and on Thursday the 24th of April he was put to the bar

CONVICT WITH HIS THUMBS TIED PREPARATORY TO THE SENTENCE OF DEATH

[*To face p.* 15.

of the Sessions House, charged with the wilful murder of Elizabeth White.[1] The evidence against him was irrefutable. Not only had he been caught red-handed, covered with blood, but passers-by in the darkness had overheard his cries of rage intermingled with the shrieks of the unfortunate woman. No one credited his defence, which was of the lamest. He protested that he was innocent, and explained that as he was walking in Moorfields he came across something lying in his way. Stirring it with his foot, he realized that it was a woman, whom he lifted up, and discovered that she had been grievously wounded. While he was holding her in his arms he was arrested.

The story had no influence upon judge or jury. Being found guilty, he was sentenced to death by the Recorder, the public executioner having tied his thumbs together previously with a stout cord as a symbol that he was to be hanged.[2] After which he was taken along the private way past the garden belonging to the College of Physicians into Newgate prison, where he was lodged in the condemned hold.

At this period the famous prison consisted of the old city gate that spanned Newgate Street, in conjunction with two spacious annexes, four storeys high, which adjoined it on either side of the roadway.[3] All three

[1] "Collection of Trials from 1706 to 1720" (Brit. Mus. 518, b.2.2.)

[2] This cruel practice, which is akin to the custom of turning the edge of the axe towards a condemned man, was continued at the Old Bailey during the greater part of the century.

[3] The gate was rebuilt in 1673, after being destroyed in the Great Fire of London. It was demolished finally in 1777.

blocks were connected together on each storey by passages and staircases. The condemned hold—a dismal dungeon twenty feet by fourteen—was on the ground floor in the southern annex, situated alongside the wall of the gateway, for it had been originally the right-hand postern leading into the city. It was divided from the main entrance hall of the gaol—an apartment known as the lodge—by a heavy door, on top of which was an aperture, protected by spikes, where prisoners could converse with their visitors. One small barred window, within the span of the gate, was its only other source of light.

Discipline in the gaol was lax in the time of John Price. Soon after his arrival he was allowed to mount to the leads on the roof of the gate, sixty feet or more above the ground, to show himself to the crowds that had collected around the portals of the lodge in the street below. Hither he was accompanied by the new executioner, one Banks, "a bailiff's follower," who had succeeded William Marvell in the previous November, when that individual lost his post owing to an arrest for debt. Clasping Banks by the hand, the condemned man hiccuped plaintively :—

"You've hanged a great many already, and now you've got to hang me."

Afterwards he was taken back to the condemned hold, where he seems to have been allowed as much liquor as he demanded, although only the debtors, and not felons, were supposed to make use of the tap-room in the lodge.

Naturally, the murder and the conviction caused a

great stir, for never before had " Jack Ketch " been in such a fix. The newspapers were filled with paragraphs, and all the principal ones, such as *Mist's Weekly Journal*, *Read's Weekly Journal*, and *Applebee's Original Weekly Journal*, were agreed that a more " hardened ruffian " or a more " outrageous villain " had never been a resident in Newgate. From the first he was impenitent and untamed, drinking spirits continually, in a hopeless state of intoxication from morning to night. The Rev. Paul Lorrain, who had been Ordinary, or Chaplain, of Newgate for twenty years, declared that he had never known such a brutal or ignorant prisoner. Frequently he fell into a fit of furious rage, when it was dangerous to approach him, although he had been put into irons. He denied his guilt, protesting that he had not had a fair trial.

The weeks passed, but no attempt was made to hasten his hour of atonement. Possibly the Rev. Mr. Lorrain was responsible for the delay, in the hope of winning over an obdurate sinner, or William Marvell, the blacksmith, his successor as common hangman—who had been deputed to make him a suit of iron, since he was to be " hung in chains " on a gibbet—may have tarried over the job in order to indulge his comrade. However that may be, nearly six weeks elapsed between his sentence and execution.

At length, on Saturday, the 31st of May, 1718, the ex-hangman was led to his doom. It had been arranged that he should suffer at Bunhill Fields instead of at Tyburn, since it was usual for a murderer of the deepest dye to expiate his crime in the place where it had been committed. So a temporary gallows was reared for him near the spot in which Elizabeth White had met her death. It was a short journey from the prison, down Newgate Street and along Cornhill, through the Old Jewry and Coleman Street and past the Artillery Ground, but to John Price the distance must have seemed interminable. Vast crowds were assembled along the route, full of glee because the chief spectacle from Punch and Judy was going to be enacted for them in reality and " Jack Ketch " actually would be caught in his own noose. The women especially were jubilant, cheering with delight while the malefactor passed along in the cart.

Throughout the ordeal Price remained as defiant as ever, being " very impudent " to everyone, so the newspapers alleged, and he still protested loudly that he was innocent. He paid no need to the unctuous voice of the Rev. Paul Lorrain, who strove to induce him to think of his spiritual welfare, but turned his back upon him churlishly. Dressed in a clean white shirt and with a large nosegay in his hands, he stood erect and fearless in the cart, bent upon making as brave a finish as any popular criminal.

His obduracy, however, forsook him in the end. Either the eloquence of the Ordinary or the sight of the gallows brought about a change of heart, and he confessed his guilt at last, with the reservation that the crime was committed when he was drunk. A further triumph for Mr. Lorrain followed immediately. At the last minute, just before the cart was drawn away, the miserable wretch begged the prayers of the multitude and hoped that they would take warning by his untimely end. At least this is the version given to the world by the reverend gentleman in his "Account of the Behaviour, Confession, and Dying Words" of the celebrated malefactor, one of the perquisites of his office, which was published in due course.

Later in the day the dead executioner was fitted into the iron suit made for him by William Marvell, and he was hanged in chains upon a gibbet near Stonebridge in the fields between Kingsland and Holloway.

In emulation of the reverend Ordinary, the inevitable poet soon composed an elegy. It was entitled, "The Sorrowful Lamentation and Last Farewell of John Price, alias Jack Ketch, who was executed at Bunhill Fields for the cruel and most barbarous Murder of Mrs. White," and it ran as follows :—

> "Behold a wicked hardened Wretch,
> Whose Neck in Justice must be stretched
> Upon the fatal Gallows Tree;
> And not a soul to pity me,
> Not one will my Just Fate bewail,
> I must be hurried from the Gaol.
> It is for Wilful Murder, I
> A Fatal Death am doomed to Die."

WILLIAM MARVELL
(1715–1717)

II

WILLIAM MARVELL

(1715–1717)

I

A GRIM and gruesome creature, William Marvell lives to fame as the executioner of the rebel lords, who were beheaded in 1716. He was called to the scaffold from the smithy, where it is easy to picture him, a lurid figure in leathern apron and open shirt, lurking in the shadows while he beat upon his anvil or blew the bellows of his fire. In all probability he was a journeyman, working for John Robbins, the City smith, since the Sheriffs were able to lay their hands on him at once when the catch-polls had arrested the drunken John Price. No doubt the Sheriffs considered themselves fortunate in their discovery, for the brawny blacksmith, with his unerring hammer, obviously was capable of being an efficient chopper-off of heads. And much horrible and vindictive business of the sort was about to take place.

It is uncertain whether Marvell was operator on the 7th of December, 1715, when nine adherents of the Pretender were hanged at Tyburn for their share in the recent rebellion; but we know that he acted as headsman in the more famous tragedy on Tower Hill on the 24th of February of the following year, when Lord

Derwentwater and Lord Kenmure were brought to the block. It was an event that thrilled the people of England, both nobles being young and attractive men, while the method of punishment had been employed seldom during the past thirty years.

James Radcliffe, third Earl of Derwentwater, had taken part in the defence of Preston with a handful of followers, but he had been of no real service to the cause nor was he one of the Pretender's military leaders. The Hanoverians, however, needed an illustrious victim as an example. Lord Derwentwater had been a marked man by the Government for a long time. His offence, since he was an English peer, was unforgivable. So, when he was condemned to death with his fellow rebel, Lord Kenmure, mercy had been refused to either in spite of a popular outcry.

Although pleading guilty at his impeachment and imploring the clemency of the King, the young Earl showed no lack of staunchness when he came to die. On the scaffold he made a brave and pathetic speech to the people, in which he declared his devotion to King James the Third and prayed that he would be restored to the throne. He seemed to have no fear of death, but knelt down serenely to try if the block would fit his neck after assuring Marvell that he forgave him. When all was ready he desired that he might be allowed a few moments to say his prayers, promising to give the signal by repeating the words "Sweet Jesus" thrice over. The new headsman did his work swiftly and well, severing the neck with one terrific blow, and Lord Derwentwater's death was instantaneous.

"He laid his head upon the block
The axe was sharp and strong;
The stroke that cut his sufferings short
His memory cherished long."[1]

Lord Kenmure was not so fortunate. Possibly the iron nerve of William Marvell had been shaken by the sight and murmur of the vast crowds, or he was overawed by the intrepidity of the two gallant noblemen. Whatever the cause, his strong arm faltered and two blows were necessary to kill his second victim.

Lord Kenmure gave his executioner a present of eight guineas, and probably Lord Derwentwater's gift was no less. So, if Marvell had acted as hangman on the 7th of December previously, when three officers of the army suffered with six other rebels, he must have collected in gratuities alone in a couple of days half as much at least as his predecessor earned during the course of twelve months. One of the debtors in Newgate, who wrote a description of the gaol about this time, had a conversation with Marvell in the Press Yard during his imprisonment, and learnt that he received a fee of three pounds from the authorities for every peer whom he decapitated. Trade had never been so brisk for "Jack Ketch" since the merry days of Charles II.

There is further evidence that the ordeal on Tower

[1] From the "Ballad of Lord Derwentwater," *Gentleman's Magazine* (1825), I., 489. The following ballad is supposed to have been written by the Earl and addressed to his wife :—

"Farewell to Lochaber, and farewell, my Jean,
Where heartsome with thee I have many days been;
For Lochaber no more, Lochaber no more."

Hill had been too tremendous even for the sturdy William Marvell, because his health broke down soon afterwards and he became dangerously ill. According to one newspaper, indeed, he was suffering from " a consumption," which made his recovery improbable. " In case of his demise," declared this authority, " several persons of Wealth and Honor are making interest to succeed him, who plead great merit at this time; one is a Wine-cooper near Austin-Friars; another a Footman in Hatton Garden; a journeyman Taylor in Puddle-dock Hill; an honest Pawnbroker in Fleet Street; two half-pay lawyers; a Hangman and an old hero woman." In a little while, however, he had disappointed the aspirants, returning to his duties apparently as robust as ever.

There was much lucrative business for the ex-blacksmith during the summer of 1716. In May two wealthy Jacobites, named Henry Oxburgh and Richard Gascoigne, were hanged at Tyburn for their share in the rebellion. In July the Rev. William Paul met a similar fate along with John Hall, a Justice of the Peace for Northumberland. No doubt gentlemen of their position slipped a purse of gold into the hangman's hands before they were turned off.

Except in the case of a few atrocious murders, like that committed by John Price, the capital convicts of the City of London and County of Middlesex were always done to death at Tyburn, a distance of two miles from the porch of Newgate. The malefactors were drawn through the streets in an open cart, with their arms pinioned by ropes and the halter that would hang them wound around their breasts. The cortege was headed by the City Marshal on horseback, followed by the Under-Sheriff with a cavalcade of peace-officers. Next in order marched a body of constables, armed with staves. Sometimes, when a criminal of importance was taking part in the show, the two Sheriffs would condescend to put in an appearance, riding in their coaches with their wands of office in their hands. Behind, lest they should come between the wind and the nobility of these great people, followed the carts containing the criminals, with more constables trudging alongside. A company of javelin men brought up the rear.

A short distance from the prison on the crest of Snow Hill a halt was made before the steps of St. Sepulchre's Church, where the sexton with bell in hand delivered a solemn admonition to those condemned to die. This ordeal was inflicted with a pious motive, a charitable Merchant Taylor, named Robert Dow, having bequeathed an annual donation in his will for this purpose.

> "All good people, pray heartily unto God for these poor sinners, who are now going to their death and for whom the great bell doth toll. You that are condemned to die repent with lamentable tears; ask mercy of the Lord, for the salvation of your own souls. . . .
>
> "Lord, have mercy upon you,
> "Christ, have mercy upon you."

Then, while the great bell of St. Sepulchre's boomed forth, the procession continued its journey down Snow Hill.

At the bottom of the steep slope the road turned sharply to the left, crossing the Fleet river—at that period an open sewer—over a narrow stone bridge. A gradual assent led up Holborn Hill and the gates of St. Andrew's Church, upon which in these days one looks down from the Viaduct, then rose high above the level of the street. Hereabouts stood several famous inns and taverns, whose windows were crowded with gentlefolk on the mornings when " the March to Tyburn " took place. Naturally, a popular criminal, such as the dashing highwayman or the daring house-breaker, was welcomed with cheers and greetings by the crowd, high-spirited girls tossing nosegays to him during the harangue of the sexton at St. Sepulchre's, ladies of the town blowing kisses to him in Holborn. But the man who had peached against a pal, or the thief-taker condemned for receiving stolen goods, was pelted with volleys of mud and garbage and sticks and stones.

In the days of Marvell the cavalcade paused usually for a few minutes at the Crown Inn near St. Giles's Pound, where the prisoners were allowed to drink a last glass, a boon that had been granted since the time when the ancient Lazar house, which stood here, used to present a bowl of ale to them. Or sometimes, when a favourite hero was in the cart, the officials gave him leave to stop at the house of a friend—if he had a friend living in the Oxford Road—for a farewell symposium.

The gallows stood between the wall of Hyde Park and the end of Edgware Road, a permanent triangular structure, formed by three tall upright posts, joined together at the top by a cross-bar. There was space for eight bodies to swing side by side from each of the beams. The carts were backed underneath, and when the Ordinary had finished his exhortations, the nooses were adjusted and the caps drawn. Lashing the horses, the hangman and his helpers put the carts in motion, leaving the malefactors dangling in the air. The grim Marvell boasted that he placed the knot " right under the left ear," and so put his patients out of pain at once;[1] but it was a slow, lingering death in most cases, although frequently the friends of a sufferer were allowed to shorten his agony by pulling his legs.

II

During the year that followed the Jacobite executions William Marvell was turned out of office, like John Price had been before him, and for the same reason. Women and wine were his undoing, and in spite of his increased earnings he fell deep into debt. One morning, on Wednesday, the 6th of November, 1717, a writ was served upon him in Holborn—which seems to have been an unlucky spot for the hangman of those times—while he was accompanying the cortege from Newgate to Tyburn to hang three condemned men. The previous arrest of " Jack Ketch " had taken place after his return from the Triple Tree when he had performed his duties. Now, however, he was apprehended on his way to Tyburn *before* he had carried out the sentence of the Court!

It was an act of flagrant effrontery on the part of the bailiffs. For a moment the Under-Sheriff and the City

[1] " History of the Press Yard " (1717).

Marshal were flabbergasted and the procession was thrown into confusion. Then the bailiff who had served the writ hastened to explain that, far from wishing to prevent the law from taking its course, he was willing to let the hangman go on his way if he would give his word to obey the summons later. Unfortunately the mob was not of the same mind. The people were resolved that " Jack Ketch " should not reach Tyburn that day if they could help it. Taking advantage of the disorder of the retinue, they pounced upon the unfortunate Marvell and made off with him. Before he could be rescued by the constables he had been mauled so unmercifully that he had lost consciousness.[1]

The Under-Sheriff was in a dilemma. He was obliged to leave Marvell behind with a guard to protect him, for it was evident that the wounded man would have to be put to bed and a surgeon brought to him; but the Under-Sheriff was obliged to get his three criminals hanged that day, so he had to proceed to the gallows in the hope of finding a deputy hangman. In this he seemed to be successful immediately. Upon telling the public of the trouble when he arrived at the Triple Tree, he was hailed by a bricklayer in the crowd, who announced that he was willing to officiate. An instant later the man must have regretted his impetuosity, for the mob turned upon him and almost beat him to death. In vain the harassed officials strove to persuade another amateur to undertake the job by the offer of a rich gratuity. The temper of the populace was too menacing, and none dare volunteer. So at length, after waiting for several

[1] *Read's Weekly Journal*, 9th and 16th November, 1717.

MARVELL, THE HANGMAN, ARRESTED ON HIS WAY TO TYBURN

[*To face p.* 30.

hours, the City Marshal was obliged to escort his three lucky gallows-birds back to Newgate, amongst the cheers of the exultant crowd.[1]

The Rev. Paul Lorrain paid a visit to the elated three as soon as they were lodged once more in the condemned hold, to assure them that, as it was improbable that they would obtain a reprieve, it would be wicked and foolish to buoy themselves up with hopes of mercy. It was a rash prophecy. On the next day they were respited for a week, and soon afterwards the capital sentence was commuted to one of penal servitude. Simultaneously it was announced in the newspapers that the Rev. Mr. Lorrain had been seized with a fit of apoplexy. It is sad to remember that one of the reprieved criminals, John Meff by name, was hanged at Tyburn four years later for committing a robbery after returning from transportation.[2]

The mishap of Marvell caused a great commotion in officialdom, the authorities being much incensed at the triumph of mob rule. It was necessary, of course, to find a scapegoat. At first the bailiff who had made the arrest was chosen for punishment, and the judge of the Marshalsea Court suspended him temporarily from his office; but when his defence was examined he was forgiven and reinstated. Then the vengeance of the Court of Aldermen fell upon the unfortunate hangman, who was accused of neglect of duty and threatened with prosecution. To be served with a writ and to be kicked and cuffed into

[1] *Applebee's Original Weekly Journal*, 2nd November, 1717.

[2] "New Newgate Calendar," Wm. Jackson (1818), I., 263.

insensibility were unpardonable offences in the opinion both of the City of London and the County of Middlesex. It was decided that the grim fellow should be dismissed, a harsh punishment on the face of it, but probably they knew at Guildhall that he had become drunken and dissolute beyond redemption. On the 16th of November his disgrace was proclaimed publicly in the columns of John Applebee's *Journal*:—

> "On Tuesday last (November 12th, 1717)—Ketch Esqre was removed from the office of Executioner-General of Great Britain; and one Banks, a Bailiff's follower, is appointed to succeed him."

To have chosen a bailiff to supplant him seems to have been rubbing it in unkindly.

Thus the numbers of the unemployed were increased by one, and Marvell must have found his situation all the more unbearable because of his recent affluence. From this time onward he became poorer and poorer, often being obliged to beg the price of a crust. He was fond of bragging of his honesty, protesting that he would rather starve than steal, and he complained incessantly that he had been treated shamefully. In addition to the odium always borne by an ex-hangman, he was reviled by the Stuart party, whose name was legion, whenever any of them recognized him in the street, because he had killed Lord Derwentwater. These were dismal days for the sombre man.

Life became a little brighter for him during May of the following year, when he secured the contract for making the chains of John Price's gibbet, but he could obtain no regular work, and sank into abject poverty. At this time he was living in a hovel in St. Stephen, Coleman Street, and in this same street the well-stocked window of Nathaniel Simms, a haberdasher, often aroused his cupidity. For many months he resisted temptation, until one afternoon on the 7th of August, 1719, when thirsty and penniless, it occurred to him how easy it would be to help himself. Entering the shop, he began to bargain for some silk handkerchiefs, and managed to slip ten of them into his pockets before he went away.

Unfortunately for the thief, the proprietor missed his property at once, and sent his daughter in pursuit, and she discovered the name of the shop-lifter. Several persons who had seen the gaunt blacksmith slouching along in his leather apron with a lock under his arm told the girl that they recognized him as the quondam hangman. The beadles were notified, and a watch was kept for the culprit. For awhile he evaded capture, but about six weeks later, on the 19th of September, the officers apprehended him. Brought before a magistrate, he was committed to prison.

The trial took place at the next Sessions, when on Thursday, the 15th of October, 1719, he appeared in the Justice Hall at the Old Bailey during the Proceedings of the King's Commission of Peace and Oyer and Terminer and Gaol Delivery of Newgate. His judges were the Right Hon. Sir John Wood, Lord Mayor of the City of London; Mr. Justice Tracy; Mr. Baron Price; John Raby, Esq., Deputy Recorder; and several of His Majesty's Justices of the Peace. He was indicted for privately stealing ten silk handkerchiefs, value 12*s.*, out of the shop of Nathaniel Simms in Coleman Street.[1]

The evidence against him was clear and conclusive, but the wily fellow showed some craft in his defence. In the hope of arousing the Hanoverian sympathies of the Bench, he alleged that he was prosecuted out of malice, the Jacobite party bearing him a grudge because he had hanged or beheaded so many of their leaders in the discharge of his duty. With even greater guile he insinuated that it was prejudice against a public hangman that had induced some of the witnesses to appear against him. Possibly his protests may have been of some avail, for he was brought in " guilty to the value of 4*s.* 10*d.*," a verdict which saved him from the gallows, but made him liable to transportation beyond the seas. In abject distress, he begged the Court not to send him into exile, but to substitute corporal punishment instead.

" I will submit to it cheerfully," he blubbered, " though I be whipped a mile."

No regard was paid to his protests, and the sentence was confirmed. Before daybreak in the early morning of Friday, the 23rd of October, he was taken from Newgate to Blackfriars Stairs, together with ninety-one other convicts. Thence he and his companions were conveyed in barges down the river to Woolwich, where they were put on board a ship bound for His Majesty's plantations. To the last he entreated that he should be flogged at the cart's tail, though he " were whipped a mile." [2]

[1] Sessions Papers, 1716–27. Vol. II. (Inner Temple Library).

[2] Newspaper paragraphs quoted by Sir Alfred Robbins in *Notes and Queries*, 10 S. VIII., 335, 353.

So, unless he died on the voyage or was taken by pirates like John Meff, he reached Virginia or the Carolinas, which for the greater part of the century were the dumping-ground of the criminal population of the motherland—a reason perhaps why the people of the South have always been so attractive. In America the ex-hangman would have to labour as " a felon hand " on a rice or a tobacco estate; and eventually, if he gained his freedom by good conduct, he may have become a landowner himself, leaving a worthy progeny behind him. Some day, perhaps, a Mr. William Marvell will be chosen President of the United States.

In one particular Marvell enjoys a distinction that is shared by only one other of the hangmen of England, being immortalized in a popular novel by a famous writer. Harrison Ainsworth has introduced him into the story of " Jack Sheppard," where he is depicted as " a tall, sinister-looking personage, with harsh, inflexible features, a gaunt but muscular frame and large, bony hands." Although a trustworthy antiquarian on most occasions, Ainsworth is incorrect in supposing that Jack Sheppard was hanged by the ex-blacksmith. When the famous prison-breaker met his death in 1724 Marvell was toiling in the American plantations. Or may be—

> " Beside the ungathered rice he lay
> His sickle in his hand."

BANKS
RICHARD ARNET
(1717–1728)

III & IV

BANKS

RICHARD ARNET

(1717–1728)

I

An unfortunate lacuna in the records of the hangmen of England occurs during the next eleven years. We know that Banks the bailiff succeeded Marvell as hangman on Tuesday, the 12th of November, 1717,[1] and there is no doubt that another hangman, named Richard Arnet, was buried on the 13th of August, 1728;[2] but at present there is no evidence to show when Banks ended his term of office or at what date Arnet stepped into his shoes. It may be, too, that between these two reigns some other "Jack Ketch" was in command of the gallows.

The report of Banks' appointment in *Applebee's Journal* was confirmed by a more instructive paragraph in the same newspaper a fortnight later :—

> "This week the new Hangman was presented to the Collegians at Newgate, who, we hear, highly approved of the choice, and 'tis expected he will this day at the Old Bailey perform some part of the Operation of his office."

[1] *Applebee's Original Weekly Journal*, 9–16th November, 1717.

[2] *Read's Weekly Journal*, 17th August, 1728; Register of St. Nicholas, Deptford.

At all events it is certain that he began to officiate during December, 1717, and apparently he gave satisfaction to all concerned.

A high-born criminal passed through his hands on the 17th of March following—no less a person than the Marquis de Paleotti, an Italian noble, the brother-in-law of the recently deceased Duke of Shrewsbury. Paleotti, an inveterate gamester and a debauchee, was a murderous scoundrel as well; and one day when his servant refused to borrow money for him he drew his sword in a fit of passion and ran the man through the body. To his intense indignation, he was condemned to death for murder, and he protested that it was outrageous to put a nobleman to death merely for killing his lackey. No reprieve, however, came for him, his crime being a dastardly one, and his sister, the unpopular Duchess of Shrewsbury, having no interest at Court. His pride remained unshaken to the last. At Tyburn gallows he requested the Sheriffs to allow him to be hanged alone, lest he should be defiled by touching any of the other criminals who were to suffer with him. And in deference to his rank the Sheriffs granted his desire.

Only one other record remains of Banks' handiwork as public executioner. As described previously, he acted as hangman on the 31st of May, 1718, at the atonement of John Price in Bunhill Fields; but although it is quite probable that he continued to ply his trade for many years subsequently, there is no certainty that he did so. The date of his death or retirement has not been ascertained. It is a calamity that so little is known of his history, because six years later the most famous criminal

JACK SHEPPARD, THE MOST FAMOUS CRIMINAL OF THEM ALL

[*To face p.* 41.

of all time ended his life at Tyburn, and at present no one can say who was the man who hanged him.

Jack Sheppard was a London thief who died before he was twenty-three years of age. Although a nimble and fearless little rogue, there is nothing remarkable in his career as a robber, and scores of footpads and house-breakers have excelled him. But, while being a mediocrity in the street, he became a genius in a gaol, for no sooner was he clapt into one than he wriggled out of it. Four times he was "jugged" and four times he made his escape, each escape being more wonderful than the last, and his contemporaries acclaimed him justly as the greatest prison-breaker that had ever been seen. Since mankind rates achievements of this sort at a high value, Jack Sheppard henceforth was assured of one of the loftiest panegyrics in the Newgate Calendar.

His first triumph was in breaking through the roof of St. Giles's Round-house, when lodged for the night there in the top storey, and getting clear away, although a hue and cry had been raised after him while he was scrambling to the ground. His next feat, six weeks later, was more remarkable still—an unprecedented escape from the New Prison, Clerkenwell, the chapel-of-ease for Newgate when the latter was crowded, where he was confined in a separate room with one of his mistresses. Having been supplied with a file and gimlets by his friends, he removed an iron bar and a stout wooden beam from the window and lowered the young woman and himself by blankets into the courtyard, twenty-five feet below. The outside wall of the prison was as high as the cell from which he had descended and crowned with chevaux-de-frise, but he climbed over it without much trouble by inserting his gimlets into the gatepost and using them as a scaling-ladder. Finally, upon reaching the top, he accomplished his most difficult task, hauling up his plump companion beside him, after which they slid down into the street.

Less than two months later, on the 14th of August, 1724, Jack Sheppard had been condemned to death, and was lying in the condemned hold in Newgate, the dismal dungeon on the ground-floor, with its spike-crested door opening into the lodge or entrance hall of the gaol. Tools, as before, were smuggled to him by his associates, and he was soon busy upon his prison bars. Almost every day friends came to talk to him through the grille above the door, on which occasions he used to saw with a file at one of the spikes. When at last he had nearly cut it through, which was not until after the " dead warrant " had arrived in Newgate,[1] and the day of his execution was at hand, two of his women friends paid him a visit after nightfall. A party of turnkeys were carousing around a table in the upper part of the lodge, adjacent to the tap, but a projection in the wall of three or four feet, which formed a porchway leading into the interior of the prison, hid the entrance of the condemned hold from their view.

Jack lost no time in taking advantage of the opportunity. Breaking off the weakened spike, he squeezed his lithe body through the narrow opening, and with

[1] The so-called " dead warrant " was merely the Recorder's " report," or list of names, of the convicts who had been capitally convicted. Those struck out from the list had been reprieved; those included in the report were " ordered for execution."

the aid of the women managed to crawl over the top of the door. Dashing across the lodge, he fled through the open gateway, unperceived by his gaolers, who did not discover his flight until later in the evening. Never before had there been such an audacious flaunting of justice. Henceforth Jack Sheppard's name was in every mouth.

It was the fourth and last escape, however, that was his masterpiece. When retaken by the turnkeys they locked him up in the Castle, one of their strongest cells, on the third floor in the centre of the gate, looking west towards Snow Hill. He was handcuffed firmly and his ankles were fastened by a heavy pair of fetters, chained to a staple fixed in the floor. Everyone believed that it was impossible for him now to break out of the gaol, unaware that it was only a question of time if he was left to his own devices. And ere long sufficient time had been given him, for his warders did not come near his cell from three o'clock in the afternoon on the 15th of October until the next morning. Six hours sufficed for his task. By nine o'clock he was a free man.

Having slipped his hands through his handcuffs, he had broken the chains upon his legs and picked the padlock that held him to the floor. Then, removing an iron bar from across the chimney by loosening the brickwork with a fragment of his fetters, he made a hole in the ceiling, through which he ascended to the room above. Here a door that had not been opened for seven years proved a stubborn obstacle, but he wrenched off the lock at last, and, bursting open another stout door at the end of the corridor, made his way into the chapel. The two gates of the spike-crested grille, which enclosed the pews of the convicts, did not check him for more than a few moments, but the last two doors in a passage leading to the leads gave him the greatest trouble, for he had to wrench the lock-box off the first and the fillet of the main post from the other. None but the cleverest of locksmiths could have done what he had done, considering that he had to work during more than half the time in pitch darkness. Besides having a highly developed sense of touch, he must have possessed a resourceful imagination to enable him to deal with countless unforeseen difficulties. The way to the leads and liberty was now open to him, but first of all he had to return to his cell to fetch his blankets, in order to lower himself from the top of the prison on to the roof of an adjoining house.

This wonderful achievement made Jack Sheppard into a national hero, and when he was recaptured, which happened about a fortnight later, men of rank and fashion flocked to Newgate to see him. William Pitt, Keeper of the Gaol, and Bodenham Rouse, the Head Turnkey, reaped such a rich harvest in fees that they came to regard the prison-breaker, who had caused them so much trouble and anxiety, as a splendid benefactor. Every day the newspapers were filled with paragraphs about the little thief, and he was the one topic of conversation among both high and low. Shortly before his execution the first painter of the day painted his portrait in the condemned hold; and when he was hanged at Tyburn on the 16th of November, every man and woman in the vast multitude that had assembled to see the last of him were full of pity and admiration for him.

It was his personality even more than his prowess that caused Jack Sheppard to make so deep an impression upon the popular imagination. He had a cheery and impudent humour that appealed to the common folk, whose love for him grew fonder when they saw that he was always merry when everything seemed most black. Sharp of tongue and quick of wit, he was a typical specimen of the Cockney gutter-snipe, and as such the great city of London took him to its heart. A morose, slow-of-speech ruffian would never have gained the affection of the people, however many times he had broken out of the stone jug. Jack's physique also was a help to his renown. A dapper fellow such as he, subtle as a panther and with muscles of steel, was naturally the ideal hero of his particular feats of skill. In popular fancy he became the will-o'-the-wisp of crime.

No malefactor ever reached his eminence. A dozen or more pamphlets chronicled his life and surprising adventures, and every print-shop displayed his portrait in line or mezzotint along with representations of his escapes. He was the subject of ballads in the street and of sermons from the pulpit, and two stage plays were made of him. In the innumerable Tyburn Chronicles and Malefactors' Registers and Newgate Calendars that appeared at intervals as the years rolled on his story was told with greater gusto than any.

Then, a hundred years later, when he seemed likely to be forgotten, Harrison Ainsworth, the writer, placed the coping-stone on his fame by weaving his story into a novel. From this time onward he continued to be the hero of hundreds of essays and romances, and his nimble little person was never long absent from the booth or theatre. For these reasons he tops the Newgate Calendar, a greater figure even than Dick Turpin or Claude Duval.[1]

II

About the time that Jack Sheppard was building up his great reputation, the condemned criminal had taken to the strange habit of going to his death at Tyburn in his shroud. It was a " whimsical humour," in the opinion of the newspapers, and the motive seems unintelligible. Perhaps it was done out of pique to annoy the authorities, or to deprive the hangman of a perquisite, or maybe the malefactors wished to indicate that they brought nothing into the world and could take nothing out of it. Anyhow, numbers went to the gallows in the depth of winter with no other garment but the thin woollen gown. There is a picture in one of the Newgate Calendars of Stephen Gardener, who was executed on a bitter morning in February, 1724, standing in the cart beneath the Triple Tree and preening himself apparently because he is dressed in a shroud. The portrait of the hangman who is adjusting the rope is so realistic, although probably it bears little resemblance to the original, that one is curious to know whether it is intended for Banks or Richard Arnet.

Seven months after the death of Jack Sheppard, a far greater scoundrel, and one of little less renown, was hanged at Tyburn. Jonathan Wild also has been celebrated in a work of fiction, but although Fielding's " Life of Jonathan Wild, the Great," is a finer work of

[1] " Celebrated Trials," III., 375.

EXECUTION OF STEPHEN GARDENER IN HIS SHROUD AT TYBURN, FEB. 3, 1724

[*To face p.* 46.

art than Ainsworth's story of Jack Sheppard, it is caviare to the multitude, and never increased the popular renown of its hero. Jonathan, moreover, is not such an attractive rascal as Jack, while Ainsworth has doomed him for all time to the rôle of the villain. Consequently, in spite of the fact that Wild made as great a stir among his contemporaries in his own particular line as Sheppard did in his, he has never occupied such a lofty pedestal in the Pantheon of crime.

Nature intended Jonathan Wild for a sleuth, and had he been born two centuries later it is probable that he would have won a responsible position at Scotland Yard. For ten years at least, from 1715 until he died, he was by far the most efficient thief-taker in England. Fear was unknown to him. He was as tenacious as a bull-dog. Whenever he had resolved to clap hands on a mill-ken or a bridle-cull—as burglar and highwayman were termed in his jargon—he ran his quarry to earth at whatever hazard. Scores of times this intrepid man arrested some armed desperado single-handed or rounded up a dangerous gang with a couple of his henchmen.

Unfortunately there was no money in sleuthdom in the reign of George I, so, like the modern Cabinet Minister, Jonathan was obliged to supplement an inadequate salary by seeking a more remunerative source of income. There was no money either to be got out of the newspapers, for descriptive journalism was as ill-paid as detective work, and the Jekylls and Hydes among politicians and schoolmasters had not begun to snatch the bread from more honest mouths. But there were other ways of dealing in stolen goods, and Wild conceived the original idea of opening a great clearinghouse, where thieves could dispose of their booty. Half the prigs in London brought their pelf to him, being allowed a fair commission on the selling price.

It was a profitable scheme for both producer and distributor, and it was successful for many years. Jonathan became commander-in-chief of a great corporation of thieves, organizing robberies and assigning the various tasks of plunder among his myrmidons. In different parts of London he had offices for lost property, where, upon payment of a fee, a stolen article might be recovered by the rightful owner. He was the most despotic of task-masters, treating his magsmen like slaves. If obedient they got a living wage and witnesses were supplied to swear to their innocence should any of them be brought to trial. But whenever one of them dared to rebel he was betrayed to the authorities at once and evidence was produced to prove his guilt. Jonathan took care that all troublesome followers should soon be "nubbed" at Tyburn.

All the time he posed as the most exemplary of citizens, and continued to help the officers of Newgate in the detection of crime. He styled himself "Chief Thief-Catcher in England," carrying a silver staff in token of his office, always wearing a laced coat. The more robberies he inspired, the more thieves he laid by the heels. He was a sort of uncrowned king in Newgate gaol, for the turnkeys were aware that none of them was his match either in knowledge or skill, and the prisoners believed that he knew enough to hang every one of them.

At last the inevitable happened, and he was found out. Indicted at the Old Bailey for a paltry fraud, he was found guilty and condemned to death. The authorities made no attempt to save him, having discovered, no doubt, and being appalled by the ramifications of his villainies. Probably they needed an example, and he was an especially suitable one, by reason of his unpopularity. So, on the 24th of May, 1725, he played the principal part in the March to Tyburn, being pelted by the mob all the way with mud and stones, and he was turned off amidst the cheers of the largest multitude that had ever gathered around the Triple Tree. The populace detested the informer and the receiver, and Jonathan Wild was the two gentlemen rolled into one. As in the case of Jack Sheppard, we do not know whether Banks or Arnet was the executioner.[1]

It seems probable, however, that Richard Arnet was the hangman who participated in the holocaust at Tyburn on the 9th of May, 1726, when Mrs. Catharine Hayes was executed for the murder of her husband. With the help of two accomplices she had battered in his skull, dismembered his body, and distributed the pieces in various parts of the town. So when brought to trial she was indicted and convicted of "petty treason," as the crime of husband murder used to be called in the old law-books, the penalty for which was to be burnt alive. In the days of George I, however, the sentence had been mitigated somewhat, as an act of grace to the condemned woman. When tied to the stake with the faggots piled around her, she was strangled by a

[1] A modern biography of Jonathan Wild has long been overdue and might be included in the *Notable British Trials* series. But it would necessitate considerable research, and must not be entrusted to the lazy or incompetent.

rope with a running noose before the fire was lighted.

But Catharine Hayes was not put out of her misery so quickly. The common hangman, who was responsible for the doing of her to death, bungled in his work. By some mischance the faggots had been kindled before the halter was fixed upon her neck, and the flames burst forth and scorched the executioner's hand, compelling him to leave go of the cord. To the horror of the spectators, the murderess was slowly roasted alive, while she shrieked in her agony and strove in vain to push the faggots away from her.[1]

Richard Arnet himself did not live much longer, dying in his gears early in August two years later at his house in Deptford. The actual street in which he lived is not recorded by the newspapers, and they made the mistake of calling him Richard Arnold. His real name appears in the registers of the parish church—the church of St. Nicholas beside the Green—where he was buried secretly at dead of night on Wednesday, the 14th of August, 1728. Owing to his calling, a hostile mob might have collected had the ceremony been performed in the day-time. The chief mourners were Mrs. Arnet, his wife, Little Tom, "his truly lamenting servant," and John Hooper, who succeeded him as public executioner.

In the days of Arnet and for many years afterwards a special torture was inflicted upon condemned prisoners in Newgate in consequence of the bequest of Robert Dow, the pious Merchant Taylor. In addition to the

[1] "Criminal Recorder" (1804), I., 442 (with portrait). Thackeray based his story of "Catharine" upon the career of Catharine Hayes.

exhortation on the church steps on the morning of the March to Tyburn, the sexton of St. Sepulchre's was required to come with his bell on the eve of each execution day and deliver another harangue at midnight beneath the archway of the gate outside the grating of the condemned hold.

> "You prisoners that are within
> Who for wickness and sin,
>
> after many mercies shewn you, are now appointed to die To-morrow in the forenoon, give ear and understand, that To-morrow Morning the greatest Bell of St Sepulchre's shall toll for you in Form and manner of a passing Bell, as used to be tolled for those that are at the Point of Death: To the end that all godly People, hearing that Bell, and knowing it is for your going to your Death, may be stirred up heartily to pray to God to bestow his Grace and Mercy upon you, whilst you live. I beseech you, for Jesus Christ's sake, to keep this Night in Watching and Prayer, to the Salvation of your Souls, while there is yet time and place for Mercy; as knowing to-morrow you must appear before the Judgment-Seat of your Creator, there to give an account of all things done in this Life, and to suffer eternal Torments for your Sins committed against him, unless, upon your hearty and unfeigned Repentance, you find Mercy, through the Merits, Death and Passion of your only Mediator and advocate Jesus Christ, who now sits at the right Hand of God to make Intercession for as many of you as patiently return to him." [1]

[1] "History of London." William Maitland (1756), I., 26.

According to other authorities the bellman used to chant a set of verses to the condemned felons at midnight before execution day :—

" All ye that in the condemned hold doth lie,
Prepare ye, for to-morrow you shall die.
Watch and pray, the hour is drawing near
That you before the Almighty must appear;
Examine well yourselves, in time repent,
That you may not to eternal flames be sent;
And when St. Sepulchre's Bell to-morrow tolls,
The Lord above have mercy on your souls." [1]

The tedious ritual that condemned prisoners had to endure previous to execution in the Georgian era, in consequence of the inordinate love of ceremonial habitual to the period, must have made the anticipation of death a hundred times more agonizing than it otherwise would have been. What the sexton did on the last night, the Ordinary at Newgate used to do every day, harping upon death and damnation incessantly. In contrast the hangman must have seemed friendly.

[1] Francis Place MSS., and MS. 27,826, No. 14.

JOHN HOOPER
(1728-1735)

V

JOHN HOOPER

(1728–1735)

I

THE zealous student of history will find it a relief to turn away from the shadowy figures of Banks and Arnet to follow the career of a hangman with a definite character, as unequivocal as that of the brutal Price or the grim Marvell. Although the world has thought fit to regard the hangman as an outcast, and would have been content to keep him on a scarcely higher level than one of the untouchables of Hindustan, the man has been able in most instances to rise above his environment and manifest an idiosyncrasy of his own. It has been made clear in his case that human nature cannot be obliterated by a pitchfork, and that a hangman is endowed with hands, organs, dimensions, senses, affections, passions, just as other men. In short, that, in spite of the contumely of mankind, he is one of God's creatures, after all, although his creation does not always reveal God at His best.

There is nothing dubious about John Hooper's temperament. He has come down to posterity as the Laughing Hangman, and was a merry soul. The ugliest being that could be imagined, with a face like a gargoyle, he made himself, nevertheless, the favourite of all by his irresistible drollery. The stranger, who was repelled at first sight by his appearance, in a little while was laughing at his jokes. For jovial Jack had the art of telling stories and possessed an inexhaustible store of anecdote. He was a born jester.

He appears first on the stage of history while he was occupying the humble position of Assistant Turnkey in Newgate. A Major John Oneby, accused of having killed a fellow gamester in a coffee-house brawl, happened to be a prisoner in the gaol, and laughing Jack was given to him as a servant. The Major was appalled by the man's forbidding countenance.

"What the devil do you bring this fellow here for?" he demanded of Mr. Pitt. "Whenever I look at him I shall think of being hanged."

In spite of the protest Jack was told to stay on, and in a short time he had propitiated his master. Delighted by his humorous yarns and his gift of mimicry, Major Oneby was never content unless his servant was at his side, declaring that he never had had such a jolly companion. And when the unfortunate officer had been brought to trial and was condemned to death, Jack did his utmost to cheer him with hopes of pardon.

It was not to be, however, and the death warrant came at last. But Major Oneby was resolved not to suffer the disgrace of the gallows. Shortly before the day appointed for his execution, on the 3rd of July, 1727 (not 1729, as most of the Newgate Calendars have it), he committed suicide in his cell. He left a scrap of written paper as his last will and testament.

> "Give Mr Akerman, the turnkey below stairs, half a guinea; and Jack, who waits in my room,

five shillings. The poor devils have had a great deal of trouble with me since I have been here."

Richard Akerman soon rose to be Head Turnkey of the gaol, and finally became Keeper of Newgate, while the swift elevation of Jack Hooper, of course, was even more remarkable. The good luck of both seems to have commenced with their attendance on the unfortunate Oneby. His bequests to them, with the quaint comment attached, certainly made them talked about.

In the following May another incident brought laughing Jack once more before the notice both of the public and the authorities. While helping to conduct a company of convicts, "cast for transportation," from Newgate to the prison barge at Blackfriars Stairs, he was attacked and felled to the ground by a man in the crowd who was endeavouring to rescue one of the prisoners. The attempt did not succeed, and the assailant himself was captured, being sent to gaol on the following morning by the Lord Mayor. Again the name of John Hooper appeared in the newspapers. He was becoming a public character before the crowning triumph of his career.

Three months later the cheery fellow had achieved the ambition of his life. In all probability it was the good nature of the man rather than self-interest or a taste for the morbid that attracted him to his new calling. Since men must be hanged, it was more humane obviously to have them put to death by a genial hangman than by a coarse and surly fellow like Richard Price or William Marvell. Conscious of his worth, he sent in his application to the Committee of Aldermen on the State of the

City Gaols as soon as he knew that the post was vacant, with the result that he was appointed Executioner for London and Middlesex.

"Captain John Hooper is made hangman," announced *Read's Journal*, approvingly, "in the room of Richard Arnold (*sic*) deceased, being a person of known probity and integrity, who merits the place by an unspotted character."

He was sworn into office before the proper tribunal on Thursday, the 15th of August, 1728; and at this period, if tradition is to be believed, the ceremony of initiation on these occasions was an awe-inspiring one. Summoned before a court of City Fathers, all in their robes of office, the neophyte chosen to be the new "Jack Ketch" was placed in front of a table, which was strewn with ropes and scourges, handcuffs and fetters, symbolical of the work that awaited him; and with a Bible in his hand he was required to take a solemn oath that he would execute every criminal condemned to die "without favouring father or mother or brother or sister or any friend whatsoever." And when he had given this horrible promise he was dismissed with the words—spoken, no doubt, by the Under-Sheriff—"Get thee hence, wretch!"

Jack was soon busy with his new task. Nine days after his installation he was called upon to execute a robber named James Haddock, and he seems to have performed his duties to the satisfaction of everybody. For the next seven years the happy soul continued to hang all and sundry with unruffled good humour, doing his business as merrily as the Ordinary or the Under-Sheriff would let him. One likes to think—but history does not record the fact—that he allowed poor Little Tom, " the truly lamenting Servant " of the late Richard Arnet, to share in his enjoyment by making him his assistant.

Shortly before the exaltation of laughing Jack to his high degree, a change that concerned his clients had taken place at Newgate. The condemned hold adjoining the lodge had been abolished and fifteen new condemned cells were built on the east side of the Press yard in an annex separated from the prison. The Press yard itself was only a narrow passage open to the sky, ten feet wide and seventy feet over its full length, extending from Newgate Street to the garden of the College of Physicians; but it contained buildings in which were the most comfortable apartments in the gaol, and they were let to rich prisoners at high prices.

The new cells, however, were not comfortable, and no word of eulogy can be said of them, for they were the most dreadful dungeons imaginable. " Prisoners shed tears upon being brought to these darksome solitary abodes," declared John Howard, speaking of them fifty years later. There were fifteen of them in all, five on every storey, one above another, occupying three storeys. Each was vaulted and nine feet high, but they measured only nine feet by less than seven, and were lighted by a small window, double grated, with thick bars. Through these the inmates could not even see " the little tent of blue that prisoners call the sky." All was in semi-darkness.

During the day-time the convicts were allowed to meet together in a large room on the ground floor, called the day-room, where they had free intercourse with one another and could be visited by their friends, but at nightfall they were locked up again in their cells. A rich man had little to complain of as regards food, for he could order almost anything for which he was prepared to pay, but the ordinary prison fare was both coarse and meagre. In these fifteen horrible dungeons in the gloomy three-storeyed annex that stood in Newgate Street on the eastern side of the gaol across the Press yard capital felons used to be incarcerated during the interval between conviction and execution for more than a hundred years. For the " new cells " were completed and ready for occupation at the beginning of 1728, and were still in use at the time when Queen Victoria came to the throne.[1]

II

Although the high spirits of laughing Jack were never depressed by an ordinary hanging, it seems probable that he was daunted a little by the terrible sentence pronounced upon a forger about two years after he had taken office. The law had not yet decided that the penalty of death should be employed indiscriminately in all cases of forgery, but endeavoured to invent various methods of making the punishment fit the crime. Thus, when Japhet Crook, alias Sir Peter Stranger, was convicted of having forged deeds of conveyance in order to appropriate two hundred acres, belonging to a Mr. Garbet and his wife of Clacton-on-Sea, he was condemned

[1] Repertory 132 f. 29 (Guildhall Record Office). " State of Prisons," John Howard, I., 152; *Read's Weekly Journal*, 30th July, 1726; *Daily Post*, 9th December, 1727; *Penny Satirist*, 20th May, 1837.

to stand in the pillory for one hour, to have both his ears cut off close to his head, to have both his nostrils slit and seared with a hot iron, to forfeit the issues of all his lands and tenements, and to be imprisoned for life. And it was Jack Hooper's job, since both pillory and whipping-post were under his charge, to see that the sentence was carried out. Yet, with his keen sense of humour, he must have realized that the whole business was theatrical and anachronistic, a sort of mediæval mountebanking.

The *auto-da-fé* took place on the 10th of June, 1731, and Japhet Crook, alias Sir Peter Stranger, who must have been a tough rascal, bore his sufferings heroically. Fortunately for himself, his crime was not an unpopular one with the mob, so they did not treat him as an Aunt Sally while he stood in the pillory at Charing Cross, as they used to treat criminals whom they disliked. He cracked jokes with the people during the whole time, and, when released at the end of an hour, he sat down unconcernedly in an elbow chair, placed in the centre of the platform, to submit to the torments that had been ordained for him.

Dressed in overalls of butcher blue, Jack Hooper came up behind him and severed his ears with an "incision knife," after which he held them aloft so that the mob could see, and then delivered them to Mr. Watson, a Sheriff's Officer. A surgeon was allowed to attend the mutilated man, and his wounds were staunched immediately. Although he endured his punishment with undaunted courage, the wretched man could not help flinching from the final act of torture. When both his nostrils had been slit with a pair of scissors and the hangman was proceeding to sear his nose, he sprang from his chair at the first touch of the red-hot iron and "left bleeding." And it is recorded that laughing Jack did not insist upon the fulfilment of the sentence.

Apparently the redoubtable Japhet Crook, fortified by his surgeon, was little the worse for his terrible ordeal. In a little while he was allowed by the complacent officials to pay a visit to the "Ship" tavern hard by, where he remained for some time, lulling his pain with strong drink, and listening proudly to the congratulations of his friends upon his intrepidity. Later in the afternoon he was taken to the King's Bench prison in Southwark, the most comfortable prison in the metropolis, "to be confined for life." History does not relate if he was ever released or if he died in captivity.[1]

Although the sufferings of this man had been so agonizing, they were nothing in comparison to what others had to endure when condemned merely to an hour in the pillory. Often, if the culprit foresaw that he would be ill-treated by the mob, he arranged with his friends to barricade the approaches to the platform with a rampart of coaches, carts and wagons in order to keep the lower classes at bay. But if the people were really angry, a device of this sort, as often as not, was no use at all. When Charles Hitchin, the Under City Marshal, who was greatly hated by the Tyburn crowd because of his office, stood in the pillory in Catherine Street, Strand, for an unpopular offence, the utmost endeavours of friendly officials failed to protect him from the fury of the mob. Leaping over the sur-

[1] *Fog's Weekly Journal*, 5th June, 1731; *Daily Advertiser*, 11th June, 1731.

rounding vehicles, the excited multitude poured volleys of stones and brickbats and broken bottles upon the man in the pillory. And when he was released at the usual time, the newspapers tell us that he was "ready to expire."

Two persons, indeed, were done to death in the pillory during the days of Jack Hooper. The first was Mother Needham, the most notorious procuress of the period, who had been in trouble with the authorities for ten years. The place of her penance was the corner of Park Place in St. James's Street, near her residence, where, in spite of the efforts of the beadles and constables to shield her, she was pelted so severely by the populace, on the 30th of April, 1731, that she died two days later.

In the following summer one John Waller was placed in the pillory at Seven Dials, St. Giles'—about the worst place in the city for an unpopular man. John Waller was particularly obnoxious to the lower orders, being a professional informer, who had sent several innocent people to their death by bearing false evidence against them. In Waller's case the beadles and constables, mindful, no doubt, of their own safety, do not seem to have made any great effort to protect him. So the unhappy creature was the target of a fusillade of large stones, pieces of bottles and dried cabbage-stalks for a whole hour. Finally a man in the crowd went up to him, pulled him down from the pillory and tore all his clothes off; after which the crowd fell upon him as he lay upon the ground, and beat him and kicked him and jumped upon him until he was dead. At the coroner's inquest on the next day a verdict was returned of "Wilful murder by persons unknown." An hour in the pillory could be the most fearful punishment in the world in the times of John Hooper.

Few of the Georgian hangmen were able to sign their names, having to be content with making their mark, but Jack could write his signature when necessary in a fine bold hand. It was not needful often, but at each Christmas he was called upon to do so in acknowledgment of a Christmas box from the Company of Barber Surgeons, to whose hall in Monkwell Street he paid a visit on every 23rd of December. Under their charter the Barber Surgeons had a right to the bodies of felons—whose sentence ordained that they should be anatomized—after they had been hanged at Tyburn. Sometimes, however, it happened that the mob did not choose that the surgeons should have a particular corpse, or the friends of the dead man managed to carry off his body, on which occasions the dissectors of Monkwell Street were robbed of their rightful booty. Frequently there were long and bloody battles around the Triple Tree between the constables and the rabble, in which, as often as not, the latter were victorious. It was wise, therefore, to conciliate " Jack Ketch," who was able to use many devices when the malefactor had been cut down in order to ensure prompt delivery at Barbers' Hall. A present of seven shillings and sixpence, given to the hangman at Christmas time, was a good investment. The receipts for this money are still preserved, and in 1730 the records contain the signature obviously written in a moment of pride—" John Hooper, executioner." [1]

Almost every hangman accomplishes a *magnum opus*

[1] " Annals of the Barber Surgeons," Sidney Young, p. 421.

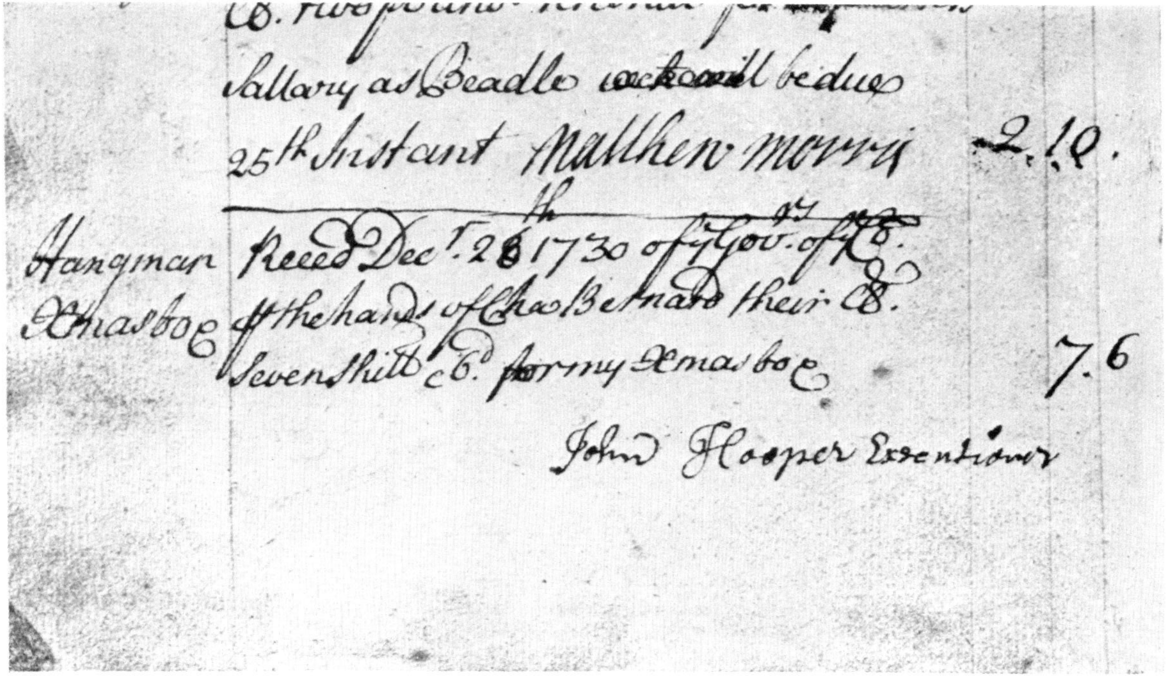
Sallary as Beadle which will be due
25th Instant Matthew Morris 2.10.
Hangman Xmas box Recd Decr 26th 1730 of ye Govr. of ye &c.
of the hands of Chas Bernard their &c.
Seven shill &c 6d for my Xmas box 7.6
John Hooper Executioner

SIGNATURE OF JOHN HOOPER, THE HANGMAN, IN 1730

[To face p. 64.

during the course of his career when he puts an end to the existence of a criminal of the highest rank, and the *magnum opus* of laughing Jack undoubtedly was the execution of Sarah Malcolm on the 7th of March, 1733. This miscreant slew her mistress and a couple of fellow servants, strangling two and cutting the throat of the third, a performance that broke the record of female thuggism up to that time. All the town was aghast at this wholesale slaughter, which for awhile was surrounded with a certain mystery, because the murderess strove to cast suspicion upon innocent men.

Sarah Malcolm, moreover, was supposed to be beloved by a young clergyman, who was convinced of her innocence, a touch of romance that added to the fascination of the crime. Many sentimentalists believed that the accused woman was the scapegoat of someone else, and regarded her as a heroine. In consequence of her notoriety, Hogarth paid a visit to her cell to paint her portrait, from which innumerable prints were engraved. It seems strange, however, that she found anyone to look upon her as a heroine, for although only twenty-five years old, the bloom of youth had vanished, and she was a sombre creature with harsh and forbidding features. According to Hogarth, her face showed that she was "capable of any wickedness." But since she continued to assert her innocence and to accuse other people, she won over a crowd of credulous dupes, like every villainess who acts as she did.

Her judges had no doubt of her guilt. When brought to trial three weeks after her arrest, she was condemned to death. It was evident that there was no chance of a reprieve, and the majority of people, who would not believe her protestations, revelled inordinately in every detail of her crime and regarded her as a great criminal. Since she had killed her victims in Tanfield Court in the Inner Temple, the tragedy was known as the Temple murder. A deed of such enormity seemed to call for special punishment, so it was decided to hang the murderess in Fleet Street, between Mitre Court and Fetter Lane, as close to the scene of her villainy as possible.

Impenitent to the last, she held herself proudly while she was being taken to the place of execution, her cheeks painted in honour of the occasion. The Rev. Mr. Peddington, her clerical admirer, who accompanied her in the cart, monopolized her attention, so hangman Jack had no opportunity to try to cheer her by his usual quips and jollities. In any case he would have found her grim and unresponsive. The famous murderess was hanged upon a gibbet, erected in the middle of the street, in the presence of an enormous crowd, but there is no evidence to show that Hooper was aware of the honour she had done him in becoming one of his patients.

When, or for what reason, John Hooper ceased to be public executioner is unknown. Perhaps some of his Methodist clients protested to the Ordinary or to the Under-Sheriff that a Merry Andrew from a booth was not a fit and proper person to dispatch them to another world. Or possibly the authorities came to the conclusion that he was apt to clown his part, a weakness of successful comedians of all ages, and he was superannuated on a pension. It may be that he spent the sunset of his life in leisured ease in the bosom of his family, with Mrs. " Jack Ketch " on the opposite side of a cosy hearth and little " Jack Ketches " playing around his knee. We do not know.

Or possibly, like Richard Arnet before him, he died in harness and was buried in consecrated ground in one of the City churchyards. Again we cannot tell. The date of his death, the place of his interment are unknown. We can point to no tombstone that marks the last resting-place of laughing Jack, the comic hangman. Of only one thing can we be certain. He was dead or had retired before the commencement of 1735, and his successor, John Thrift, was carrying on his work far less humorously.

JOHN THRIFT
(1735–1752)

VI

JOHN THRIFT

(1735–1752)

I

An important official, when asked his opinion of John Thrift, the public executioner, made reply, " He is a good sort of man," and this seems to have been the verdict of most of his contemporaries. Of nervous temperament, impulsive and easily perturbed, it was inevitable that Thrift should be more readily affected by his environment than a person of his occupation had any right to have been. There is no doubt that he was not of tough enough mould for his particular business. It is strange that he should ever have sought the office which he held. It is more wonderful still that he should have been able to hold it, and with credit, for so long a period as seventeen years. Indeed, both on account of the quantity and quality of his work, he has some claim to be considered a great hangman.

Although he had not a scrap of the humour of John Hooper, being incapable of bringing a smile to a patient's lips by jest or story, he appears invariably to have been as kind and considerate in his methods as circumstances would allow. Undoubtedly he was even more humane than laughing Jack, who was apt to be brusque and slap-dash in spite of his geniality. Taking him all in all, it may be assumed that John Thrift was the most polite hangman who had been born into the world hitherto. Nevertheless, this well-meaning creature was in hot water perpetually. The victim of a too highly-strung temperament, he was his own worst enemy. A simple, illiterate soul, he could not even write his name.

Even on the day of his initiation, he got into trouble, though it must be confessed that there was an excuse for him. The date was the 11th of March, 1735, and he had been required to turn off no fewer than thirteen malefactors before a critical Tyburn crowd, an ordeal that should never have been imposed upon a debutant, and the task was beyond his powers. Yet, considering that two well-filled carts had to be used and two of the cross-beams of the Triple Tree brought into action, his blunder might well have been more serious.

The Rev. James Guthrie, the Ordinary, had finished his admonitions, and the unhappy thirteen were standing in the carts with their faces uncovered, singing the Tyburn hymn, or offering up distracted prayers. Had he observed the ritual, the hangman should have requested his congregation to pull down their caps, but fussy John Thrift, in the excitement of his first hanging—and that such an orgy of its kind—forgot this part of the ceremony. So one of the carts moved away before all the caps had been lowered, and the faces of several of the men were exposed to the crowd.[1] For such a grave offence against decency the careless hangman was sure to receive a tempestuous scolding from the Under-Sheriff.

[1] *The Old Whig*, 15th March, 1735.

During the next year the unlucky Thrift got into a fresh scrape. A charge of theft was brought against him by a woman named Mary White. According to her account, he burst into her house on Monday, the 24th of May, soon after his return from an execution at Tyburn, and, after knocking her down, robbed her of a striped ticken pocket, containing three shillings and sixpence, which he had cut off while she was lying helpless on the ground. Since she swore to the facts on her oath, the magistrate, always prone to commit in those days on slight evidence, ordered the hangman to be taken to Newgate.

It proved, however, to be an entirely false accusation, a wicked concoction on the part of Mary White. It was discovered that no pocket had been stolen, or, if it had, that Thrift was not the thief. In a few days he was bailed out by the Sheriffs and set at liberty, while the woman herself was sent to prison on a charge of malicious prosecution.[1]

His second misfortune during the same year was of a different kind. On this occasion he became the victim of mob violence because of his supposed relentlessness to one of his gallows-birds. Thomas Reynolds, a "turnpike leveller," had been hanged at Tyburn and cut down as usual, but whilst the undertaker's men were fastening him in his coffin he thrust back the lid, much to their annoyance, and sat up. In obedience to orders, the hangman was proceeding to hang the man over again, when the crowd, forgetting that Thrift was merely

[1] *Daily Journal*, 25th and 31st May, 1736; *Gentleman's Magazine*, 1736–, p. 291.

carrying out the instruction of the Under-Sheriff, made an attack upon him and almost beat him to death. " Jack Ketch " always took his life in his hands whenever he went to Tyburn at this period. A party of footguards with loaded muskets frequently attended at executions to protect him from the mob.

In a little while Thrift had recovered from his wounds, and it was a long time before another mishap befel him. When it came at last, it must have vexed him sorely, since it involved him in a dispute with his excellent patrons, the Worshipful Company of Barber-Surgeons. A serious accusation was made against him. According to the beadles, the hangman not only had " obstructed the bodies being brought from Tyburn to the hall for dissection," but had also threatened to prevent the Company from obtaining them in future. Summoned to Monkwell Street at once, Thrift was reproved severely by the indignant chirurgeons, who reported the matter subsequently to the Lord Mayor and Court of Aldermen. No grudge, however, appears to have been borne on either side, since Thrift continued to receive his Christmas boxes as usual.[1]

It is difficult to imagine that an obsequious person such as Thrift should have run any risk of offending the Barber-Surgeons' Company by embarrassing their beadles wilfully. Probably the dispute arose out of a misunderstanding. It has been shown previously that an unseemly scuffle, which frequently became a fierce battle, always took place when the felons were cut down

[1] " Annals of the Barber-Surgeons," p. 358.

from the Triple Tree. The friends of the dead men fought to save them from dissection, the emissaries of the Surgeons strove to seize their lawful prey, while "Jack Ketch" was determined to keep the clothes of his victims. In addition, there were many turbulent free-lances, who tried to snatch a body to sell on their own. Usually the corpses were stripped naked at the foot of the gallows, and almost all the combatants had a broken head. No doubt it was in a scramble of this kind that John Thrift managed to annoy the Beadles of the Barber-Surgeons' Company.

The case of Thomas Reynolds, "the turnpike leveller," proves that it was possible for a man to survive the usual period of hanging at Tyburn. Several instances of resuscitation have been recorded, but the most famous of all is that of William Duell, who passed through Thrift's hands on the 24th of November, 1740. Although only sixteen years old, Duell was a cruel young scoundrel, who had been convicted of rape and murder and ordered to be anatomized. During the journey to the dissecting hall he had shown no sign of life, but when placed on the table it was seen that he was breathing still. By way of experiment the surgeons endeavoured to revive him, being successful in a very short time, so that he was able to sit up and drink some warm wine. In spite of the fact that he was taken back to Newgate, he had recovered completely in three or four days. According to his account the process of hanging had not been painful, bringing merely peace and unconsciousness in the midst of a beautiful dream. Others of the initiated, however, have not endorsed his opinion. At the next

Sessions at the Old Bailey he was ordered for transportation, and possibly may have founded a family in Dixie-land.[1]

II

Of the scores of people hanged at Tyburn by John Thrift in the course of his busy career, four only occupy a prominent place in the Newgate Calendar, a famous scholar and three highwaymen. The first of these, one Usher Gahagan, was an Irishman of good birth. He seems to have possessed the not uncommon temperament of scholar and debauchee. Highly educated, with a Latinity of rare excellence, he alienated both his parents and his young bride by his dissolute habits. Upon coming to London to seek his fortune, he continued to lead a double life, wasting his health and his money in every form of vice while earning a good income by editing a beautiful edition of the classics. Finally he took to filing guineas and selling the gold dust.

For a time he found it a lucrative business, but discovery was inevitable, and upon being brought to trial he was convicted and condemned to death. His plight aroused much pity, for he was a fastidious poet, and some of the verses which he wrote in the condemned cell touched the hearts of all who read them. Nevertheless, they failed to move the great persons to whom they were addressed, and on the 20th of February, 1749, poor young Gahagan was hanged at Tyburn. One may be sure that John Thrift, who always had much com-

[1] "Tyburn Tree," Alfred Marks, pp. 223–4.

miseration for gentlefolks, treated him as kindly as possible.

Thrift's highwaymen were capital rascals of their kind, who rode the high toby in gallant fashion, and any hangman might have been proud of attaching three such scalps to his girdle. Their names were Henry Simms, known as "Gentleman Harry," James Maclean, "the Gentleman Highwayman," and William Parsons, a son of a baronet. All won celebrity at their trade, although the gentleman of the road had lost much of his glamour since the palmy days of Charles II.

Simms began life as a footpad, and, having learnt to ride by becoming apprentice to a post-master, he stole a horse and set up as highwayman on his own. A sentence of transportation followed, and he made the voyage in a convict ship to Maryland. Escaping before long, he worked his passage back to England, whereupon he enlisted on a man-of-war, and in due course gained the rank of midshipman owing to his good conduct. But the lure of the high toby was irresistible. Deserting from his ship, he stole a horse and took to the road once more, becoming in a short space of time famous all over England. Hertford and Northampton were his favourite hunting-grounds.

Like most of his kind, his halycon days were short. When captured at last, his fate was sealed, for a gentleman of the road was never pardoned. Although not unnecessarily malevolent as a robber, he became a savage ruffian while a prisoner. Having thrice made murderous attacks upon his gaolers, he was chained down to the floor. They hanged him at Tyburn on the 16th of June, 1747.

There was only one circumstance of note in connection with his passing. Three days after the event an advertisement appeared in the *Daily Advertiser*, announcing that John Thrift, the executioner, was ready and willing to testify on oath that Henry Simms, known as Gentleman Harry, assured him, a few minutes before the cap was drawn over his eyes, that, as he hoped to be saved, he had not given any account of his life except to Mr. J. Nicholson, the printer in Old Bailey. It may be assumed that the Rev. John Taylor, the Ordinary, was neither surprised nor distressed to hear that the man whom he had shrived should bother his head at the last moment about such a mundane matter. Being as prolific an author of Dying Speeches and Confessions as Paul Lorrain himself, he must have guessed that money had passed between the printer and the hangman.

James Maclean, who was John Thrift's second highwayman client, achieved far greater renown than Henry Simms. Although his career on the road lasted for less than two years, he made as much noise in the world as any other high tobyman of the eighteenth century. No great feat of daring, indeed, lies to his credit, but he possessed a plausible Irish tongue and won repute as a lady-killer in early youth. Ostentatious and overdressed, he strutted from spa to spa, posing as a man of fortune and proclaiming openly that he was in search of a bride, arousing hopes in scores of gentle breasts in consequence. When he took to the highway he was well known in Bath and Tunbridge Wells and the West End of London, and women of rank and fashion, who imagined that he was going to prove a second Claude Duval, followed his adventures with breathless interest.

For a while he made a brave show, stopping the mail on two occasions, holding up unprotected travellers by post-chaise, almost blowing out the brains of Horace Walpole by accident. It seemed as though a brilliant future lay before him, but, to the disappointment of his admirers, the handsome Irishman was not clever enough to evade the thief-takers for long. He was arrested in his lodgings in St. James's Street and lodged in the Gatehouse near the Abbey.

Almost two months passed before he was brought to trial, during which period he was kept in Newgate. Since the time of Jack Sheppard no prisoner had received more attention. Men and women of the highest position came to see him, and the day after he was condemned to death no fewer than three thousand persons passed through his cell. One of his constant visitors was a famous high-born beauty, who strove in vain to procure him a pardon. It is difficult to account for this universal adulation, considering that his exploits on the high road had been few and mediocre, but he was a good-looking young man, only twenty-six years of age, and he had moved in good society during his prime. He died at Tyburn, an exemplary penitent, on the 3rd of October, 1750.

The third and last of Thrift's highwaymen did not cut such a dash in gold lace, nor was he able to win so much success with the ladies, but, being a baronet's son, he was entitled to call himself William Parsons, Esq., and his prestige was increased through his connection with several noble families. Eton was his school, and he had held a commission in the army. So when he began his career upon the road there was no question about his right to the title of gentleman highwayman. Naturally his exploits excited the greatest interest.

It soon became known that a robber of more than usual intrepidity was working the country round Hounslow Heath—that favourite resort of the marauder—and when it was discovered that he was an old Etonian and a man of high birth, his fame was established. Every one of his exploits aroused fresh admiration; his valour and recklessness were greatly exaggerated; and the women, who dearly loved a knight of the road, were ready to believe that the country had never seen such a gallant highwayman.

When it came to fighting for his life, however, Parsons did not prove at all gallant. Arrest and condemnation followed, and he ended his days at Tyburn on the 11th of February, 1751. The print shops were filled with his portraits, as they had been with those of Maclean before him. Pamphlets also were published describing his life and adventures. In the opinion of his contemporaries, he was a distinguished member of his profession.

The execution of four such famous criminals would have been sufficient to make the reputation of any hangman. But it is the Jacobite rebellion of '45 that has caused the name of John Thrift to live in history. Like Marvell before him, he was compelled to act as headsman. He disliked such employment intensely. Being no politician, he could not understand why a beaten enemy should be made to endure the Caudine Forks. He disapproved of archaic punishments like the axe and the block, as every good hangman should, believing that a stout hempen rope afforded ample protection both for Church and State. And his nervous, simple little soul was thrown into an agony of consternation by the fuss and panoply always associated with the chopping off of heads. One motive only induced him to perform his distasteful task. Like Marvell, he could not resist the purses of gold which Jacobites usually gave to their executioner.

The uncongenial work of butchery began on the 30th of July, 1746, when nine unfortunate gentlemen, who had been in the service of the Pretender, were drawn on hurdles from the New Gaol, Southwark, to the gallows on Kennington Common to be hanged, drawn and quartered, as the sentence of the court had ordained. The most famous among these were Francis Towneley, Thomas Deacon, and the romantic Jimmy Dawson. Their story has been told by Ainsworth in his novel "The Manchester Rebels," in which the manner of their cruel death is described.

A pile of faggots and a butcher's block stood beside the gallows, and while the prisoners were being placed in the carts beneath the cross-beam the fire was set alight. Towneley was cut down five minutes after he had been turned off, unconscious but still alive—showing that to be hanged by the neck was by no means a swift death—and when his body had been stripped it was laid upon the block that awaited it. Here the nauseated Thrift had to sever the head with a cleaver, being obliged, moreover, to disembowel the corpse and cast the heart and entrails into the flames. Glancing up at the eight figures swinging comfortably above his head, he must have wondered why his tiresome taskmasters could not leave well alone. However, he succeeded in treating the rest of the rebels as he had dealt with

Towneley; and when he had blundered through his gruesome work, he managed also to bellow to the crowd—as they had told him to do—" God save King George."

An even more awe-inspiring experience befel him on the 18th of August in the same year, when the paramount tragedy of the rebellion took place and Lord Kilmarnock and Lord Balmerino were beheaded on Tower Hill. It was on the eve of the execution that General Williamson, Lieutenant of the Tower, informed Lord Kilmarnock that Thrift was " a good sort of man," whereupon the young earl had replied that he was sorry to hear it, because a fellow of a rougher nature and a harder heart probably would do his work more quickly. The surmise seemed likely to be correct. Poor Thrift was in a dreadful state of panic. When they dressed him all in white and brought him to the scaffold—which was caparisoned in black and surrounded by a dense multitude—and stood him beside the block, he was so dismayed by the terrific spectacle that he fainted away. After a draught of wine he recovered and was able to stand at attention, although trembling still, when Lord Kilmarnock arrived. It was observed that he held the axe behind him so that the doomed man should not see it.

The officials must have endured great anxiety lest he should fail them. It seemed doubtful whether he would have courage enough even to cut off one head, let alone two. The appearance of the young and comely nobleman distressed him so deeply that he burst into tears, in an agony of compassion. Once more he was revived with a glass of wine, but when led forward to beg his victim's forgiveness according to custom he fell upon his knees and wept bitterly. Lord Kilmarnock spoke to him gently, while he slipped into his hand a more effective restorative than strong drink, a purse full of guineas.

At last the hangman-headsman recovered his self-control. He stood at attention once more with the axe in his hand, and he had sufficient presence of mind to ask Lord Kilmarnock after he had knelt down to remove his hands from the block, "lest," as he said, "they should be mangled or intercept the blow." Fortunately, too, his nerve did not fail him when he came to perform his task, for he struck boldly and well, severing the head with a single stroke.

As soon as the scaffold had been strewn with fresh sawdust and Thrift had put on another suit of white clothes, Lord Balmerino was brought out to die. A brave old swashbuckler, "treading like a general," his intrepidity seemed to unnerve Thrift as much as the humility of the other rebel lord. Moreover, he was unable to administer the same powerful remedy as Lord Kilmarnock, having only three guineas to present to his headsman. Upon kneeling down he vaulted from one side of the block to the other, and gave the signal by throwing up his arm as though he were going into battle. These incidents combined seemed to bring back all Thrift's trepidation. He swayed, as though terrified, his arm trembling obviously as he raised it. The blow that he struck fell feebly, and to the horror of everyone the neck was only lacerated. Two more strokes were necessary before it was cut through.

A similar scene was witnessed on the 8th of December following, when Charles Radcliffe, youngest brother of the unfortunate Earl of Derwentwater, was decapitated for his share in the rebellion of 1745, just as his brother had been for that of 1715. Although Radcliffe gave his executioner a present of ten guineas, Thrift was unable to behead him in less than three blows. It is true that he operated more skilfully upon Lord Lovat on the 8th of April, 1747, but no one had any pity for the poor old rascal, so Thrift felt no qualms of conscience in using his axe. Nevertheless, whenever his compassion was aroused by the youth or valour or noble birth of one of his victims, he was an unreliable headsman.[1]

III

There is no doubt that life was never the same for Thrift after the ordeals of Tower Hill. Every Jacobite in London now loathed him with the deadliest hate, seizing every chance of showing their detestation. Since Marvell no hangman had been so greatly detested. His existence was made miserable in countless ways, and the nerves of the excitable little man fell to pieces. People reviled him as he passed along in open daylight; they mingled stones and brick-bats with their curses after nightfall. Crowds gathered in the streets whenever he chanced to be recognized, following him with groans and hooting. He could not take a walk abroad without hearing malicious shouts of " Jack Ketch." A constant echo pursued him everywhere—" Jack Ketch, Jack Ketch."

[1] Thomson's " Memoirs of the Jacobites "; " An Account of the Behaviour of the late Earl of Kilmarnock " (1746), pp. 26, 35, 36, 37.

One evening in March in the year 1750, about six o'clock, he was walking from St. Giles's Church to his home in Coal Yard, Drury Lane, an alley running parallel to High Holborn, when a party of men hailed him by the hateful name and pursued him menacingly. He hastened his steps to escape from them, but they followed him to his door. And at the sound of the shouts of " Jack Ketch," a crowd began to gather.

Mrs. Thrift was sitting at the door, awaiting the coming of her husband, like a dutiful wife—for even hangmen have someone to love them—and she began at once to scold at the people who mocked him.

" You pack of thieves ! " she cried. " Suppose it is ' Jack Ketch ' ! Do you want to rob him ? "

What followed is obscure, owing to conflicting testimony. There is no doubt, however, that the crowd increased both in numbers and ferocity, and that John Thrift, in terror of his life, rushed into his house for a weapon with which to defend himself. A moment later he had reappeared in the doorway with a drawn cutlass. Throwing off his coat and hat and wig—for he was somewhat of a beau—he brandished his blade and ordered his tormentors to disperse.

Apparently some of the ringleaders fled at the sight of cold steel, with Thrift in hot pursuit, since he was too excited now to realize what he was doing. And a little farther on, in Short's Gardens, beyond Drury Lane, he became concerned in actual murder. For one David Farris was cut down and killed in the open street, and several persons who saw the deed declared that the slayer was " Jack Ketch," the hangman. Justice Fielding was informed almost at once, and John Thrift, who surrendered at Bow Street in due course, was committed to prison.

He was indicted at Justice Hall in the Old Bailey on Friday, the 27th of April, 1750, for the murder of Farris on the 11th of March previously, before the Right Hon. Sir Samuel Pennant, Lord Mayor of London, the Right Hon. the Lord Chief Justice Lee, Sir Thomas Abney, the Hon. Mr. Baron Clarke and Richard Adams, Esq., Recorder.[1] The defence was a complete denial of the charge, the prisoner declaring that a friend, named Enoch Stock, had snatched the hanger from him and struck the blow in order to save the lives of both of them. Stock corroborated this explanation to some extent, but had little recollection of what occurred, having been knocked down by the mob and stunned.

A clever counsel, no doubt, would have been able to urge successfully this plea of self-defence, but in those days the law would not allow a counsel to any prisoner, the presiding judge being supposed to act in that capacity for all. From the evidence as it stood Sir William Lee and his colleagues had no hesitation about their decision, bringing in a verdict of guilty, and Thrift was condemned to death. The Court was aware that if the Mayor and Aldermen of the City of London considered their hangman worthy of a reprieve they would be able to obtain one for him.

From the first there was no doubt of the attitude of the Corporation. Pro-Hanoverian to a man, they were resolved that " Jack Ketch " should not go to Tyburn for having rid the town of a cursed Jacobite. So,

[1] Old Bailey Sessions Papers—25th to 30th April, 1750, p. 75; *General Advertiser*, 28th April, 1750.

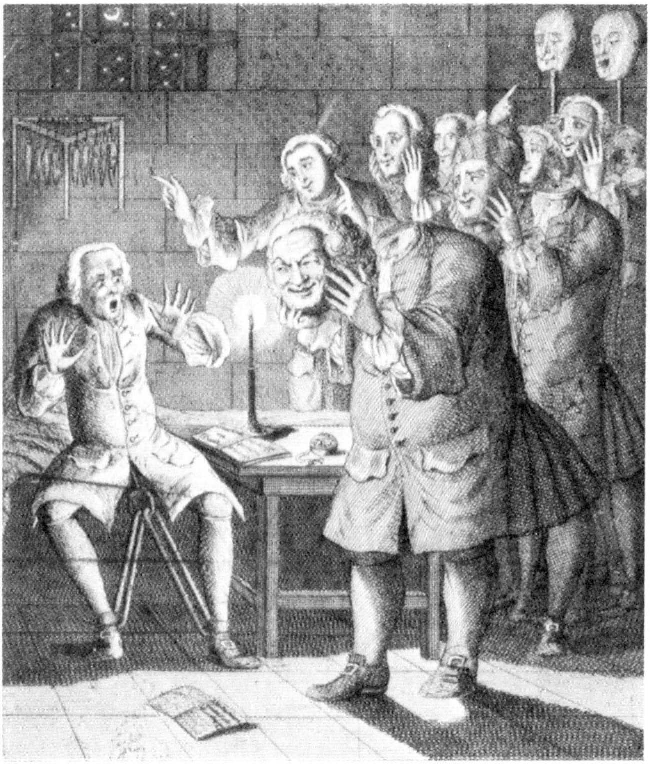

THRIFT, THE HANGMAN, TERRIFIED BY THE SPECTRES OF THE REBEL LORDS AND OTHERS IN THE CELLS OF NEWGATE, APRIL 1750

[*To face p.* 86.

although he was included in the Recorder's report of the 10th of May, he was respited at once for a fortnight, at the end of which time he was granted a further respite during His Majesty's pleasure. On the 26th of May it was arranged that he was to be transported to the American Colonies, where he also might have had the opportunity of becoming the ancestor of a prospective President.

It was not to be, however. The officials had decided that he was too valuable a man to lose, while the City Corporation was aware that a free pardon would exasperate the adherents of Prince Charlie. As soon as possible, therefore, he was released from the condemned cells, where he had lain in horrible suspense for many weeks, and when the free pardon at last was granted he was allowed "to enter again upon his office as executioner." Apparently he had resumed his work about the middle of September.[1]

The misery and hardships of these dreadful experiences affected Thrift's health very grievously. Although he continued to "hang on," accomplishing two of his most notable achievements, indeed, when he dealt with James Maclean during the next month and William Parsons in the following February, his eventful life was fast drawing to a close. He was able to fulfil his duties only for about eighteen months longer, dying in his home in Coal Yard, Drury Lane, on Tuesday, the 5th of May, 1752, after acting as public executioner for nearly eighteen years. Some time before the end his place had been taken by a substitute.

[1] *Whitehall Evening Post*, 18th September, 1750; *London Magazine*, 14th September, 1750.

Trouble, which had been his lot through life, followed him to the tomb. No funeral could have been more tumultuous. It was arranged to bury him in the churchyard of St. Paul's, Covent Garden, where on Saturday afternoon, the 11th of May, his body was brought in a hearse without any coach in attendance, in order not to attract attention. News of the occurrence, however, had been noised abroad and a great concourse had assembled.

The people were furious, showing their displeasure in the fashion of the mob of those days by throwing dangerous and unsavoury missiles. Volleys of stones and offal were hurled at the undertaker's men, and at one time it seemed as though the body would be torn out of the coffin. The presence of the new hangman, whose name appears in the journals as Tullis, added to the indignation of the multitude. Finally, at the suggestion, no doubt, of the Rev. Charles Tough, rector of the parish, the coffin was carried into the church. It was a successful manœuvre. In a little while the crowds had dispersed, and about eight o'clock in the evening it was possible to place Thrift in his grave.

It was imagined by some that the riot had occurred because the public disliked the idea of burying the common hangman in consecrated ground. Such an explanation attributed too much piety to the lower classes. The resentment was wholly parochial. Naturally, the inhabitants of St. Paul's, Covent Garden, were indignant that a man who had lived and died in the parish of St. Giles'-in-the-Fields should be interred in their burying-ground. As it was, there was not enough room in the churchyard for themselves. Of late years the soil had been so much raised, owing to the great number of burials, that it had reached the height of the parlour windows of the houses that surrounded it.[1] The parishioners of St. Paul's, Covent Garden, had an earnest objection to the bodies of strangers.

All trace of the grave of John Thrift is now lost. The churchyard has long since been paved and levelled and all the tombstones have been removed.

[1] Register of Burials at St. Paul's, Covent Garden; *London Daily Advertiser*, 14th May 1752; *Covent Garden Journal*, 16th May, 1752.

THOMAS TURLIS
(1752–1771)

VII

THOMAS TURLIS
(1752–1771)

I

WE now come to a very great hangman indeed. In fact, taking into consideration the length of his service and the magnitude of the work that he accomplished, it is not improbable that he is the greatest of them all. He held office for twenty years, passing through the tempestuous period of the Wilkes agitation, a time of riot and turbulence that must have tried the stoutest official nerves. He executed many supreme criminals, one of them being the only peer of the realm who has been hanged for murder. Moreover, the golden age of the gallows was dawning during his reign, since forgeries of all kinds were now capital offences, and thus the hangman was given more opportunities of achievement. For these reasons the figure of Thomas Turlis seems to stand out in greater prominence than that of any of his predecessors since the dawn of the century.

In the newspaper Press he is often called Tullis or Tollis, as many pronounced the name, but he spelt it Turlis when he wrote his signature in his neat and not uncultured hand. Every picture of him shows an alert, sharp-featured face, belonging evidently to a resolute man; and all the evidence that has come down to us indicates that he was a zealous, energetic, efficient executioner, imperturbable at a crisis, undismayed by brickbats and dead cats.

Unlike Thrift, he was seldom in trouble with the authorities, but there was one occasion—after he had been hangman for eleven years—when he might have been indicted on a capital charge. In January, 1763, he was caught stealing coals from a neighbour's cellar, whereupon he was taken into custody by the constables, who hauled him before the nearest magistrate. Too sensible to extenuate his guilt or deny it, he pleaded poverty as an excuse, declaring that he was in need of bread for his wife and children. Upon inquiry this was found to be true. Hanging had been a poor trade lately. For the moment the "Ketch" cupboard was bare and "Jack" himself had empty pockets.

Officialdom was sympathetic. Ashamed apparently that a valued servant should be reduced to such an extremity, the Sheriffs of London not only obtained a pardon, but also took steps to relieve Turlis from his financial embarrassment. He was appointed Finisher of the Law for the County of Surrey, a post that had become vacant recently owing to the death of one Jones, its previous occupant, the duties of which he could combine with those of hangman for the City of London and County of Middlesex.[1]

A little later in the year another unprecedented adventure befel him when he was engaged in a terrific scuffle with an Amazonian Irishwoman, named Hannah Dagoe, who was one of his clientèle at Tyburn. When the cart was drawn beneath the gallows she tore off the rope that bound her arms and threw her gloves, bonnet and

[1] *Lloyd's Evening Post*, 15th January, 1763.

cardinal—which were the hangman's perquisites—to a friend in the crowd. Turlis promptly pinioned her again, but once more she got loose from her cords, and struggled fiercely when he made another effort to fasten her, cursing him in the foulest language, daring him to hang her. Still the staunch Thomas refused to be intimidated. Although she dealt him a blow which almost knocked him out of the cart, he closed with her again. The rope that had pinioned her was lost in the fight, but he snatched off his garters and succeeded at last in binding her wrists. Daunted now by the implacable executioner, Hannah Dagoe made no further resistance. Yet, when the noose was slipped around her neck, she hurled herself out of the cart in a fit of rage before the signal was given, dying, so the press-men tell us, without a struggle.

During the whole of the adventure the constables seem to have made no attempt to assist, leaving Turlis to deal with the situation single-handed.

In the following December Tom's intrepidity had a still more severe test. At noon on Saturday, the 5th of December, 1763, it was his duty as common hangman to burn the *North Briton*, No. 45, in front of the Royal Exchange. Number 45 was a seditious publication, written by John Wilkes, Member of Parliament for Aylesbury, but the Government had fallen into disrepute, and Wilkes, being against it, had been acclaimed a popular hero. The Ministers, too, had made a martyr of him by an injudicious persecution. So the multitude that gathered in front of the Royal Exchange was a hostile one, prepared to go any lengths to thwart the authorities.

Sheriff Thomas Harley was in attendance in his chariot, with a great array of constables, and a small bonfire was laid and kindled, ready for the work in hand. Taking the copy of the *North Briton* from one of the officers, Turlis stepped forward to commit it to the flames. Then the mob arose in its might. Having pelted the officials with showers of dirt, it charged down upon them, putting everyone to flight. The windows of Sheriff Harley's coach were smashed to atoms by a faggot of wood, and he himself was wounded before he could escape. For a few moments the indomitable Turlis stood his ground. Although covered from head to foot with the filth that the crowd had showered upon him, he managed to thrust the *North Briton* into the fire. A moment later a workman had sprung forward and rescued it, and the hangman was swept aside. Most of the constables now had been put to flight, their staves broken and many of their heads too, so Turlis, realizing that he might be beaten to death if he stayed, followed the example of the Sheriff and took refuge in the Mansion House.[1]

For many years the London mob was apt to demonstrate tumultuously on behalf of Wilkes, who, having been expelled from Parliament and convicted in a court of law, was obliged to flee the country to avoid imprisonment; and thus officialdom invariably ran the risk of personal injury whenever a crowd gathered together. Naturally, the public executioner suffered most of all from mob violence. The danger seemed very frequent during 1768 and 1769, when Wilkes, having been elected

[1] *Public Advertiser*, 5th, 6th, and 7th December, 1763; *Gentleman's Magazine*, 1763, p. 614.

member of parliament for Middlesex upon his return from exile, was not allowed by the Government to take his seat in the House of Commons. At this period the collection of a crowd invariably resulted in a wild demonstration on behalf of the popular idol, and many public executions were carried out by " Jack Ketch " at the peril of his life.

Two extracts from the *Public Advertiser* are sufficient to show how hazardous it was in those days to be an executioner.

> " *Wednesday*, 20*th April*, 1768. Turlis, the Common Hangman was much hurt and bruised by the mob throwing stones at the execution of three malefactors at Kingston."
>
> " *Monday*, 6*th March*, 1769. On Friday, a tradesman, convicted of wilful and corrupt perjury, stood in and upon the Pillory in High Street, Southwark, and was severely treated by the populace. They also pelted Turlis, the executioner, with stones and brickbats, which cut him in the Head and Face in a terrible manner."

But we never read in any of the newspapers that the intrepid Tom ever played the part of a craven.

Sunshine comes, however, even into a hangman's life, and unpleasant jobs have their compensations. It must be allowed that the office of executioner at this period had become a lucrative one. Tom Turlis was public whipper as well as public hangman, and whippings had never before been so numerous. A receipted bill, signed by Turlis in June, 1767, proves that he earned the sum of four pounds in two months by his flagellations.

APRIL SESSIONS, 1767.

	£	s.	d.
Horsewhipping May the 4th.		7	6
For whipping of George Cane at Isleworth.		10	0
For whipping of Elizabeth Fletcher.		5	0
For whipping of George Cane at Isleworth.		10	0
JUNE SESSIONS.			
For whipping of Sarah Johnson.		5	0
For whipping of Anne Eaton.		5	0
For whipping of Timothy McCarthy from one end of the Haymarket to the other end.		5	0
For whipping of Mary Dolley, from Cavendish Square to Duke Street, Tyburn Road.		10	0
Horse hiring, June the 10th.		7	6
For whipping of Abraham Johnson from Mile End Turnpike to London Hospital.		10	0
For whipping of Jane Hodgson from one end of Nightingale Lane to the other end.		5	0
For a Quarter's wages due at Midsummer.	2	10	0
	6	10	0

Received June the 30th, 1767, of the Sheriff of Middlesex the sum of six pounds ten shillings by the hand of Mr. George Scarth in full of the Demands.

*£*6 10*s.* o*d.* THOMAS TURLIS.[1]

The whipped ones were tied to the cart's tail, which accounts for the hiring of a horse, but no mention is made in the above bill of any gratuities received from persons who had been hanged, which was a separate matter.

II

During his long tenure of office Turlis witnessed many essential reforms in the ceremonial of Tyburn that added to its solemnity and impressiveness. Of these most important by far was the removal of the Triple Tree, the permanent triangular erection which had stood

[1] "Notes from a Collector's Catalogue," A. W. Oxford, p. 31.

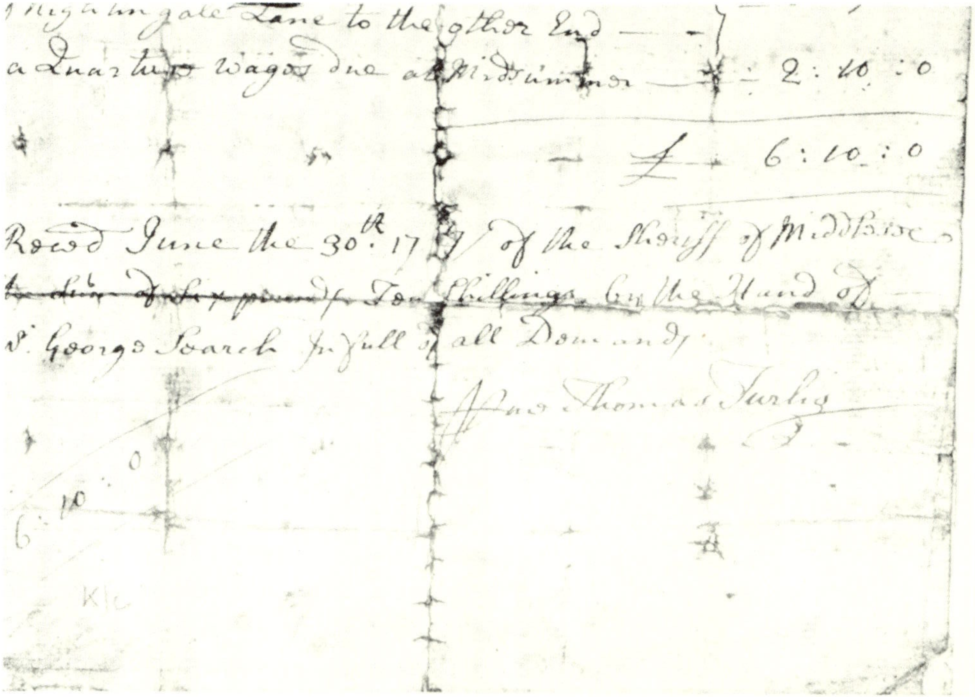
Nightingale Lane to the other End —
a Quarters Wages due at Midsummer — : 2 : 10 : 0
£ 6 : 10 : 0
Recd June the 30th 17[illegible] of the Sheriff of Middlesex
[illegible] Ten Shillings by the Hand of
Mr George Search in full of all Demands
Thomas Turlis

SIGNATURE OF THOMAS TURLIS, THE HANGMAN, IN 1767

[*To face p.* 98.

where it was for centuries. Traffic was increasing along both the Edgware and the Tyburn roads, making it necessary to clear away all inconvenient obstacles. So, some time between the 18th of June and the 3rd of October in the year 1759, the ancient landmark was pulled down. In its stead a "new Moving Gallows" was conveyed in a cart to the place of execution on every hanging-day.[1]

The business of setting up the gallows, with its slow, inexorable progress, perhaps impressed the crowd more forcibly than the old familiar spectacle of the Triple Tree, and certainly it gratified the passion of officialdom for dramatic effect. Soon after the institution of the "new Moving Gallows" the Sheriffs of London began to take more interest in hanging-days, attending the executions frequently in person. The pageantry of the March to Tyburn was augmented by the presence of the chariots of the Shrievalty. It was the Hon. Thomas Harley and Richard Blunt, whose year of office coincided with the early riots in favour of Wilkes, who were the first Sheriffs to superintend an execution since the punctilious Alderman Janssen fourteen years previously. On the 12th of October, 1763, they accompanied the procession in their coach and sat on horseback while the criminals were being turned off. To add to the solemnity of the scene, they had ordered that the tumbrils in which the condemned men were conveyed from Newgate should be draped in black cloth.[2]

[1] "Tyburn Tree," Alfred Marks, pp. 69, 70; *The London Chronicle*, 22nd September, 1759.

[2] *St. James's Chronicle*, 13th October, 1st and 22nd November, 1763.

It was about this time also that the custom was revived of permitting a malefactor of importance to ride to Tyburn in a mourning coach instead of in an open cart like the common folk. This privilege, indeed, had been granted to William Baker, a sugar refiner, hanged by Thrift for forgery on the 31st of December, 1750, but it had fallen into disuse ever since. On the 15th of January, 1767, however, one Samuel Orton, Clerk of the Court of Requests in Southwark, condemned for forging letters of attorney, went to his death in a coach of his own; and from this time onward any person who could afford the expense was allowed a similar luxury.

It was on an occasion of this kind that Turlis took part in the most magnificent procession that has ever made the March to Tyburn. The cortege commenced its journey from the Tower of London, where the chief actor of the day was imprisoned, since he was a criminal of the highest rank, Laurence, Earl Ferrers, by name, who had been condemned by his peers to be hanged for murder. His crime was brutal and commonplace, for he had shot and killed his steward in a fit of frenzy, and should have been locked up in a madhouse long before as a homicidal maniac. In deference to his station in life, the Sheriffs had suggested that he should ride in a mourning coach like Mr. William Baker in the years gone by, but he declined the offer, requesting instead that he should be allowed to use his own landau. The boon was granted, and bearing in mind that a peer of the realm might never again pay a visit to Tyburn, the officials determined to make the most of the opportunity of pageantry.

The execution took place on the 5th of May, 1760,

seven months after the abolition of the Triple Tree, so the Sheriffs were able to mark the importance of the occasion by preparing a new and elaborate scaffold. It was proposed also that a silken rope should be used, but this was found to be impossible, there not being time enough to manufacture one. The Ferrers landau, drawn by six horses and attended by liveried servants, in which the Earl was seated dressed in a white satin wedding suit, provided a suitable nucleus around which to construct the pageant. First marched a very large body of constables from the county of Middlesex, preceded by one of the high constables. Then came two parties of the Grenadier Guards, one mounted, the other on foot, followed by Sheriff Errington in the official chariot. Next in order was Lord Ferrers' carriage and six, surrounded by a company of horse soldiers and more of the Grenadier Guards. Sheriff Vaillant followed in his public carriage, and the rejected mourning coach brought up the rear, along with a hearse and six horses, which was to convey his lordship's corpse to the dissecting-room at Surgeons' Hall. It took nearly three hours for the procession to travel from the Tower to Tyburn.

The new scaffold was a novel structure, consisting of a wide platform across which extended a stout beam, supported on either side by a tall post. Beneath the cross-beam there was a little raised stage which could be lowered at will, leaving the criminal suspended. All was covered with black baize and there were black silk cushions to kneel upon during prayers. When the landau arrived at the gallows Lord Ferrers was received by both the Sheriffs, who led him up the steps with stately deference.

The poor madman refused to have any religious services except the Lord's Prayer, and, this being finished, he asked to see the executioner in the approved fashion, as though he was a rebel earl. Turlis came forward at once, brisk and business-like and begged for pardon, whereupon Lord Ferrers replied :—

" I freely forgive you, as I do all mankind, and hope myself to be forgiven."

Taking five guineas from his pocket, he offered them to the hangman, but the assistant executioner pressed forward at that moment and snatched the money away. The company manners of Tom Turlis were not proof against such an outrage. Angry as a butcher when the cur steals a prime joint from the counter underneath his nose, he turned upon " Jack Ketch " junior, and, calling him all the names he could remember, he demanded restitution. Sheriff Vaillant had to intervene to make peace.

No doubt the under-hangman was compelled to restore the gratuity, for Turlis proceeded to perform his duties without further protest. Lord Ferrers was guided to the raised stage beneath the fatal beam, his neckcloth was removed, and a white cap, which he had brought in his pocket, was put upon his head. Then, when his arms had been bound with a black silk sash, for a common cord could not be used upon a man of his rank, the noose was placed around his neck.

" Am I right ? " he asked Turlis, who told him that all was in order.

Upon the signal being given, the raised stage sank a few inches, but the mechanism was faulty, and it did not fall low enough, so that the toes of the hanging man still

EXECUTION OF LORD FERRERS AT TYBURN

[*To face p.* 102.

touched the boards. Rushing to his side, Turlis and his mate strove to put him out of his pain by pulling his legs. But four minutes had gone by before he was dead.

No greater crowd had ever been present at an execution or lined the streets to watch the procession. The trial for murder of a peer of the realm by the House of Lords in Westminster Hall, the imprisonment of the convict in the Tower of London, the passage to Tyburn of the condemned man in a landau and six dressed in his wedding suit, the unconventional scaffold and the rumour that his lordship would be hanged with a silken cord—all these uncommon occurrences united to form a combination of circumstances which excited popular curiosity to the highest pitch. The people were not at all incensed against Lord Ferrers, who, on the contrary, was a popular criminal. Indeed, everyone was grateful to him for providing an entertainment far better than any circus.

Another quarrel between Turlis and his henchman took place after the body was cut down, both executioners fighting for the rope, and, according to an eye-witness, the one who lost it burst into tears. No name is mentioned, but certainly the tearful one was not intrepid Tom, who was hardly the sort of man to be humiliated by an understrapper.

III

Undoubtedly the Ferrers drama was the greatest incident in the career of Turlis, and it must have consoled him for not having hanged Eugene Aram of Knaresborough—the most illustrious criminal of his age—who passed through the hands of the Yorkshire executioner in the previous year. But there were several other very conspicuous persons whom Turlis sent to another world during his long term of office. The chief of these were a Jacobite rebel, two famous forgers, and a murderer and a murderess.

The rebel was poor Dr. Archibald Cameron, one of those " out in '45," who was condemned to be hanged, drawn and quartered when they caught him at last, although eight years had passed since the rebellion. He was one of the most humane and benevolent of men, but no mercy was shown to him, unless indeed the omission of dismemberment can be regarded as an act of mercy. All the rest of the horrible sentence was carried out. On the 7th of June, 1753, the unhappy physician was dragged to Tyburn on a hurdle, and after hanging by the neck for twenty minutes—another favour—he was taken down and disembowelled. Turlis had only held office for twelve months, but seems to have done his duty efficiently and shown a tenderness to the unhappy man that was commented upon by the Press.

The two forgers were celebrities of their kind. John Ayliffe, the first of them, who was hanged at Tyburn on the " new Moving Gallows " on the 19th of November, 1759, had not embezzled a large amount of money, but he became almost a popular hero because it was believed that he had been prosecuted unjustly by the unpopular Henry Fox, the Paymaster-General, owing to a private grudge. Ayliffe was a man of some position, having a right to the title of Esquire; and, being a reprobate as well, the common people regarded him as an attractive criminal. In consequence of his behaviour in Newgate, he had been suspected of pusillanimity, the curiosity of the public becoming more intense in consequence. Still, no one could have shown more courage on the fatal day, and he gave Turlis no trouble. Ever afterwards Fox was regarded as his murderer.

John Rice, the second of Tom Turlis's great forgers, was a defaulter of some magnitude, for he stole Government securities amounting to nearly £70,000 by forging powers of attorney. A stockbroker with a considerable business, he owed his ruin to speculation and extravagance. Great excitement was caused in the City when the extent of his defalcations became known, and when it was ascertained furthermore that the swindler had absconded to Flanders. Pressure was put upon the Government by the Bank of England to commence negotiations with the view to an extradition, to which the Court of France eventually agreed.

Such a transaction had not occurred within the memory of man, and there was much excitement when the British Government succeeded in dragging the forger away from his refuge. Crowds met him on his arrival at Dover. Whenever his post-chaise halted at an inn during the journey to London everyone in the place flocked to see him. Naturally, there was no chance of saving his life. The sum total of his thefts was unprecedented, and stern example was necessary. When brought to trial he was condemned to death.

John Rice proved a gentle and penitent criminal on his day at Tyburn, which fell upon the 4th of May, 1763. The enormous mob had been attracted by his notoriety, but during the final scene its attention was diverted from him by his two companions. One of these was Hannah Dagoe, the rebellious Irish-woman, who attracted every eye during her bout of fisticuffs with Turlis. And the other was a flamboyant young highwayman, named Paul Lewis, with gold lace and a nosegay, who played bombastic antics all the way down the Oxford Road. Nevertheless, Rice won sympathy from the better portion of the crowd by his "pious conduct," and we are told that there was much weeping. He is said to have been the only stockbroker who was ever hanged, which suggests that lucky escapes have been prevalent. Or perhaps Providence has not always attended to business.[1]

Tom's first-class murderer was an artist, named Theodore Gardelle, a Swiss by birth, who painted miniatures. He was a gentle, inoffensive soul, fond of a pretty face and prone to gallantry. Happening to take lodgings in Leicester Square at the house of Mrs. Anne King, who was a buxom and attractive woman, his "amorous propensities" became excited and he resolved to be her lover. Mrs. King, however, rated herself highly and spurned the poor painter.

Naturally, her obduracy increased Gardelle's passion. In the belief that it was useless to sigh at the feet of his mistress, he made up his mind to lay forcible siege to her person, and one morning he entered her room while she was still asleep. Awakening in alarm, Mrs. King put up a stout resistance. She was a big powerful woman and gave her assailant a buffet in the chest that sent him reeling backwards. Then, enraged at the insult offered to her, she sprang out of bed and beat him with all her might.

[1] For the cases of Ayliffe and Rice see "Trial of Henry Fauntleroy and Other Famous Trials for Forgery" (*Notable British Trials*), pp. 156–72.

TURLIS HANGING A CRIMINAL AT SMITHFIELD IN 1761

[*To face p.* 106.

Staggered by the unexpected attack and almost stunned, Gardelle fancied that she was going to kill him. Scarcely knowing what he was doing, he caught up the nearest weapon, which happened to be a heavy poker, and struck a blow at the angry woman. Unfortunately the blow was more vigorous than he intended, and, falling upon her head, it felled her to the floor, where she lay senseless, with the blood pouring from a gash in her temple. Gardelle believed that he had killed her. It seemed that his only chance of concealing the crime was to dispose of the corpse. In a wild panic he severed her head with his clasp knife. Later he dismembered the body.

There were no other lodgers in the house, and having discharged the only maid-servant upon a plausible pretext, the murderer was able to proceed with his horrible work without interference. For the next five days he laboured frantically to remove every trace of his crime, burning some portion of the body in the parlour fire, hiding other parts in the garret or in outhouses or throwing them down the privy. Eventually the neighbours became suspicious. They could not understand why Mrs. King's house remained shut up. They wished to know the cause of the dense smoke that was pouring from the chimneys. In due course a warrant was obtained, and the constables caught Gardelle red handed.

All crimes in which the body of the victim had been dissected and dispersed invariably cause the greatest excitement and indignation, and the murder in Leicester Square became a popular horror. Gardelle was regarded as a monster of cruelty, the vilest of the vile. Yet crimes of this sort, revolting though they appear, in most cases are unpremeditated. A man who plans a murder beforehand is not so shortsighted as to embarrass himself with the cutting up and concealment of the body. The deliberate criminal chooses poison as a weapon, or arranges an alibi, or provides means of flight. On the contrary, the man with no intention of doing bodily harm, but who becomes a murderer through a chance blow, is the man who is obliged to dispose of the body by dismemberment. Gardelle, who never intended to kill, is surely a less detestable wretch than the poisoner.[1]

He was hanged as high as Haman on the 4th of April, 1761, in the Haymarket at the corner of Panton Street, as near as possible to the scene of his crime, for he could not suffer in Leicester Square, because it contained a royal residence. An indignant crowd attended the scene, and greeted the culprit with groans and hisses. Afterwards he was hung in chains on Hounslow Heath.

The next famous criminal to be executed by Turlis was a midwife named Elizabeth Brownrigg, who was hanged at Tyburn on the 14th of September, 1767, for flogging to death a female apprentice. Corporal punishment was the lot of children of the period, and had Mrs. Brownrigg been content to truss the girl, although she was sixteen years old, and birch her soundly she would have done nothing unusual. But it is not improbable that the woman was insane, her cruelties being so abominable. Whenever the apprentice committed the least fault she was stripped and horsewhipped, and was kept continually without food and made to sleep half naked in a coal cellar. Savage floggings with a broomstick or the

[1] "Memories of William Hickey," 115–19. Hickey gives the most rational account. He was a lawyer.

butt end of a whip were inflicted upon the unhappy Mary Clifford several times every day.

At last the girl died, and Mrs. Brownrigg was arrested for murder. From the first she was the most unpopular of criminals, cruelty to an apprentice being one of the most odious offences in the eyes of the common folk. Her condemnation was hailed with joy by the crowd in the Sessions House yard, and she made the journey to Tyburn through an exulting mob. After she was hanged her body was dissected at Surgeons' Hall in the Old Bailey, where her skeleton was preserved for many years. In spite of this emphatic warning it is a curious fact that a milliner in Bruton Street, named Sarah Metyard, was executed in the following summer along with her daughter for almost a similar crime.

Turlis lived for three years after the Metyard sensation. His end came suddenly, as he, in common with most men, would have wished it. On the 27th of March, 1771, he hanged five malefactors, one of whom struck him a blow in the face, when being led to the cart. It was his last execution at Tyburn, and it is characteristic of his stormy life that there should have been turmoil. A few days later the efficient fellow was dead, dying " on the road " on his return from a hanging at Kingston.[1] The newspapers do not state whether he passed away in the room of an inn or, more appropriately, in the cart that was bringing him back to London.

His memory survived him longer than that of any hangman since the days of Jack Ketch. It was still green six months after his death, which is indicated by a

[1] *Public Advertiser*, 12th April, 1771; cf. Musgrave's Obituary, VI, 131.

facetious letter, purporting to have been written by him, printed in the *Public Advertiser* of the 25th of October, 1771. And forty years later, a satirical magazine made an attempt to establish his name as a generic term for all Finishers of the Law by referring invariably to the hangman of the day as Mr. Thomas Tollis.[1] Which shows what subtle pitfalls lie in the paths of the adventurous historian.

[1] *The Satirist or Monthly Meteor*, VII, 221–3, 272, 310, 332, 371; XI, 18–24.

EDWARD DENNIS
(1771–1786)

VIII

EDWARD DENNIS

(1771–1786)

I

Taking all things into consideration, there is no doubt that Turlis was followed by a worthy successor, one who has many claims to be considered a great hangman. Edward Dennis seems to have fulfilled most of the requirements necessary to such a reputation. The length of his service was fifteen years, a sufficient test of his capabilities. Although it was not his lot to hang such a picturesque criminal as Lord Ferrers, he had to deal with four others infinitely more famous than any four of whom Tom Turlis could boast. And he has a unique achievement to his credit, being the only chief hangman in the category who carried on business both at Tyburn and the Old Bailey. For he was hanging for twelve years at the gallows in the Oxford Road, and he went on hanging still when the place of execution was removed to Debtor's Door, outside Newgate prison. In addition, he has another claim to distinction, since during his reign the gaol itself, including the Old Gateway, was pulled down and an immense new building erected on the same site.

In character Dennis appears to have been wholly dissimilar to the neurotic Thrift or the alert Turlis. One visualizes him as a stubborn creature, plodding along obtusely in his own way, a steady and industrious workman, but rather stupid now and then, with little more imagination than the horse that pulled his gallows-cart. It is this occasional stupidity that has prevented him from reaching the highest place in his profession, and is the reason why he must be ranked below Tom Turlis and William Marwood.

During his first year of office he took part in an execution which, although no famous criminal was concerned in it, has remained one of the most memorable, because it is one of the most pitiful, in the annals of Tyburn. It happened on the 16th of October, 1771, and a handsome young woman was its unhappy heroine, Mary Jones by name, who had been condemned to death for stealing four pieces of muslin, worth £5 10*s*., from a shop on Ludgate Hill. Since nearly two hundred persons had been tried for larceny of various kinds at the last Sessions, stern examples were deemed necessary, but the youth and good looks of Mary Jones might have gained her a reprieve "had she not behaved in court with great insolence, cursing the Judges."

Contemporary press-men are unanimous as to her beauty, writing of her fair complexion and wealth of golden hair. All are agreed, too, that the crime was her first one, to which she had been driven in desperation. For a press-gang had carried off her husband, and she had been reduced to poverty, and had committed the theft to buy food for her two babies. The parish officers corroborated her story, but her conduct in court had outweighed all considerations of mercy, and it was decreed that the sentence of the law should be fulfilled.

She was carried to Tyburn with four male felons, but

in spite of her youth and beauty the crowd in the streets does not seem to have pitied her overmuch, although, according to one account, which, happily, is uncorroborated, she rode in the fatal cart with her baby at her breast. It was the same at the gallows. No one appears to have felt much sympathy for the poor girl. A penitent thief, who delivered a long and sanctimonious address, and an obstreperous sailor, who dealt Edward Dennis a lusty blow when he was about to adjust the noose, interested the mob far more than the young mother. The illustrious Mr. Wilkes, also, who was present in his capacity of Sheriff, was not shocked in the least by the sad tragedy.

Five years later, however, the whole nation was roused to pity by the remembrance of her cruel death. During a debate in the House of Commons Sir William Meredith told the story of Mary Jones in a speech of passionate eloquence, moving his callous hearers as seldom they had been moved hitherto. And henceforth the sad tale has served as a classic instance of the iniquity of the bad old laws.[1]

Before Ned Dennis reached the culminating point in his career, when he was called upon to operate on criminals of the highest rank, he hanged one very notorious person, who is entitled to Class Number Two in the Newgate Calendar. This individual was John Rann, a highwayman of some renown, with the nickname of Sixteen-string Jack, owing to his habit of wearing breeches with eight strings at each knee. Like so many other high-tobymen—although his deeds were worthy only of the low toby—he had graduated as a

[1] *Notes and Queries*, 11, Series IV, 414; Parl. Hist. XIX, 237–8.

gentleman's servant, acquiring horsemanship through being groom, post-boy, and coachman. But his riding was neither fast nor furious. His deeds of plunder were not very audacious or very clever. Most of his renown was earned by a flashy costume and bombastic swaggerings.

Two circumstances only make him worthy of remembrance. Not long before Sixteen-string Jack was arrested and condemned he attended an execution at Tyburn. Forcing his way through the ring of constables around the gallows, he asked that he might be allowed to stay there. "For," he continued, "perhaps it is very proper that I should be a spectator on this occasion." Which shows that the rascal had humour. The fame of a mistress whom he left behind when he met the fatal accident at Tyburn has cast a lustre also upon his memory. This Laetitia Darby grew more fastidious in her choice of lovers after his death, becoming, under the name of Smith, one of the most prominent of the frail sisterhood. Her first achievement was to captivate Frederick, Duke of York, son of George III, whose friendship with her lasted for several years; and subsequently she managed to persuade Sir John Lade, the sporting baronet, to make her his lawful wife. She was a skilful whip and a good judge of horseflesh, and better known on the turf than any woman of her day.

Not long after the execution of Jack Rann, an under-hangman, named William Brunskill, was appointed by the Sheriffs to assist Dennis. Proving himself a zealous, amenable collaborator, he was retained in his post, staying on until after the death of his chief, whom he succeeded in his office. He is the only other hangman, besides Dennis, who acted as executioner both at Tyburn and in the Old Bailey, though, of course, in the former place he officiated only as a subordinate.[1]

II

The two first criminals of real eminence to be hanged by Ned Dennis were the twin brothers Robert and Daniel Perreau, who suffered at Tyburn on the 17th of January, 1776. The former was an apothecary with a good business, a respectable married man and the father of a family; the latter was a wastrel and ne'er-do-well, living by his wits and upon the earnings of a dissolute mistress. In addition to these immoralities, David Perreau was also a gambler in the Funds, and he induced his brother Robert to take part in his speculations. Losing money and being on the verge of bankruptcy, they forged bills of acceptance for many thousand pounds.

When detected and brought to trial, there were two reasons that made their case into a *cause célèbre*, which created more excitement throughout the British Isles than any since the affair of Lord Ferrers. Many persons believed that Robert Perreau had been an innocent dupe, and were shocked that a man of his respectability should be in such a position. But what gave far greater piquancy to the crime was the personality of Mrs. Margaret Caroline Rudd, the mistress of Daniel Perreau, who was accused by both the brothers of being the forger and the instigator of the forgeries. She was a lovely woman, as well as a most clever one, and for several months it was doubtful whether she or the Perreaus would go to the gallows.

[1] Rep. 219, f. 510 (Guildhall Record Office).

In the end the case was decided in her favour. The brothers were tried and convicted on the clearest evidence. Mrs. Rudd was tried and acquitted, the verdict obviously being a just one. Following this result the Perreaus, who had been respited until now, were both ordered for execution. Great efforts were made to save Robert, but it was decided that they must die together.

It was a memorable execution day. Deep snow lay upon the ground and there was a keen frost. A fog hung over the house-tops. The two brothers rode to Tyburn in a mourning coach. They were preceded by an open cart, which was covered with black baize, containing an impudent boy highwayman in a crimson coat and a gold lace hat and two tatterdermalion Jews, condemned for housebreaking. Two wretched creatures, whose crime was coining were drawn along on a hurdle afterwards. Never before, even on the atonement day of Lord Ferrers, had such a stupendous multitude lined the streets. "The unfortunate brothers" were a popular attraction.

The gallows on this occasion was a double one, the cross-beam on the left-hand side being reserved for the Jews and that on the right for the five Christians. Upon the arrival of the cortège the Jews were placed in one cart and the coiners and the highwayman in another, made specially broad for occasions like this when several convicts had to be hanged together. While their companions were being tied up the Perreaus were allowed to remain in their coach, where they sat calm and imperturbable, regarding the awful spectacle without a tremor. When at last they, too, were wanted, Edward Dennis, whom they had appeased with a gift, approached with an abrupt bow, and, opening the door of the coach, beckoned to them to descend. Then, guiding each in turn, he helped them to climb into the spacious cart beside the three others. Both remained unshaken to the end, joining fervently in prayer with the Rev. John Villette, the Ordinary, and continued to protest that they were innocent. When all was ready Dennis made a last inspection of the halters and pulled down the caps, while Brunskill attended in like manner to the Jews. As the cart drew away from beneath their feet the hands of the unhappy brothers were clasped together, remaining so for a full half-minute while they swung side by side, until they passed away into unconsciousness.

The execution of the Rev. William Dodd, D.D., on the 27th of June, 1777, made an even greater hubbub. Dodd was a popular preacher and a man of some ability, known to everyone as the "Macaroni Parson," owing to his foppery. Extravagance caused his ruin. He fell into debt and committed forgery to save himself from a temporary embarrassment. Unlike the Perreaus, however, he did not exist by swindling for many years. His forgery was a single one, the passing of a bond drawn upon a favourite pupil, and immediately the fraud was detected he was able to offer a complete restitution.

Although tried and convicted, it was never believed that he would be brought to the gallows. He had done many good works during his life; his preaching had attracted fashionable congregations. There was a great popular outcry for a reprieve, and Dr. Johnson made strenuous efforts on his behalf. It seemed certain that he would gain a pardon. Then hopes of mercy grew fainter and fainter as the days passed by without result, while an atmosphere of melancholy seemed to settle upon the whole of London. Meanwhile, in the gloom and loneliness of one of the condemned cells in Newgate, the miserable Dr. Dodd was setting down his "Thoughts in Prison," a work that was destined to live long after him.

When at last the ministers of the Crown proved inexorable, and it was decreed that the unfortunate man must die, his friends began to plan fantastic schemes to resuscitate him after he was cut down from the gallows. It was arranged that he should be taken with all speed to the house of an undertaker in Goodge Street, off the Tottenham Court Road, where a distinguished surgeon—either Percivall Pott or William Hunter—would be ready with every expedient known to medical science. It was whispered that Dennis had been bribed to use the doctor as tenderly as possible, and had promised to adjust the noose in such a manner that the hanged man would be able to survive. Rumours were spread also that a silver tube was going to be inserted in his throat.

There had been enormous crowds at the executions of Jack Sheppard and Jonathan Wild, Lord Ferrers and the brothers Perreau, but the crowd that assembled when Dr. Dodd was taken to Tyburn was the greatest that had ever been known. Fearing a rescue, the authorities had brought two thousand soldiers into Hyde Park. The doomed man was allowed to make the journey in a mourning coach, accompanied by a clerical friend and by the Rev. John Villette, Ordinary of Newgate, who held office from 1773 until 1799, and is perhaps the most famous Ordinary of them all. Every window along the route of the procession was filled with spectators; the people stood, many rows deep, from Newgate to Edgware Road. Never before was there such universal sympathy. There were few dry eyes as the unhappy clergyman passed along to his death.

For it was the day of his death, since all the preparations to save his life were unavailing, although Dennis seems to have done his best—as far as he was able, with the eye of the Under-Sheriff upon him—to help the conspirators. Having arranged the halter with the utmost care, he descended from the cart in order to lead away the horse himself, lest there should be a sudden jolt. Just before the fatal moment Dodd was observed to bend down to whisper earnestly to his executioner, causing all those who had heard rumours of the intended resuscitation to imagine that he was asking that his legs should not be pulled. This was not so. He had stooped to listen to what the hangman was saying to him.

"You must not move an inch," muttered Dennis.

Anxious that his knot should not be disarranged, he was giving a last injection to the prisoner.

"You must not move an inch," said Dennis.

And when the cart drew away he ran back immediately, taking hold of the doctor's limbs as though to steady him.

Skilful craftsman though Dennis was, the task imposed proved beyond his powers. Perhaps a shrewd and resourceful hangman such as Tom Turlis might have hoodwinked the Under-Sheriff, cutting down the body at the end of half an hour on the plea that the clocks were slow, or making Brunskill hold it up as long as possible under the pretence of leg pulling. Hangman Ned unfortunately had no initiative. In all probability Dr.

Dodd was dead when cut down at the end of an hour, but certainly life was extinct when he reached the house where the surgeon awaited him. Through some mischance it was a long time before he was put into the hearse. Owing to the press of the crowd the journey in search of medical aid was a slow one. Although the doctors used every means in their power, it was impossible to restore animation.[1]

The next and third *cause célèbre* in which Dennis took part also concerned a clergyman. It was a case of murder too, and a *crime passionnel*—so made greater commotion than mere forgery—the crime of the Rev. James Hackman, who shot Miss Martha Ray, the mistress of Lord Sandwich, First Lord of the Admiralty, in the portico of Covent Garden theatre after the conclusion of the performance of " Love in a Village," just as she was stepping into her coach. Many circumstances combined to excite public interest. The charm of poor Miss Ray, the high position of her protector, and the infatuation of the love-sick Hackman, who had slain his victim through jealousy—these among other reasons helped to inflame the curiosity of everyone.

Hackman, of course, was condemned to death, and was hanged at Tyburn on the 19th of April, 1779. That a clergyman should be brought to the gallows for murder seemed a most frightful thing, and a greater crowd than ever attended the execution. Except for the fact that James Boswell accompanied Hackman in

1 For the cases of the Perreau brothers and Dr. Dodd see " Trial of Henry Fauntleroy and other Famous Trials for Forgery " (*Notable British Trials*), pp. 173–95 ; " Tyburn Tree," Alfred Marks, pp. 261–3.

the mourning coach, there was nothing remarkable about the final scene. The murderer was penitent enough to satisfy even the Rev. Villette, and Dennis was adroit, although he does not appear to have received any gratuity, as he did when the Perreaus and Dr. Dodd met their doom. Probably he was dissatisfied, since it is the common fault of hangmen to be too expectant. And the unimaginative fellow could not console himself with the knowledge that during the past three years his dealings with great criminals had written his fame amidst the stars.

III

The new gaol of Newgate was now complete. Its foundation stone had been laid in the year 1770 by William Beckford, then Lord Mayor, and it was finished seven years later, when the Old Gateway that spanned Newgate Street was pulled down. Sentimentalists will regret that the ancient landmark was not preserved. It would have made an imposing entrance to the new prison, and the roadway might have been diverted to pass around it.

The new prison was belauded by admiring contemporaries as the finest in Europe. Its façade extended for one hundred and seventy feet down the Old Bailey and one hundred and twenty feet along Newgate Street. Everyone of the former buildings had been demolished, except the Press yard and the condemned cells. Within there were light and airy rooms and two spacious quadrangles for the prisoners to take exercise. Externally it was a massive and imposing pile. Even John Howard the philanthropist admitted that it was a great improvement on the old gaol.

Three years, however, after it was finished, this new Newgate was destroyed for the most part during the Gordon Riots. It happened on the evening of the 6th of June, 1780, when the mob made an attack upon the prison in order to release some of their fellow rioters, who had been arrested for burning and pillaging the houses of Catholics on the previous day. The Keeper's residence in the centre of the façade in the Old Bailey was set on fire, the flames spreading to other parts of the building. Faggots and brushwood were piled against the great gate, which at last was burnt to tinder and fell with a crash into the quadrangle. Through the open door debtors and felons to the number of three hundred rushed forth in panic.

Their escape was only just in time, for the prison soon became a burning fiery furnace. The flames spread through the passages and corridors, engulfing the chapel on the top storey, spreading swiftly from cell to cell. Soon the whole of the interior was gutted, only the outside walls, uninflammable masses of stone, resisting destruction. Inside everything was obliterated, and the prison, which had cost £140,000, had to be rebuilt entirely. But the façade, both in the Old Bailey and in Newgate Street, was uninjured, remaining just the same as it was when George Dance, the architect, had designed it, until it was demolished finally in 1904, after an existence of nearly one hundred and thirty years.

The name of Edward Dennis has been associated for all time with the Gordon Riots, because Charles Dickens has made him a principal character in the story of "Barnaby Rudge," in which he is represented as one of the ringleaders in the attack on the gaol. The Ned

Dennis of the book, however, does not bear the least resemblance to the Ned Dennis of real life. The real Dennis had no reason for wishing to destroy the prison, which, indeed, was necessary to him in earning his daily bread. Nor did the real Dennis perish on the gallows to which Dickens consigned him, but died in his bed some years later. He played a minor part in the riots certainly, and got into trouble in consequence, but the trouble came about in a different manner.

On Wednesday, the 7th of June, the day after the destruction of Newgate, he was walking along Holborn between six and seven o'clock in the evening to his house in Newtoner's Street. Tumultuous crowds were parading the streets still, pillaging and destroying, and fires were blazing in many parts of the town. The rioters continued to attack the houses of known Catholics. Passing by New Turnstile, a passage leading to Lincoln's Inn Fields, Dennis noticed that a mob had collected in front of a chandler's shop, and he approached to discover what was happening. The shop belonged to Edmund Boggis, who was believed to be a Catholic, so the people were looting it.

A passion for destruction is latent in the hearts of all uneducated folks. No sooner did Dennis perceive what was going on than he took a hand in the impious work. He carried out furniture and he tore down pieces of wainscoting, casting them into a fire that was kindled in the street. People saw him and recognized him, and were glad to betray him to the authorities. In a little while it was common gossip that "Jack Ketch" had been helping the rioters. Greatly to his astonishment, Dennis was placed under arrest.

There are three possible explanations of his behaviour, for, not being a bigoted Protestant, it is certain that he was prompted by no anti-Catholic animosity. Either he was tipsy, or it was a piece of stupid horse-play, or he had acted as he did because he was compelled to do so by the mob. The last was a somewhat fantastic explanation, although not altogether incredible, and is the one which he chose for his defence when put upon his trial before James Adair, the Recorder, at the Old Bailey Sessions on Monday, the 3rd of July.[1] Two notable counsel appeared for the Crown, William Howarth, M.P., one of the most able men at the Bar, and William Norton, son of the late Speaker. There were five credible witnesses for the prosecution, all of whom told the same tale, viz. that Dennis had taken an active part in the work of pillage.

The Recorder was sympathetic towards the prisoner, admitting that there was no improbability in his statement that the mob had closed around him with the clamour, "Here's bloody 'Jack Ketch'; let's make him carry some to the fire," threatening to burn him unless he consented. The Recorder also acknowledged that the witnesses for the prosecution may have been prejudiced against the accused man "on account of the odious light in which Dennis stood as executioner." Nothing could have been more fair or more impartial than the summing-up. The jury, nevertheless, preferred to believe the evidence for the Crown. They were tradesmen of the neighbourhood, who had suffered loss and inconvenience during the late turmoil, and were indisposed to

[1] Old Bailey Session Papers (Guildhall Library); *Morning Chronicle*, 4th July, 1780; *Gazetteer*, 4th July, 1780.

give any accused " rioter " the benefit of the doubt. So they brought Dennis in guilty, and the Recorder was obliged to sentence him to death.

The poor stupid fellow lost all self-control. Throwing himself upon his knees, he howled for mercy.

" My will was innocent," he cried, " my body was compelled."

And he appealed to the Sheriffs, Aldermen and Lord Mayor to vouch that his behaviour had always been that of a quiet peaceable man.[1]

Newgate not being available, the condemned rioters were distributed among the other prisons of the metropolis. Dennis and his fellow convicts were lodged in the Tothillfields Bridewell, beyond the Horseferry Road. Here Mr. Smith, the Keeper, placed the hangman in a separate room, fearing, with justice, that he would be torn to pieces if left alone with his fellow prisoners. The wretched man appeared to abandon all hope of pardon when he found himself in a condemned cell. In a petition to the authorities he begged that his son might be allowed to succeed him, " a youth of sobriety and abilities, who would be a credit to the position "—which caused a jocund journalist to point out that, if the request were granted, the son would have to hang the father.

" Poor ' Jack Ketch,' " wrote the Rev. Dr. Warner to his friend George Selwyn, who had much regard for hangmen. " He who has swung so many must at last swing himself."

Ned Dennis, however, was not destined for the gallows. His suspense, too, was soon over. Two days after his

[1] *Morning Post*, 4th July, 1780; *Public Advertiser*, 7th, July, 1780.

condemnation the Recorder made his report. The name of Dennis was included in the list of capital convicts, but he was not ordered for execution. Later in the day it was announced that he had been respited, and in due course he received a free pardon, " so that he could hang his fellow rioters."

IV

It is uncertain when he resumed his duties, and the doubt involves another mystery. For during the next two or three weeks there were mishaps at several executions, the hangman bungling in his work deplorably. On one occasion no caps had been provided, and the ceremony was delayed while they were being found. At another time the executioner " rubbed off " the cap of a convict in full sight of the spectators as he was cutting him down. When Jonathan Stacey and George Staples were hanged at Moorfields for demolishing the Catholic chapel there, the gallows was conveyed to the wrong place, and when it had arrived at last the two convicts " struck against one another with great violence " after the cart drew away. At the execution of William Brown a fierce altercation arose between the hangman and the constables, the latter protesting that the rope was not adjusted properly. " Who ought to know best, you or I ? " retorted the hangman, refusing to alter the noose; and when the unfortunate Brown was turned off " he was twenty minutes dying."

" The present ' Jack Ketch ' is a disgrace to his office," wrote a correspondent in the *Public Advertiser* on the 11th of August. " He handles the unhappy convicts with as little concern as a butcher would a sheep or a bullock. . . . On Wednesday last he was much hooted by the populace."

It would be satisfactory to know the name of this persistent bungler. Had a new hangman been employed, or was it Brunskill who was proving inefficient, or had Dennis returned to his duties with shattered nerves and bewildered wits, thinking to gratify his employers by his ruthlessness? As we have seen, he could be very stupid on occasions.

A newspaper paragraph at this date gives complete information about the hangman's wages. Apparently the salary amounted to £30, with 6*s.* 8*d.* for each person executed and 5*s.* for every public whipping. Probably the earnings for the latter employment were no less than those of Turlis, or £2 a month, and, as thirty persons on an average must have met their deaths at Tyburn, Kennington Common and Kingston Hill during the course of the year, the fees for executions should have yielded an income of another £10.[1] Thus, the salary of £40, received by Price and Marvell, appears to have risen to £60 in the days of Dennis.

Dennis's last famous client was William Wynne Ryland, the engraver, who was hanged for forgery on the 29th of August, 1783. Although the case did not make the great popular appeal that those of the two clergymen had done, it caused much excitement in the world of art. For the prints of Ryland, both in stipple and mezzotint, were familiar to every collector, and he had been engraver to the King. The crime, too, for which he suffered was an artistic performance—the fabrication of one of the East India Company's bills of

[1] *Public Advertiser*, 14th July, 1780.

exchange—for the copy was a perfect replica of the original. When arrested poor Ryland had failed in his attempt to commit suicide, a circumstance that aroused sympathy still more.

Nothing noteworthy occurred at the execution of the unfortunate artist, except that the gallows was placed fifty yards nearer than usual to the wall of Hyde Park, while a thunderstorm delayed the ceremony for half an hour. Two carts were used to turn off the sufferers, six in all. Ryland met his death with dauntless courage, giving Dennis no trouble.

There were not many more executions at Tyburn, that of John Austin on the 7th of November of the same year being the last which took place there. Ever afterwards the felons convicted of capital crimes committed in the City of London or County of Middlesex were hanged on a scaffold in front of Newgate. The change was inevitable. The March to Tyburn had become an obstacle to traffic and a hindrance to business. The assemblage of unsavoury mobs was looked upon with fear and disgust in the West End of the town. The neighbourhood that had owed its renown to the Triple Tree for centuries was now a fashionable part of London, whose ungrateful residents did not approve of a gallows in their midst.

The change had one staunch opponent. "The age is running mad over innovations," grumbled Dr. Johnson. "All the business of the world is to be done in a new way; men are to be hanged in a new way; Tyburn itself is not safe from the fury of innovation . . . it is not an improvement: they object that the old method drew together a multitude of spectators. Sir, executions

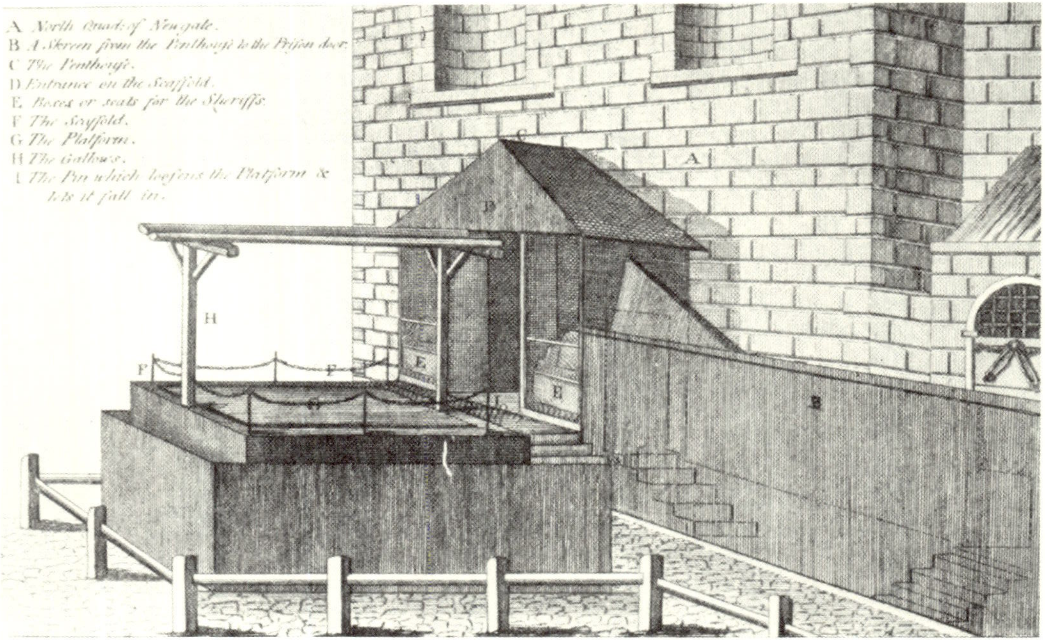

"THE NEW DROP," NEWGATE PRISON, 1783

[To face p. 131.

are intended to draw spectators. If they do not draw spectators they don't answer their purpose. The old method was most satisfactory to all parties; the public was gratified by a procession; the criminal was supported by it. Why is all this to be swept away?"

The new gallows at Newgate was a solid structure with two parallel cross-beams, a platform and a falling drop. Housed in a shed within the prison, it was dragged out by horses into its proper position in the street when it was needed. While in use it stood just outside the Debtor's Door, at right angles to the prison wall, its front projecting horizontally into the Old Bailey facing Ludgate Hill. On this scaffold a dozen prisoners could be executed together. In late years the houses which had divided the Old Bailey into two narrow lanes had been pulled down, making one broad thoroughfare at the northern end. On hanging days the spaces in front of the gaol and all adjacent streets from which a view was obtainable were packed with a joyful multitude. A hundred thousand people are said to have been present on several occasions. Dennis performed his first execution here on the 9th of December, 1783, when he and Brunskill hanged ten malefactors.

His days of usefulness were now nearing their close. He survived less than three years longer. One of the last occasions on which there is anything of note associated with him was in the year 1785, when the Sheriffs presented—or are said to have presented—a robe to him, which robe he "laid by on account of its inconvenience." History does not say how or why the robe was given to him, and there was probably some *jeu d'esprit* connected with it, but it is related that he sold the garment to a fortune-teller of the period, named Old Cain, soon after he received it.[1]

In the following year he died, passing away on Tuesday, the 21st of November, 1786, "in his apartments" in the Old Bailey, whither he had removed from Newtoner's Street to be nearer his work. There were numerous Press notices, in which he is styled—in addition, of course, to Jack Ketch and Finisher of the Law—by various facetious titles, such as Surveyor of the New Drop, Apparator of the Necklace and Yeoman of the Halter. Once again he is said to have recommended his son as his successor, declaring on his death-bed that the young man was "fit for that or any other office in which His Majesty might employ him." In another ribald publication he is made to boast that he has "never wanted for gin, tobacco, nor a woman," which possibly may be the lampoon of an enemy, although it must be acknowledged with regret that hangmen do not always observe the seventh commandment as obediently as they should.

Still, whatever may have been his moral imperfections, he was received into a burying-ground of the Church of England according to all the rights and ceremonies of the Church of England, the funeral taking place on the 26th of November, when he was buried at St. Giles'-in-the-Fields.[2]

[1] *The Attic Miscellany*, I, 167.

[2] *Morning Chronicle*, 24th November, 1786; *Morning Post*, 25th November, 1786; *Public Advertiser*, 25th November, 1786; *Rambler's Magazine*, IV., 447, 479; *Register of Burials*, St. Giles'-in-the-Fields.

WILLIAM BRUNSKILL
(1786-1814)

IX

WILLIAM BRUNSKILL

(1786–1814)

I

On Wednesday, the 22nd of November, the day after Edward Dennis died, William Brunskill was called upon to carry out an execution by himself in the Old Bailey. It was a formidable début for the new hangman, in spite of his dozen years experience as deputy, since seven malefactors had to be disposed of and there was a large and critical crowd, who knew that he had never taken the leading part before. Everything passed off without a hitch. Although extremely nervous, Brunskill acquitted himself as dexterously as his former chief could have done, and the seven penitents cannot have perceived any difference.

But after the bolt was shot there was a startling innovation in the ceremonial. The drop had fallen with the usual crash, and the seven white-capped bodies had sunk through the platform as far as their knees, swinging by seven stout ropes side by side like seven great pendulums, when the hangman advanced to the front of the platform in the manner of the star actor, and making a profound bow to the people, with his hand on his breast, seemed to inquire how they approved of his first performance. Now that his task was finished William Brunskill was overwhelmed by stage fright, and did not realize what he was doing.[1]

The incident, nevertheless, reveals much of the man's character. Throughout his long career as "Jack Ketch" he seems to have been an apologetic, rather cringing sort of person, ordering himself lowly and reverently towards his betters, always humble and long-suffering and intensely anxious to please. As a craftsman he was not in the first rank, and bungled things on more than one occasion, but he was painstaking certainly, and sober until his latter days, which unhappily cannot be said of every hangman.

In the first year of Brunskill's reign a new colony began to be used as the habitation of criminals who were "cast for transportation." Since the American rebellion in 1775 the Southern States had not been available for the reception of our convicts, who accumulated at home, in consequence, for several years, until another region could be found for them. At length, in 1785, it was decided to send them to Botany Bay in Australia. Before the end of the year no fewer than fifteen hundred, both male and female, and including husbands and wives, had been selected to make the voyage, and ships set sail with them periodically in due course. Thus, Virginia, Maryland and the two Carolinas ceased to provide a home for a most robust section of our population, after having profited exceedingly from their invasion, both physically and morally, for more than sixty years. What was America's loss became the profit of New South Wales.

Unluckily for Brunskill, the hangman's earnings fell

[1] *Morning Chronicle*, 23rd November, 1786; *Sussex Weekly Advertiser*, 4th December, 1786.

considerably during his first years of office. According to a sympathetic journalist, he was " not rewarded according to his merits," his wages being so trifling that he can hardly keep body and soul together. With the outbreak of the French war a large part of the criminal population was swept into the Services by the press-gangs or the militia ballot, and both whippings and executions were fewer in number. A general rise in prices, too, affected " Jack Ketch's " domestic expenditure adversely. In due course he was obliged to address a humble petition to the Court of Aldermen—the first of its kind, apparently, from such a source—which, although it does not appear in the Minute Books at Guildhall, was printed in the *Times* newspaper.

In this petition, set forth with his habitual humility, Brunskill entreated their lordships to grant him relief, pointing out that, being public executioner, he could not get any other employment, and explaining that he was obliged to keep an assistant, though his allowance was so small and his income so trifling as to be insufficient to maintain himself and his family. In the version published by the *Morning Post*, then a more ribald journal than the *Times*, he is made to allege, as a reason for demanding higher pay, that his family was large and that " business is bad." The Court of Aldermen is said to have referred the matter to the Sheriffs.

II

A most barbarous custom was forbidden by law in the early days of Brunskill's tenure of office. Until 1790 women were not only burnt at the stake for husband murder, but for coining or debasing the coinage as well, and an execution of this kind had taken place in front of Newgate shortly before the death of Edward Dennis. It happened on the 21st of June, 1786, when Phœbe Harris, a coiner and the daughter of coiners, was the victim. She was led through the prison door a quarter of an hour after the drop had fallen with six male felons, but the sight of the horrible scaffold and the six swinging figures with their heads on one side can have caused her no terror. For she was swooning with fear already and trembling in every limb, and had to be carried forth by the Sheriff's men, a "well-made little woman" of about thirty, with pleasant features. A stout post about eleven feet in height had been reared in the street between the scaffold and the pump, with a curved piece of iron projecting near the top, from which a rope and a noose were dangling. When she was tied up the low stool upon which she had been standing was taken away, leaving her to be strangled with her feet about twelve inches from the ground. Then, all signs of life having vanished, two cartloads of faggots were piled around her and she was burnt to ashes.

The last execution of this kind occurred on the 18th of March, 1789, on which date Christian Murphy was put to death in the same manner in the Old Bailey. She also had been convicted of coining, and the sentence pronounced was that she should be "drawn to the place of execution and there burnt with fire till she was dead." The distance was too short, however, to bring the criminal to the stake on a hurdle, and she was able to walk from the prison, dressed all in white, in token of her innocence. They treated her in the same manner as Phœbe Harris, but in her case the faggots were heaped

REV. JOHN VILLETTE, ORDINARY OF NEWGATE

[*To face p.* 139.

over her head, so that the whole of her body was covered entirely. In the following year the savage law was erased from the statute book.

About this time Brunskill was allowed to engage an assistant, named John Langley, a humble labourer, but a loyal fellow unmistakably, for he served his chief faithfully for the next twenty-four years.[1] He gave no trouble, keeping modestly in the background, on one occasion only—and that undoubtedly much against his will—figuring prominently in public. It was at the hanging of Martin Clench and James Mackley, on the 5th of June, 1797, that Langley had this conspicuousness thrust upon him. And it was through one of Brunskill's periodical bunglings that it came about.

The two criminals were standing on the scaffold beneath the cross-beam when the event occurred. While the hangman and his mate were fixing the halter, and the Rev. Mr. Villette, Ordinary of Newgate, and a Roman Catholic priest—who is described as a "very lusty fellow"—were administering to the doomed men according to their respective creeds, suddenly and without warning the platform gave way. Clench and Mackley were precipitated to their deaths, half-shrived and without their caps, and down went the two padres and the executioners through the open trap-door in a struggling heap. Villette escaped with a few bruises, but the priest, being a man of full habit, suffered severely when a couple of heavy hangmen fell on the top of him. Brunskill, of course, should have satisfied himself that the bolts were secure, and would have to answer for his carelessness to the Under-Sheriff. The incident came to be regarded

[1] Rep. 221, f. 368 (Guildhall Record Office).

with superstitious awe, since not long afterwards it was believed that Clench and Mackley were innocent of the murder for which they were convicted.

Naturally, during his long years of office Brunskill hanged more criminals than any of his predecessors, but only a few of his executions call for special notice. That of Governor Wall, on the 28th of January, 1802, is one of the most remarkable, involving as it did a miscarriage of justice. Joseph Wall's crime had been committed twenty years before, when he was Governor of the island of Goree, near Cape Verde. In order to suppress a mutiny amongst the garrison, most of which consisted of ex-convicts, he had flogged three soldiers, all of whom died subsequently, succumbing to dram-drinking in hospital rather than because of their punishment. Nevertheless, Wall was taken into custody on a charge of murder two years later, after his return to England, by order of the Privy Council.

Had he stood his trial then, while all the witnesses were alive, in all probability he would have been acquitted. Unfortunately for himself he ran away, crossing over to France, where he lived for nearly twenty years. When at last, compelled by poverty, he was obliged to return to England, a combination of circumstances brought about his condemnation. His chief witness proved unreliable, militarism was regarded with disfavour now that peace with Bonaparte had been declared, and the Attorney-General, who prosecuted for the Crown, treated him with rancour. Moreover, when efforts for a reprieve were made the authorities were afraid to be lenient, because mutinous seamen had been hanged recently at Spithead. Lest it should be said that there was one law for the officer and another for the men, the brave Colonel Wall was sent to the scaffold.

His execution took place in front of Newgate soon after eight o'clock in the morning. He was sixty-five years of age and six feet four inches in height, but had become weak and emaciated owing to his long imprisonment. As was the custom of the period, since his crime was one of murder, he had been fed on nothing but bread and water since his conviction. Neither his grey hairs nor his courage nor his splendid record as a soldier gained him any pity. On account of his supposed tyranny the mob hated him, hailing his appearance on the scaffold with terrific cheering. Apparently the ebullition made Brunskill nervous. He arranged the noose around the Colonel's neck, then took it off again and replaced it. It was now the practice invariably to pull the prisoner's legs, which the assistant hangman was able to do out of sight of the spectators underneath the scaffold. Wall, however, had exacted a promise that his legs should not be pulled, an omission that may have worried the executioner still further. Whatever the cause, this was one of Brunskill's bad days, and he bungled his work shockingly. When the drop fell the knot of the rope slipped behind the soldier's neck, so that he hung for a quarter of an hour in convulsive agony. In the end both hangmen had to throw their weight upon the poor wretch's body in order to put an end to his life.

Colonel Despard, who was hanged for high treason on the 21st of February, 1803, was another of Brunskill's celebrated victims. He suffered on a scaffold built on the top of Horsemonger Lane gaol—known as the New

Gaol in the Borough—for the gallows at the south-west corner of Kennington Common was used no longer.[1] Like Wall, he had been a brave soldier, but, being the ringleader, in a plot to assassinate the King, he had been condemned to death along with six associates. All were sentenced to be hanged, drawn and quartered, but instead of being dismembered, it had been decreed that they should be beheaded after death.

Nothing could have been more absurd than the first part of the punishment. When their irons had been knocked off, the criminals were placed in turn, two at a time, in the body of a small cart without wheels and dragged solemnly by a pair of horses across the outer courtyard of the prison as far as the lodge, where there was a staircase leading up to the scaffold. Despard was the last of the seven to be treated thus.

"What nonsensical mummery!" cried the old soldier, when they put him into the cart, while Brunskill and Langley, each with a drawn cutlass in his hand, took a seat on either side of him.

This time there was no mishap on the scaffold. The bodies were allowed to hang a full hour before the horrible sequel. Then a man in a mask appeared, said to have been a surgeon of some ability, and the head of each criminal was cut off. As each was severed Brunskill held it up for the people to see, exclaiming, "This is the head of a traitor."

The execution of John Holloway and Owen Haggerty on the 23rd of February, 1807, marks another of Brunskill's red-letter days. The two convicts were disreputables of the worst type, but there was some

[1] The gallows stood on the site of St. Mark's Church.

HORSEMONGER LANE GAOL, SURREY

[*To face p.* 142.

reason to believe that they were innocent of the murder for which they had been condemned. Which occasioned much sympathy and the assembling of an enormous throng in the Old Bailey to watch the execution. In parts of the street people were packed so tightly that they could not stir.

Through some cause or other panic seized the crowd. Those behind began to press upon those in front, and soon many had been knocked down and trampled upon. A fierce tumult took place, everyone fighting to escape from the crush, and more fell never to rise again. Even before the criminals appeared on the scaffold the multitude had commenced its mad struggle. Until the bodies were cut down an hour later the dense masses swayed and fought with insane rage, amidst the shrieks and groans of the sorely wounded.

When at last the crowd dispersed a little and the constables were able to clear the street, it was found that thirty persons had been killed and great numbers had suffered grievous bodily harm. Thus the hanging of two uninteresting and commonplace murderers remained more memorable than that of many other far more distinguished malefactors. The Haggerty-Holloway disaster was remembered as long as public executions continued to take place in the Old Bailey.

III

There was another place of execution in the City of London besides Debtor's Door. All persons condemned for crimes committed at sea were hanged at Execution Dock, which was situated at the bend of the river between

Wapping New Stairs and Wapping Dock Stairs, where a gallows consisting of two posts and a cross-beam was erected upon the uncovered foreshore at low tide. Here many notorious sailor criminals had met their doom during the latter half of the eighteenth century—Captain James Lowry on the 25th of March, 1752, for flogging a seaman to death; Captain John Lancey on the 7th of June, 1754, for scuttling the brig *Nightingale*; and Captain David Ferguson on the 4th of January, 1771, for the murder of a cabin boy. In the time of Thrift and Turlis, who executed these malefactors, the body was kept hanging until three tides had swept over it, but in the more civilized days of William Brunskill, at the dawn of the new century, this custom had become obsolete, and the dead man was cut down after the water had risen as high as his feet. It was at Execution Dock on the 29th of June, 1809, that Brunskill was called upon to hang Captain John Sutherland, who had stabbed his young negro servant in a drunken passion. The case had made a great noise because of Sutherland's position in the merchant service, while most sailors thought it unfair that an English seaman should die on account of a nigger boy.

The procession from Newgate to the waterside, through Cornhill, Whitechapel and the Commercial Road, was an imposing one. First came the Marshal of the Admiralty in his carriage, preceded by the Deputy Marshal bearing the Silver Oar—the ancient emblem of the authority of the Civil Court over persons afloat—and followed by the two City Marshals on horseback. The prisoner rode in an open cart, with Brunskill and Langley beside him, and a great array of Marshal's men and Sheriff's officers marching in the rear.

The stretch of beach was occupied by an enormous multitude. Scores of small boats had collected on the river in front of the gallows, which had been set up a few yards above the low-water mark, while behind there was a row of barges packed with spectators. The riggings of every ship were filled with seamen. Crowds filled the windows of all the houses on shore.

Poor Captain Sutherland was humble and contrite. He had pleaded that he was drunk when he struck the boy, protesting further that the wounds were insufficient to cause death, which must have been brought about through want of proper care. Upon reaching Execution Dock his hands were tied, after which he was led down the slip to the platform beneath the gallows, where he prayed fervently with Mr. Ford, Ordinary of Newgate. Just before he was turned off he gave his prayer-book to Brunskill, who, since there is no evidence that he was a religious hangman, probably sold the book for the price of a noggin of gin.

The last celebrated criminal to be hanged by Brunskill perhaps was the most illustrious in his list. John Bellingham, who was executed in front of Newgate on the 18th of May, 1812, was the murderer of Spencer Perceval, the Prime Minister, in the lobby of the House of Commons, so was the author of a unique crime. The man was a maniac with a grievance against the Government, but there was never any chance of a reprieve on account of his insanity. Even the humane Romilly acknowledged that " it was a species of madness which, probably for the security of mankind, ought not to exempt a man from being answerable for his actions."

Retribution followed him rapidly. Tried on the 15th

of May, three days after he had shot Perceval, he was executed three days later. Like all capital convicts who were guilty of murder, he was allowed no food or drink but bread and water, even a cup of tea being refused him. He remained dauntless to the end, and while expressing sympathy for his victim, he rejoiced that he had been able to strike a blow against the Ministry.

Perceval and his Government were not beloved by the common folk, so Bellingham proved a popular criminal. When he appeared on the scaffold the people cheered, many calling to him "God bless you!" Although the morning was stormy, there was an immense crowd, who hooted Brunskill. By this time, however, he should have been used to these demonstrations. In those days the hangman, like the actor, must always have been prepared to "take the bird."

Brunskill had now reached the allotted span. He was thirty-one when he became Dennis's mate and forty-three when he succeeded him, and he had been chief executioner for twenty-six years. Only two years before he had been seriously ill, being even now somewhat feeble. It was rumoured in the Press that he had been obliged to tipple more than usual on the Bellingham execution day in order to get through his task. The hostile attitude of the crowd unnerved him, and the image of the hanged man haunted him afterwards in his sleep.

"I dreamed," he used to relate, "as how Bellingham came to my bedside with a great horse pistol in each hand and swear'd as how he'd make a Mr. Perceval of me." [1]

[1] *The Satirist or Monthly Mirror*, VII., 272, 310; XI., 18–24.

The journalist who tells the story made an attempt at the same time to persuade the world that the hangman's name was Thomas Tollis, either forgetting that he was called Brunskill, or trying to convert the name of the great Tom Turlis into a synonym for all executioners, like that of " Jack Ketch."

Brunskill did not remain " hanging on " much longer. Two years later he had a seizure. After November, 1814, he seems to have operated no more, and John Langley succeeded to the vacant throne. But it was not until the next year that he sent in his formal resignation, when he realized at last that he would never be able to officiate again, having learnt, moreover, that Langley had engaged an assistant hangman named James Botting.

It was on the 9th of May, 1815—the month before the Battle of Waterloo—that the humble petition of William Brunskill, public executioner, was presented to the Court of Aldermen at Guildhall. It related that the petitioner had served the office of executioner for upwards of forty years, being now in the seventy-third year of his age, and had unfortunately been afflicted with a paralytic stroke and rendered totally unfit for business. It concluded as follows :—

> " That your Petitioner, has been informed that James Botting, the assistant executioner, has petitioned the Honourable Court for the full allowance of wages, therefore your Petitioner thinks it his duty hereby to present this Honourable Court his reignation." [1]

No address is given, and as there is no signature, it

[1] Rep. 219, f. 510; cf. Rep. 219, f. 471 (Guildhall Record Office).

may be presumed that William Brunskill, like some of his immediate successors, was unable to write his name. Fortunately for him the Court of Aldermen was in a generous humour. Mindful of his long and faithful service and his invariable docility, they granted the old man fifteen shillings a week, which was a handsome pension for a hangman in those days.

JOHN LANGLEY

(1814–1817)

X

JOHN LANGLEY

(1814–1817)

I

THE choice of William Brunskill's successor, when the old hangman became moribund, did not cause the Sheriffs of London a moment's hesitation. Obviously, John Langley's faithful service as mate for nearly a quarter of a century gave him a paramount claim to take command, so they chose him at once without considering the credentials of other applicants. He was now forty-eight years old, with a wife and three children.[1]

Unfortunately there is little evidence, either documentary or traditional, that sheds a light upon the man's character. We know whom he hanged and how he hanged, because that is related in the newspapers and chap-books and Newgate Calendars, but whether he was a sour man or amiable, a faithful husband or a breaker-up of homes, are details that have never been revealed to us. He may have had a happy disposition like Jack Hooper or have been a mercurial impressionable person like John Thrift, but we do not know. There is nothing to indicate what he was. He remains a nebulous and elusive hangman, sandwiched between five predecessors with distinct and definite temperaments, and a couple of successors, about whose personalities there is not the slightest mystery.

[1] Rep. 221, f. 368 (Guildhall Record Office).

Jemmy Botting, for instance, who became assistant executioner to Langley in November, 1814, and eventually succeeded him, was a coarse, unfeeling ruffian after the style of the functionaries of a hundred years before.[1]

From time immemorial it had not been etiquette for the executioner to appear in Newgate prison on a hanging day. On certain occasions we read that he was admitted within the gaol, as when Bellingham was executed, but usually he had to wait outside on the gallows. The pinioning of the prisoners was done by one of the Sheriffs' officers, specially deputed for the purpose, who had been dubbed long ago the Yeoman of the Halter, and it was done immediately after the prisoner's irons had been knocked off by the blacksmith.

The dismal scene that took place inside the Press yard on every execution morning has been described by many pens. Upon being led from their cells the convicts were conducted to the apartment on the ground floor which the condemned felons used as a day-room, and was now known as the Large Room. Here a small crowd was assembled, a dozen or more newspaper reporters, the Sheriffs and their myrmidons, and a party of the Sheriffs' friends, invited specially to witness the entertainment. The coming of the doomed men was announced by the clanking of their fetters some time before their entrance.

A block with a small anvil stands near the door, and as each culprit is brought in he is taken to the smith, who relieves him of his iron chains. Afterwards he is passed over to the Yeoman of the Halter, who binds his arms close to his body above the elbow with a length of cord. The strangers, who have been warned previously by the

[1] Rep. 219, f. 471; Rep. 219, f. 510 (Guildhall Record Office).

Under-Sheriff, speak only in whispers, but there is no need for such solicitude, since the blows of the smith's hammer echo through the room, extinguishing all other sounds. One by one the prisoners are taken apart and seated on a low bench, where the Ordinary awaits them to offer religious consolation, and all the time until the last of them has been freed of his fetters the voice of the clergyman is drowned by the clang of beaten iron.

At length the last rivet has fallen, and for a while there is no sound except for the unctuous intonations of the Reverend Ordinary or the sobbing of one of the malefactors. Presently the Sheriffs approach the bench at the far end of the room to ask the unhappy occupants in turn whether they have any message to send or any request to make, while the guests and the press-men, anticipating that the fatal moment is at hand, begin to murmur to one another. In a moment or two the Under-Sheriff refers to his watch and exchanges significant glances with his superiors. The Sheriffs answer with a nod, moving forward towards the door, bearing their wands, followed by the clergyman, open prayer-book in hand. Next come the culprits with the warders around, the visitors jostling after them.

"Don't press upon the sufferers," says the Under-Sheriff in a hoarse whisper.

The procession moves slowly along the dark stone passages, the deep tones of the Ordinary interspersed with the sighs and lamentations of the moribund, while the tolling of St. Sepulchre's bell becomes audible as they draw nearer to the gateway of the prison. In a few moments they have reached the small entrance hall, whence the Debtor's Door opens into the street. The flight of stairs leading up to the scaffold comes into view beyond the threshold. The doomed wretches stumble up the steps to the platform, where the hangman and assistant are awaiting them.

A universal roar arises from the vast multitude, which stretches the full length of the Old Bailey from St. Sepulchre's church as far as Ludgate Hill.

" Hats off, hats off! "

For everyone is anxious that his view shall not be obstructed. And thousands of heads are bared and thousands of faces are upturned as soon as the first of the prisoners appears on the platform. Langley and Botting are swift and skilful. Each victim in turn is tied up in a few seconds, while the Ordinary continues to intone the prayers for the dead. All being ready, the hangmen descend from the scaffold, and the Under-Sheriff, probably intercepting them on the stairs, gives them a last injunction to pull the bolt out smartly. In another moment the drop has fallen.[1]

II

In the year 1815 John Langley had one famous case which dwarfs every other during his tenure of office. It concerned an interesting young woman of twenty-one, who was tried and condemned to death for attempted murder, and more than half the people of England believed that she was innocent.

Eliza Fenning, the daughter of a soldier, was in service as cook with Mr. and Mrs. Turner, who kept a law-

[1] " Life in London," Pierce Egan, Book II, Chap. V; " Many Coloured Life " (Hugh Cunningham, 1842), pp. 36–48; " Life of Calcraft, the Hangman," pp. 6, 7, 11–14; *The Penny Satirist*, 20th May, 1837.

stationer's shop in Chancery Lane. There was one other female servant in the house, besides two boy apprentices.

It was in connection with the two latter, apparently, that trouble befel Eliza in the first instance. It is said that she was detected by her mistress when going into the young men's bedroom "partly undressed," receiving a severe scolding in consequence. Henceforth it is supposed that she bore rancour against Mr. and Mrs. Turner, becoming sulky and churlish, and her fellow servants believed that she was brooding over some act of revenge. Such was the motive alleged against her when she was indicted at the Old Bailey before Sir John Sylvester, the Recorder, on the 11th of April for administering arsenic to her employer's family with intent to murder.

Although proof of motive was not a strong part of the case, there were grave suspicions against her. For on the 21st of March she had made some dumplings for the parlour dinner, in the cooking of which no other person had been concerned. Everyone who ate them became violently sick, and continued ill with symptoms of arsenical poisoning for many hours. A quantity of arsenic also was missing from an open drawer in the office, where it had lain in a packet labelled "poison," kept there to kill mice. Most suspicious of all, Eliza had served up the dumplings, although they were black and heavy and had not risen as they should have done.

In spite of the accumulation of suspicious circumstances, the prosecution certainly failed to establish its case. It is impossible that Eliza Fenning could have been convicted in the present day. No arsenic was ever traced to her possession. It was not proved that the sick persons were suffering from arsenical poisoning. There was no proof that the dumplings really contained arsenic. The attempts made to indicate the presence of the poison were crude and unscientific, the most contemptible rule of thumb. The evidence of the only medical person to appear at the trial—half apothecary, half surgeon—was wholly unconvincing.

Nevertheless, the prejudice brought into the case was fatal to the prisoner. The weight of suspicion against her overwhelmed all contradictory testimony. Every one of the five witnesses, who belonged to the Turner household, might have been schooled beforehand, since each told the same tale. From the commencement of the trial the Recorder was hostile to the prisoner, and his summing-up was fatal. After hearing his interpretation of the evidence, the jury had no option but to return a verdict of guilty, so, as attempted murder was a capital crime, the poor girl was condemned to death. We are told that she " was carried from the box convulsed with agony and uttering frightful screams."

An extraordinary interest had been taken in the trial, and a storm of protest burst forth. Efforts were made at once to procure a remission of the sentence. Unhappily for Eliza Fenning, the nation was at death-grips with Napoleon at the time, and the Battle of Waterloo was fought in the midst of the agitation against her conviction, otherwise it is probable that the anger of the people would have been more manifest. Under the circumstances a sense of gratitude deterred the general public from joining in a clamour against a Government which had rid the country of the peril of the Corsican Ogre. It was unfortunate for her also that the wrong people were prominent in the agitation for a reprieve, since it fell into the hands of the extreme Radicals and root-and-branch party.

The authorities refused to over-rule the verdict. The Recorder, convinced that the girl was guilty, used all his influence to prevent a pardon. Lord Sidmouth, most implacable of Home Secretaries, was guided by the opinion of the presiding judge. Lord Chancellor Eldon, after examining the evidence twice over, declined to interfere. In spite of the fact that many circumstances had been discovered favourable to the prisoner, she was ordered for execution.

Professional lawyers are fond of insisting that it is necessary to see the actual witnesses and to watch their demeanour in court in order to form a correct judgment in every trial of law, forgetting how many subtle actors there are in the world, unmindful of the fact that the most innocent folk often seem to be the most guilty liars under cross-examination. Moreover, if this opinion of the professional lawyer is accepted, a revision of any case, either by a contemporary court or by posterity, would be impossible. The truth, of course, is that every cause must be decided by facts, and facts alone, whatever the faces of the people in the witness-box may look like. "Data, data, data," Sherlock Holmes used always to insist upon. In such manner we can decide that Mary Blandy was convicted justly and that Madeleine Smith very properly was given the benefit of a slight doubt, and by such a test also it is safe to say that there is no conclusive proof that Eliza Fenning was guilty.

The unhappy girl was hanged in the Old Bailey on the 26th of July, 1815. She was dressed in a white muslin gown with a high waist, tied with a satin ribbon after the fashion of the day, and a white muslin cap on her head, a pair of high-laced lilac boots giving the only touch of colour to her attire. Comely and graceful, with a small but shapely figure, she was the most attractive perhaps of all the poor young women who have suffered as she did. When summoned to her doom her courage in the Press yard was undaunted. Evidently on this occasion Langley was admitted into the prison, and while he was binding her elbows to her sides and fastening her hands together in front—acting instead of the Yeoman of the Halter—she did not show the slightest trace of fear. Even when he wound the halter around her waist according to custom she remained firm and unwavering, without a quiver on her lip or a tear in her eye.

It was the same upon the horrible scaffold in the midst of the great multitude, all full of grief on her account. She stood calmly and patiently with the Rev. Horace Cotton, the Ordinary, and her own priest beside her, while the hangman tried to adjust a white cotton night-cap, which he was unable to draw over her head because of the muslin cap she was wearing. Failing in his purpose, Langley bound a muslin handkerchief over her face, and since this was not sufficient cover, he substituted a dirty pocket handkerchief. For the first time she began to rebel.

"Pray do not let him put it on, Mr. Cotton," she implored in disgust. "Pray let him take it off; pray do, Mr. Cotton."

"My dear," stammered the perplexed Cotton, "it must be on—he must put it on."

And so, since they could think of no other expedient, it had to remain.

VIEW OF AN EXECUTION BEFORE THE DEBTOR'S DOOR AT NEWGATE

[*To face p.* 159.

Langley appears to have been unmoved by the sadness of the occasion or the solemnity of the vast crowd. Whatever else he may have been, he was a stolid fellow, at any rate. Having placed the rope around the girl's neck, he ascended a pair of steps, and, throwing the end of the rope over the beam, he fastened it with several knots. Next the other two criminals who were to suffer with the girl were tied up in turn likewise, the first an unsavoury creature named Oldfield, guilty of an odious crime, hysterical and sanctimonious, who had been granted permission to die beside her. Meanwhile, poor little Eliza Fenning continued to pray with her priest, brave and tranquil to the end. Her last words were, " I am innocent."

Happily she died without a struggle.

III

The peace with France, following the Battle of Waterloo, did not bring peace at home to England. The industrial machine of a country becomes disorganized during a long war, and time must elapse before it works smoothly again. Prices were high and wages low, and there was much unemployment. Mechanism, too, was supplanting hand-labour in every manufacture, and naturally the workers were the chief sufferers. There was discontent throughout the length and breadth of the country. And the discontent was increased and multiplied by the speeches and publications of clever marplots of communistic principles.

Under these circumstances it was inevitable that there should be riot and disorder; and a year after the Peace of

Paris a tumult burst forth in the city of London, which, but for the prompt action of the authorities, might have proved as serious as the Gordon Riots. This disturbance occurred on the 2nd of December, 1816, and was known as the Spafields riot. It was, however, by no means confined to Spafields, which was merely the original meeting-place of the mob, attracted thither by seditious handbills. Here thousands of desperate men gathered together to protest against the condition of society, and, having been instigated by an inflammatory speech of a young man named Watson, they set off in all directions through the city, eager for red revolution. "Arms! arms!" was the cry, and the shops of the gunsmiths were ransacked.

Part of the mob spread through the Minories, others made a demonstration against the Tower of London. The Royal Exchange was attacked, and the insurgents spread along Fleet Street and the Strand, pillaging the shops and taverns as they went. From noon until nightfall the town was in the hands of the rioters. Fortunately the disturbance was suppressed before darkness. The military had been called out, and gradually the mob was dispersed and its ringleaders were arrested. Strange to say, the riot did not cause the loss of a single life. The display of force had not been postponed unduly.

Only one life, too, was demanded in expiation by law, a show of mercy not often to be observed in those robust days, but there is much that is ironical in this leniency when the facts of the case are taken into account. For the scapegoat selected by the authorities was a battle-worn sailor named John Cashman who had served with credit in the navy all his life, a happy-go-lucky fellow, an

Irishman, and somewhat of a buffoon. Convicted of having plundered the shop of Mr. Beckwith, a gunsmith, this hero of a hundred fights was hanged on the 12th of March, 1817, in Skinner Street, Snow Hill, opposite the scene of his crime.

Naturally he was a popular criminal, the mob cheering him uproariously while he was being taken through the streets to his death. Cashman behaved with the greatest levity, and his sanity appears doubtful. From the first he had protested his innocence. The gallows was surrounded by an enormous crowd, who hooted Langley and Botting, and no doubt would have pelted them with stones but for the array of constables and soldiers.

This was Langley's last important execution. For some time he had been unwell and was an out-patient of the London Hospital, but during April he became so ill that they gave him a bed in one of the wards. Here he did not trouble them for long, dying late at night on Sunday, the 27th of April, 1817, at the age of fifty-one. Thinking perhaps that it would be too crude to state that he died "of death," the astute old leeches entered in their Record Book that he had died "of mortification." In his case the Court of Aldermen did not prove very generous. When petitioned for assistance by Elizabeth Langley, the widow, who declared that she was "now thrown upon the world with their children," they only granted her the salary of her husband " due next Mid-summer."[1] He had been chief hangman for two and a half years, a shorter period than any since William Marvell.

[1] Record Book of the London Hospital for 1817; *Bell's Weekly Messenger*, 4th May, 1817; Rep. 221, f. 368 (Guildhall Record Office).

JAMES BOTTING
(1817–1820)

XI

JAMES BOTTING

(1817–1820)

I

James Botting was a self-assertive type of hangman, who never lacked anything through not asking for it. Having a strong objection to be "put upon," he was not afraid of grumbling to his superiors whenever he fancied that he had a grievance. Less than five months after his appointment as assistant to John Langley we find him appealing to the Court of Aldermen for an increase of salary.

It does not seem to have been an unreasonable request, since, as he told "their lordships," he was paid only the "small sum" of ten shillings and sixpence a week; and he reminded them further, in the faulty but habitual phraseology of the hangman seeking a boon, that "the unpleasant nature of your petitioner's employment and from the prejudice of the public against him . . . render it impossible for him to obtain regular employment." Jemmy, as he was now known to everybody, was then living at No. 4 Badger's Court, Harlow's Rents, Shoreditch, and it was certainly true that his neighbours had no great love for him. Whether or not he obtained his rise in wages we do not know, for the Aldermen merely referred the matter to the Sheriffs.[1]

[1] Rep. 219, f. 471 (Guildhall Record Office).

Two years later, on the 13th of May, 1817, after Botting had risen to chief command upon the death of John Langley, he was soliciting his employers again, this time trying to persuade them to allow him an assistant. Naturally he was anxious to have an assistant, like every one of his predecessors. An assistant was useful to fetch and carry and go messages and do any rough work that came along. An assistant adds to the dignity of a hangman. Thus Botting instigated one Henry Small to petition the Court of Aldermen to be appointed deputy executioner "in the room of John Langley, deceased." The Court, however, refused the request, resolving "that an assistant to the public executioner is unnecessary."[1]

During the following year, on the 24th of November, 1818, Botting sent in the third of his humble petitions, setting forth a list of grievances such as no hangman had ever submitted to the Aldermen before.

> "Your Petitioner, James Botting," he declared, "succeeded to the office of executioner on the demise of John Langley, the late executioner, who, as his predecessor had always received small fees from the undertakers and friends of the criminals executed,[2] also the privilege of rubbing persons afflicted with wens, for which it was usual to receive 2*s*. 6*d*. for each person. That the late John Langley at the time of the Sessions received 2*s*. 6*d*. per day for his attendance, whereas your Petitioner has the

[1] Rep. 221, f. 368 (Guildhall Record Office).

[2] The father of Eliza Fenning had to pay fourteen shillings and sixpence as "executioner's fees" before he could obtain the dead body of his daughter for burial.

duty of two persons, there being no assistant executioner as was always before, and your Petitioner has only 1*s*. a day.

"That your Petitioner from the demise of John Langley until within a few weeks received the usual fees and payments with his weekly pay. He was fully satisfied, and always endeavoured to discharge his duty with diligence and attention.

"That your Petitioner understands he no longer receives the fees and emoluments due to him.

"That your Petitioner prays your consideration as regards the loss of his fees, for his small salary is insufficient to support him."[1]

The screed concluded by reminding the Court that "the office of executioner was one of great personal danger." It is dated from Shoreditch again, and shows that Jemmy was illiterate, his signature being indicated by a mark.

It is not on record that the Court of Aldermen agreed to all these suggestions, but it is certain that the position of the hangman, both financially as well as socially, began to improve considerably about this period. From now onwards he received a fixed weekly wage of one pound, which was handed to him over the prison gate in the Old Bailey, indicating that he was recognized as a salaried servant of the establishment. The "great personal danger," too, was removed, because the authorities always provided sufficient forces at every execution to protect their officials. And the hangman, although still unpopular with the mob, was beginning to be sought

[1] Rep. 223, f. 19 (Guildhall Record Office).

after by the flash men and "the fancy," who were glad to beguile him into a tavern or ale-house for a gallows-chat over a tumbler of "blue ruin" or "belch." Tom and Jerry, whose motto was *humani nihil a me alienum puto*, were by no means ashamed to be seen hob-nobbing with "Jack Ketch."

Since he reaped the benefit of all these unaccustomed advantages, it is a pity that Jemmy Botting was not a more amiable character. But it must be confessed with regret that he was one of the most unsavoury and repellent of hangmen. Apparently he delighted in his gruesome work, loving hanging for hanging's sake, always acting his part at an execution—so they used to say of him—"with something more than indifference—something very like levity." He never spoke a word to the "*party*," as he used to call the convict, handling him as though he were a beast at the shambles.[1] Thrift certainly—and perhaps Turlis and Dennis as well—had been a self-respecting, well-groomed hangman, but Botting might have passed for Dirty Dick of Leadenhall Street. Moreover, he was a surly, taciturn fellow, from whom no one expected anything but a grunt. No wonder that the common people did not love him.

Occasionally he seems to have displayed a ghoul-like wit, but it always had reference to his grim calling. Once upon a time, before the death of Langley, when he was still assistant executioner, he happened one morning to be passing by a public house, against which some loafers were propping themselves. According to custom, they began to ridicule him unmercifully, taunting

[1] "Many Coloured Life," (Hugh Cunningham), 1842, p. 15.

him about his profession. He listened passively without saying a word in reply.

"Why don't you answer them back, Jemmy?" said an onlooker.

"Nay, nay," growled Jemmy. "I never quarrel with my customers."

One of the most aggressive of his revilers on this occasion was a man named Falkener, who, strange to say, was hanged by Botting at Horsham only two or three months afterwards, being executed on the 12th of April, 1817, for a rape near Hove.[1]

II

The services of the Newgate executioner were now utilized all over the country, and he went a-hanging through the home counties and even into the Midlands and the west. Naturally the various authorities found this method cheaper than retaining a "Jack Ketch" themselves. In Lancashire and Yorkshire, however, where there was a sufficiency of gallows-birds to justify the extravagance, the stubborn parochialism of the people made them insist upon doing their own hanging, and a local man was always employed. At Lancaster a villainous fellow named Edward Barlow—yclept "Old Ned"—held office during the whole time that Botting was in full vigour; while at York the famous John Curry was appointed in 1802, and remained hangman until his death in 1836. In Scotland also they took good care that "Jack Ketch's" fees should not be appropriated by a stranger. There was a permanent hangman

[1] Bishop's "Peep into the Past," pp. 203–4.

at Edinburgh and Glasgow and at Perth and Inverness; and although the first of these, one John Foster by name, was dismissed in 1818 because of his outrageous mismanagement of the execution of Robert Johnstone, and the latter, a man called Donald Ross, was exasperating his patrons by annexing some new perquisite every six months, the whole of North Britain nevertheless remained a closed province to the English practitioner.[1]

The *magnum opus* of James Botting was accomplished on the 1st of May, 1820, when he hanged the five leaders in the "Cato Street Conspiracy" in front of Debtor's Door. Arthur Thistlewood, the author of the plot, was a remarkable character. Sprung from a yeoman stock in Lincolnshire, he was in conflict with his environment at an early age, having become demoralized by reading the works of Tom Paine. Travelling first to the United States, and thence to revolutionary France before the fall of Robespierre, he returned to his native land a rabid republican. Three events, however, soon contributed to the sobering of him. He obtained an ensigncy in the militia, which he afterwards exchanged for a lieutenancy in the regular army, and some years later he married a lady of fortune.

Affluence did not long remain with him. His wife died and her income reverted to her relatives. Soon afterwards Thistlewood lost a large sum at the gambling table, reducing himself to penury. He was now thirty-four years of age, and, having resigned his commission, had no means of subsistence. Proceeding to London,

[1] "Lancaster Castle," J. Hall, 1843, pp. 55–6; "Criminal Chronology of York Castle," W. Knipe, pp. 139, 197; *Bell's Weekly Messenger*; 8th November, 1819; *Bell's Life*, 5th January, 1834.

he joined the Spencean Society, a revolutionary organization whose aim and object was to establish socialism. In a little while he had become a marked man by the Government.

It was at his instigation, aided and abetted by a kindred spirit named James Watson, that the Spafields' disturbance was planned. He had hoped for a general uprising of the people like that which had brought about the storming of the Bastille, and believed that the Tower would surrender to the mob. When the tumult was suppressed he went into hiding, but, being captured in a little while, he was put into prison pending the result of the trial of his colleagues. Watson, however, was acquitted, owing to the mistake of charging him with high treason instead of with exciting a riot, and the proceedings against Thistlewood were dropped in consequence. Keeping him under careful surveillance, the Government was content to let him have as much rope as he would take.

Henceforth he drifted away from the less truculent members of his party, like Henry Hunt and J. T. Wooller and Richard Carlile, who were content to advocate constitutional reform. Having adopted the slogan of "Socialism in our time," he was convinced that it might be achieved by desperate measures. His mind was full of plots for the assassination of Ministers, to be followed by an armed insurrection. Had he possessed funds or been assisted by capable associates, he might have caused a serious rebellion.

Still at the best it would have been only a temporary rebellion. Thistlewood did not understand that his aspirations would never be realized completely. In

France, as he had seen, a blood-stained revolution had been carried out with the support, or at least with the acquiescence of the middle class. But in England the middle classes had no desire to emulate the French, preferring to wait for their revolution until it could be effected by Act of Parliament.

Nevertheless, the state of the country was serious. In the Midlands and the industrial north the people were seething with discontent, caused by want and privation. Nearly every artisan believed that all his woes would be removed by parliamentary reform, making riot and holding meetings everywhere to petition for what he desired. Such a one was the mass gathering in the August of 1819, when the yeomanry attacked "the reformers" in St. Peter's Field, Manchester, causing the slaughter of many inoffensive citizens. The whole country was aghast at the tragedy. It seemed to Thistlewood that the hour had come when the nation would respond to the lead of a strong man, so he determined to strike his blow.

His scheme, although a crude one, lacked nothing in ferocity. He proposed to massacre the Cabinet Ministers while they were dining at Lord Harrowby's house in Grosvenor Square, and then to seize the Tower and the Bank and the Mansion House by force of arms. What was to happen subsequently was left in a great measure to chance, but Thistlewood hoped to establish a provisional government in the midst of the confusion that would follow the extinction of Lord Liverpool's administration. He over-estimated entirely the number of his adherents. He was unaware that his most trusted lieutenant was a spy in the service of the Government.

Although a man of ability, he was fanatical and unreasonable, and seemed to care little whether his plot succeeded or failed as long as it was the prelude to red revolution.

When the authorities thought fit and proper to deal with the conspirators, they were attacked in their lair in Cato Street, Thistlewood and four of his chief followers being arrested and brought to trial. The evidence against them was clear and conclusive, and although defended ably by John Adolphus, the chieftain of Old Bailey advocates, they were found guilty of high treason and condemned to death. In spite of the fact that they had been under Government espionage for so long, it is idle to pretend that such desperadoes had been inspired by an *agent provocateur*.

At the execution in the Old Bailey every one of them displayed undaunted courage, tinged in most instances with bravado. Several spoke jestingly to Botting on the scaffold, but did not succeed in chaffing him out of his habitual moroseness. On this occasion the hangman was not admitted into the prison, the pinioning in the Press yard being done by Slarke, the appointed Yeoman of the Halter. Many revolutionaries had come to watch the spectacle, and the "conspirators" were cheered by numbers of their sympathizers. While the horrible ceremony of decapitation was being performed, and when the severed head of each of the criminals was held aloft in turn by the executioners, the mob showed its disgust by hissing and hooting and yells of protest. It is said that the surgeon who performed the operation was the same person who had done the like to Colonel Despard.[1]

[1] *Morning Chronicle*, 2nd May, 1820, "Old Stories Retold," Walter Thornbury.

Botting had no more opportunities of obtaining another famous scalp. Not long after the execution of Thistlewood he seems to have ceased to be hangman. Whether he lost his position through misconduct or because of ill-health is not mentioned in the archives at Guildhall, but it is written in the Minutes of the Court of Aldermen on the 17th of February, 1824, that James Botting, "late hangman," was living in the debtors' prison for London and Middlesex. The Corporation granted him one freedom at the rate of five shillings a week, besides instructing their solicitor to take the necessary steps to procure his release. Two years later, on the 24th of February, 1826, another freedom of the same value was assigned for his benefit, the proceeds to be paid to him by the Keeper of Guildhall.[1] And when this sum was exhausted the pension was continued.

III

About this date Jemmy migrated from Shoreditch to Brighton, where he was born. His father—James Botting also—had possessed a small property there, known as "Botting's Rookery," the resort of tramps and harlots, situated at the back of West Field Lodge, immediately to the west of the bottom of Cannon Place. From its position close to the Metropole Hotel it must be a valuable site in the present day. Jemmy now had difficulty in getting about, a stroke of paralysis having disabled him. He hit upon the device of using a chair, supporting himself when moving by leaning on the back as though it was a crutch, sitting down upon it when

[1] Rep. 228, f. 393; Rep. 230, f. 247 (Guildhall Record Office).

tired. And whenever the gruesome old cripple was seen shuffling up the street, pushing his chair along beside him, the people fled from him as though he had a writ for them. He was one of the familiar figures of Brighton in the second decade of the nineteenth century, and one of the least loved. The clatter of his chair upon the stones had the same effect as a leper's bell.[1]

Once upon a time James Foxen, his successor as public executioner, called upon him to ask his opinion with regard to the decrease of capital punishment since George IV had come to the throne. He wished for advice also in drawing up a petition, aware that Botting was an expert in petitioning the Court of Aldermen.

" I don't know," said Jemmy, " as how you can say anything better than that His Majesty has got so gallows-merciful there's nothing left for a hangman to do, and beg them to give him a hint it's time to begin to do a bit of justice again."

It was on the 22nd of March, 1830, that Botting, true to his motto of " ask and ye shall receive," sent in his own last petition to his late employers. It was terse and emphatic, representing that the Freedom of twenty-five pounds granted him in April, 1828, was exhausted, and praying for the same relief to be continued. It was dated from Brighton and signed James Botting, " his mark," and resulted in the pension of five shillings a week being made permanent. It was not much to demand, but he knew that it was all that he would get.[2]

There soon came a time when the clatter of Jemmy's

[1] " History of Brighthelmston," Erridge, pp. 335–6.
[2] Rep. 234, f. 463 (Guildhall Record Office).

chair was heard no longer in the streets of Brighton, and the shambling hangman was never seen in public any more. Stricken by another paralytic stroke, he was scarcely able to crawl across his room. Thus, bedridden for most of the twenty-four hours, there was nothing for the illiterate old ruffian to do but to lie and think. And his thoughts were the most horrible that ever tormented the brain of a human being. Both asleep and awake the pictures in his mind were nearly always the same. He beheld a ghostly procession passing incessantly along the foot of his bed, the spectacle of one hundred and seventy-five "parties," who moved slowly by, wearing white caps and with their heads on one side. They were the ghosts of all the people whom he had hanged.

In vain he cursed and swore at them and strove to frighten them away. Except for the brief moments when he was free from hallucination, the silent company was always there, haunting him by day, coming back to him in his dreams. One hundred and seventy-five "parties" in white caps, carrying their heads on one side. He shook his fist at them and scolded.

"Damn their eyes!" he used to vociferate. "If they'd only hold up their heads and take off their night-caps I wouldn't care a blast about any of them."

He was lucky enough to have a landlord and a landlady who would give him board and lodging in exchange for his meagre stipend, although their house was a hovel and the food of the coarsest. It is not improbable that they were able to earn a few pence now and then by making a show of the old hangman when he was engaged in altercation with his "parties," the fame of whom had spread far and wide. But Jemmy himself had nothing to contribute save the five shillings a week from the Corporation of the City of London.

During his last years he was completely paralysed and could not leave his bed. Although so greatly disturbed by the ghosts of the past, the only thing, oddly enough, that seemed to give him any pleasure was the execution of a notorious criminal. A good murder, followed by the hanging of the murderer, always raised his spirits amazingly. The case of James Greenacre, once a prosperous London tradesman, who was executed for the murder of a mistress on the 2nd of May, 1837, afforded the old hangman the greatest enjoyment. He followed the incidents of the affair from day to day. When the result of the trial was known he calculated how long the criminal had to live, gloating over every detail exultantly. On the fatal morning Jemmy was awake early, quivering with excitement. As the clock struck eight he gave a growl of triumph.

"That's the time o' day!" he cried. "I'm blest if he an't a-coming out to nap it."

Jemmy did not survive much longer himself, dying on Sunday, the 1st of October of the same year. He had lived in retirement for seventeen years, a longer time than any other hangman. The news of his death was communicated to the hall-porter at Guildhall by his landlord, who stated that "the deceased had met his end like a Christian person, although he sometimes was troubled with fancies about the offices he had performed," the letter concluding with the request that "as, like some other ministers," Mr. Botting had "died poor," the corporation would be so good as to " grant the price of a shell for a departed brother."

The Police Committee of the Corporation contributed two pounds towards the expenses of the funeral.[1]

[1] *Morning Advertiser*, 7th October, 1837; *Morning Post*, 9th October, 1837; " Many Coloured Life " (H. Cunningham), p. 16.

JAMES FOXEN

(1820–1829)

XII

JAMES FOXEN
(1820–1829)

I

It has been pointed out frequently that it is possible to commence a political career late in life and achieve the highest success. This is true also with regard to the hangman. A man may enter the House of Commons at the age of two score years and ten and reach Cabinet rank. A man may have never tied a noose until he is fifty, and yet attain a European reputation. So it was with James Foxen. He had lived for nearly half a century when he was appointed assistant to Botting in 1818. At his death, eleven years later, he had a " better Press " than any previous executioner. His name had been for long a household word, as familiar to the tongue as those of Tom Cribb or Grimaldi.

It does not follow that he deserved this celebrity. Greatness was thrust upon him adventitiously. It was his good fortune to be associated with several criminals of high degree. All over the country his services were more in request than those of any of his predecessors. Whenever a man had to be executed in the provinces it was found most convenient now to employ " the Newgate practitioner." Even at Lancaster, since old Ned Barlow was no more, James Foxen made several appearances.

Socially Foxen was no great improvement upon Botting. A little less of a sloven, perhaps, but still careless and unkempt in his attire, he was true to the type of hangman that had arisen since the removal of the gallows from Tyburn, a fellow without any regard for ritual, who did not care how his work was done as long as it was got through expeditiously and there was no absolute hitch. Like all the new hangmen, he had a bad bedside manner. He loved his profession and was proud of his renown, but there was no ingenuity about the man, and his methods were clumsy and elementary. Not so surly by any means as Jemmy, he did not resent the overtures of strangers, though his small talk was almost non-existent and was concerned wholly in "shop." Oddly enough, the press-men were apt to misspell his name, calling him Foxton.

James Foxen had many famous affairs during his first years of office, but his first superlative criminal was Henry Fauntleroy, the banker, who was hanged for forgery in the Old Bailey on the 30th of November, 1824. It was a tragedy that thrilled the whole nation, because Fauntleroy was a gentleman of position and his frauds were the most colossal ever known. From first to last he robbed the Bank of England of more than a quarter of a million pounds. There were other reasons why the crime should fascinate the public. For the banker had been a well-known man about town for many years, apparently a person of influence and power, with a house at Brighton and a villa on the Thames and a succession of pretty mistresses. In reality his firm had been insolvent ever since the management had been thrust upon him seventeen years before, when he was only twenty-three—a sort of "Voysey Inheritance." At the time of his detection he was a handsome debonnair man of forty, and most people were sorry for him.

The British public was beginning to wonder whether capital punishment was not too severe a penalty for the crime of forgery, however mean or flagrant that forgery might have been. From the moment of Fauntleroy's arrest it was clear that he would be convicted, since the proofs were evident and he avowed his guilt, and it was certain that he would be condemned to death. Consequently nearly everyone sympathized with him, heedless of the poor depositors who had lost their savings when his bank suspended payment, forgetting also that he had treated his unhappy wife with heartless cruelty. In the City of London, however, the plunder of the Bank of England was regarded as sacrilege, while it was the opinion of the financial world that commercial credit would receive an irreparable blow unless Henry Fauntleroy was executed.

The forger was sentenced to be hanged on the 2nd of November, whereupon there ensued a strenuous struggle during the next four weeks to preserve his life. His friends were hopeful, since King George IV was disposed to be merciful to those condemned to death for crimes less than murder. But the Bank of England exerted all its influence to punish its despoiler in the good old-fashioned way, and was supported tacitly by the Court of Aldermen and the Common Council. The newspapers, also, for the most part were hostile to Fauntleroy. So the appeal for mercy was drowned in an angry growl for severity, and severity prevailed. Fauntleroy's forgeries had been so enormous that the authorities were agreed that it would be impolitic to suspend the law in his case.

On the day of his execution the greatest multitude that had ever been known was gathered together in the Old Bailey. All the windows in the houses facing the prison had been let at high prices, for Lord Tom Noddy and his companions always patronized these entertainments, and the house-tops also were full to overflowing. Most of the people believed that the banker would be reprieved at the last moment. Nearly fifty years had passed since a gentleman of position had suffered death in the street at the hands of the common hangman. It was incredible that the genteel Henry Fauntleroy, who lately had been a slap-up Corinthian, should be hanged like a common criminal. So many imagined that a pardon must arrive and that Jim Foxen would be baulked of his prey.

Nothing of the sort, of course, happened. The banker was brought upon the scaffold at eight o'clock on a bitter winter morning, and Foxen performed his task with his usual brutal indifference. Nothing untoward took place. Poor Fauntleroy met his death with courage and humility. His executioners were merciful and expeditious. Nevertheless, such is the credulity of mankind, many persons believed that he was resuscitated by the surgeons when cut down and lived long afterwards on the Continent.[1]

II

A little more than two years later, on the 2nd of January, 1827, Foxen had the most frightful experience

[1] See "Trial of Henry Fauntleroy" (*Notable British Trials*), Hodge & Co., Edinburgh.

of his life, when it was his duty to hang a man called Charles White, who had been a bookseller of repute, carrying on business in Holborn. He was only twenty-three and in prosperous circumstances, and there was no apparent motive for his attempt to burn down his house in order to defraud the insurance company. Probably he was too young to realize the enormity of his offence, and did not foresee the appalling punishment. When found guilty and condemned all sense of manliness seems to have left him.

All day long he brooded continuously upon his doom, cursing his cruel fate and protesting his innocence. He paced his cell from morning till night without ceasing, crying upon man and God for mercy, raving against the injustice of his judges. He concocted elaborate plans of escape, but was frustrated by the gaolers. There was no hope of reprieve for him, since arson was regarded as the next serious crime to murder.

While being pinioned in the Press yard on " the fatal morning," he struggled frantically all the time that Foxen was binding the cords around him, fighting again with both executioners when he was being tied up on the scaffold. No sooner had the hangman left him than he managed to free his arms and tear off his cap. A couple of assistants, provided beforehand as a precaution, rushed upon him, replacing the cap and securing his arms and wrists once more in spite of his struggles. The last scene, described by a contemporary reporter, was a horrible one.

> " The accustomed signal having been given, the drop sank; but the wretched man, instead of falling

> with it, suddenly jumped upon the platform, and seizing the cord around his throat with his hands, which he had sufficiently loosened by the violence of his struggles, he made an effort to prolong that life to which he seemed to be so strongly attached. At this moment the spectacle was horrifying in the extreme. The convict was partly suspended and partly resting on the platform. During his exertions his tongue had been forced from his mouth and the convulsions of his body and the contortions of his face were truly appalling. The cries from the crowd were of a frightful description, and they continued until the executioner had forced the wretched man's hand from the cord and having removed his feet from the platform, had suffered his whole weight to be sustained by the rope. The distortions of his countenance could even now be seen by the crowd, and as he remained suspended with his face uncovered, the spectacle was terrific. The hangman at length terminated his sufferings by hanging to his legs, and the unhappy wretch was seen to struggle no more."[1]

It must have been a long time before Foxen forgot the execution of Charles White. It is evident that he was beginning to lose his efficiency.

In the following year he was anxious to resign his post. Capital punishment was now rarely inflicted for the smaller forgeries, and the hangman's trade had suffered in consequence. There was a loss of fees for delivering the bodies of criminals to their friends and

[1] "Chronicles of Crime," Camden Pelham, 1887, II., 144.

relations. George IV, in the words of Botting, had become "so gallows merciful." Foxen also suffered from weak lungs, the result of long exposure in all weathers while performing his task. On the 13th of May, 1828, he addressed "The Humble Petition of James Foxen, one of the Executioners at the Old Bailey, for relief" to the Court of Aldermen from his home at 19 Booth Street, Hoxton.

The petitioner stated that he had been one of the executioners at the Old Bailey for ten years, that he was now in a very infirm state of health and not able to perform the duties allotted to him, being now at the age of sixty and upwards, and was at present confined to his bed. He prayed that he might be allowed a pension, as other executioners had been favoured, and signed the petition with "His X Mark," being illiterate, like Jemmy Botting.[1]

Probably the arrival of warm summer weather healed his weak chest and induced him to withdraw his resignation. Three months later he officiated at the hanging of William Corder for the murder of Maria Marten in the Red Barn, an event that caused as great an uproar as the execution of Henry Fauntleroy, and is remembered more vividly in the present day. For ever since that stupendous crime a favourite melodrama, called "The Murder in the Red Barn," has held the stage in hundreds of other barns, and during a hundred years has been the most popular tragedy in the repertory of the barnstormer.

William Corder was a well-to-do young farmer of Polstead in Suffolk, who shot an importunate mistress

[1] Rep. 232, f. 535 (Guildhall Record Office).

and hid the body in one of his barns. Eleven months passed without suspicion being aroused, it being supposed that Maria was living with her lover in another part of the country, since he had told everyone that they were going to elope. Then the girl's mother dreamt three times in succession that her daughter was buried in the Red Barn; and, search being made there, her remains were discovered in a shallow grave, just as the dream had foretold. In due course Corder was arrested and brought to trial at Bury St. Edmunds. His plea that the death of Maria Marten was caused by the accidental discharge of a pistol had no weight with the jury, who, after a consultation of little more than half an hour, brought in a verdict of guilty.

The date of execution was fixed for the 11th of August, 1828. Convinced that the accused man would be convicted, the local authorities sent a " retaining fee " to James Foxen—five guineas and expenses, or perhaps ten—before the verdict was pronounced, in order to make sure of procuring an experienced hangman; and Jim had arrived at Bury St. Edmunds with a double set of " furniture," as he called his ropes, long before the trial was over. The scaffold was erected outside the prison wall, overlooking the open country, half the county of Suffolk, apparently, flocking thither to watch the ceremony.

Corder, who was only twenty-four years old, bore himself valiantly. When he had been pinioned, he insisted upon being taken around the gaol to bid farewell to the other felons, after which he walked without faltering to the gallows. Here an unpleasant incident occurred. While Foxen was adjusting what he always described as " the mysterious knot," either the Under-Sheriff or the governor of the prison happened to suggest that he had given the criminal too much fall. There is nothing, of course, that a hangman resents more bitterly than any interference in the midst of an operation, when he is apt to be nervous and preoccupied. Foxen was furious, his ill-temper being apparent to everybody. Shortening the rope with a gesture of annoyance, he tied up " his gentleman "—as he always called the victim—carelessly and roughly; and clambering down from the platform, he released the drop before the signal was given.

Afterwards there were many complaints of his brutality and awkwardness, while he, on his part, was loud in his grumbles.

" I never like to be meddled with," he growled, " because I always study the subjects which come under my hands, and, according as they are tall or short, heavy or light, I accommodate them with the fall. No man in England has had so much experience as me, or knows how to do his duty better."

He must have forgotten all about John Curry of York, who, though he had not the prestige of Newgate behind him, had been hanging busily for a quarter of a century.

Later in the day Foxen visited the Shire Hall, where the body of the dead criminal was on view, in order to claim Corder's trousers as his perquisite. Pointing to the mark of the rope upon the criminal's neck, he asked exultantly if he had not " done the job in a masterly manner." Jim Foxen, indeed, was almost as much a ghoul as Jemmy Botting. He got the trousers, which he claimed as his " undoubted right," and the stockings as well. The rope, too, which was cut up into small pieces, sold for a considerable sum, the proceeds of which went also into the hangman's pocket. When asked how much it realized, Foxen refused to give the information.

"What I got, I got," he replied brusquely, "and that's all I shall say, except that are a very good rope."[1]

From all that we can learn of him it is evident that the company manners of James Foxen never showed any amelioration in consequence of the improved status of the public hangman.

Once upon a time a City contractor, who had shown Foxen some favours, said to him :—

"Supposing I were condemned to death, would you have the heart to hang me ?"

"Well, Mister," answered the executioner, scratching his head, "somebody'd have to do it, so why not me, because I know how to do it more comfortably than anyone else ?"

III

Foxen's last notable execution took place on the 8th of December of the same year, when Joseph Hunton, a Quaker, was hanged with three others in the Old Bailey. Hunton's crime was forgery to a considerable amount, but death was regarded now by most people as too great a punishment for the offence, so there was much sympathy for the culprit. He was a diminutive person with eccentric manners, and in his prime had been a wealthy man. Although the greatest efforts were

[1] "The Murder of Maria Marten," J. Curtis, 1828, pp. 297, 301, 302, 304, 306, "Life and Recollections of William Calcraft," p. 19.

made to procure a pardon by the Society of Friends, the "hanging judges" of the Privy Council set their faces against mercy.

The cold weather had brought back the old hangman's cough, and he was in a bad state of health all winter. Nevertheless he was more efficient than usual on this occasion. Not only were his "gentlemen"—he was not so impolite as to speak of them as "parties," like James Botting—tied up more rapidly than usual, but all four had a speedy death. The rope with which Hunton was hanged was longer than the rest because he was such a remarkably small man, and he appeared to die instantly.

Two months later James Foxen was dead also, succumbing to the effects of a chill, after a brief illness, on the 14th of February, 1829. All the newspapers printed obituary notices of various lengths, everyone of them making the mistake of calling him Foxton. Never before had the decease of a hangman been reported to the same extent in the public Press. Each of the accounts paid tribute to his fame, but some appeared suspicious of his craftsmanship, referring to "his *supposed* skill." One of them, indeed, declared, in reference to the usual character of his executions: "It is painful to witness the extreme and disproportionate sufferings of many of the victims of the law." Which indicates that the opinion was prevalent that James Foxen had not been a great artist.

The journalists were agreed that the dead hangman was sixty-one years of age, but most of them were mistaken with regard to the duration of his term of office, stating usually that he had been executioner for sixteen years. This assertion, of course, is contradicted by his petition to the Court of Aldermen in May, 1828, which proves that he became assistant to Botting only ten years before.

Alone among the Hangmen of England since the death of John Price he was the subject of an Elegy, composed in his memory by Jack Scroggins, the poet of *Bell's Life in London*. It ran as follows:—

" Jack Ketch, farewell! thy mug no more
We'll see upon the town;
Now all thy pleasant pranks are o'er,
For Fate has *cut you down*.

" Never again at heads and tails,
For pints of beer you'll toss;
Your death each Newgate bird bewails
It is a *gallows* loss.

" Swift was the progress of disease,
Its course no art could stop,
Thy sufferings nothing could appease,
And you were doomed to *drop*.

" Thy worthy actions to recite
Exceeds these powers of mine,
How many a staunch and sturdy wight
You've troubled *with a line*.

" Ages to come shall sing thy praise,
And fame be thy reward,
While Scroggins tries in simple lays
Thy merits to record." [1]

---

[1] *Bell's Life in London*, 15th and 22nd February, 5th April, 1829; *Gentleman's Magazine*, 1829, Pt. I., 282; *The Englishman*, 15th February, 1829; *Observer*, 15th February, 1829; *Morning Post*, 16th February, 1829; *Morning Chronicle*, 19th February, 1829; *Weekly Despatch*, 22nd February, 1829.

THOMAS CHESHIRE (Assistant)
(1808?–1840)

XIII

THOMAS CHESHIRE (ASSISTANT)
(1808 ?–1840)

I

THE fame of Thomas Cheshire was earned entirely as deputy hangman. It is stated on good authority that he assisted at an execution now and then as early as 1808. Nearly thirty years later he was still employed to help William Calcraft, who was then Finisher of the Law, after Queen Victoria had ascended the throne. It has not been clearly established, however, that he took part in hangings during four successive reigns, and the first actual and reliable records of him that we possess are when he was acting as mate to James Foxen between the years 1820 and 1829.[1]

According to some authorities, he succeeded to the post of chief hangman after Foxen's death, but if this were so his tenure of office must have been a brief one, nor does it appear to have received the sanction of the Court of Aldermen. The truth is that Cheshire was incapable of undertaking a position of responsibility for any length of time. With a despotic hangman as his superior officer he could get through his work expeditiously, if not with credit, but when left to his own

[1] *Notes and Queries*, 2 Ser., XI., 315; Vol. 155, *The Penny Satirist*, 19th August, 1837; *Bell's Weekly Messenger*, 16th February, 1829; *Gentleman's Magazine*, 1829, Pt. 1, 282.

devices he was not to be trusted. His mother, a zealous Methodist in her sober hours, is said to have divided her time between preaching and drinking. The son cared nothing about preaching.[1]

He fell into a fit of temper, so they say, when the news of the sudden death of his colleague, Foxen, was brought to him.

" Very well," he snarled. " How the devil could I help it ! "

His irritation was not unnatural. Foxen and he had worked in perfect harmony for many years, but Tom was not so sure that a new hangman would be as tolerant of him. Realizing his own defects, he knew that he would not be made chief himself, and he wondered how he was going to like the new " Jack Ketch." His real opinion of Foxen was expressed a little later, when he learnt that no new executioner would be appointed immediately and that he must " carry on " in the meantime.

" Take him all in all," he remarked of his dead C.O., " we ne'er shall look upon his like again."

Few hangmen in the calendar have been more unsavoury and repellent than James Botting and James Foxen, but both of them were decent members of society compared with Thomas Cheshire. Everyone seems to have agreed that no fouler specimen of humanity ever existed. " Horrible stories are told," writes a contemporary in *Notes & Queries* on the 20th of April, 1861, " of the fiendish delight, even when a feeble old man, which he seemed to take in his wretched office.

[1] *Morning Advertiser*, 7th October, 1837; " Chronicles of Newgate," Major Arthur Griffiths, II., 412.

The basilisk gleam of his eye, the stealthy cat-like clutch with which he pounced upon his victim—foh! I saw Cheshire once and while memory holds its seat I never will forget the occasion." Still, he is said to have been a chatty fellow on the scaffold all the same, and, unlike Botting, always gave courage in a whisper "when making a neck ready for a start." He was an old soldier, who delighted in administering a flogging. Everyone spoke of him as "Old Cheese," or "Cheesy," and because he always wore a snuff-coloured coat reaching to his heels he was known also as "snuffy skull-thatcher." Nearly always a crowd of small boys pursued him with hooting and hisses when he walked down the street.[1]

II

In spite of being only an assistant, Tom Cheshire hanged a supreme criminal "all on his own" during the régime of his master, James Foxen. On the 9th of January, 1824, he superintended the execution of John Thurtell for the murder of a fellow gamester named William Weare in Gill's Hill Lane, near Elstree. It was the fashionable crime of the moment, making as great a noise as that of William Corder. The newspapers were filled with columns of lurid details. Little else was talked of from Land's End to John o' Groat's.

Yet it had been a most cowardly and sordid murder, its object being the money which the victim was supposed to carry on his person. Having consented to go into the country with his friend for a few days' shooting,

[1] "Heroes of the Guillotine and Gallows," p. 6, from "Curiosities of Street Literature," Reeves & Turner (1871); *Bell's Life*, 15th and 22nd February, 5th April, 1829.

the unhappy Weare set out with Thurtell in a dog-cart one dark night along the St. Albans road from London to Gill's Hill cottage, which was to be their headquarters. When nearing the end of the journey Thurtell shot his companion, whose body he rifled and concealed in a pond. Unfortunately for the murderer, he had two accomplices, named Probert and Hunt, who turned King's evidence against him. The corpse was discovered, the assassin arrested, and he was brought to trial eventually at Hertford.

The crime itself was commonplace enough, but the personality of the criminal gave zest to the tragedy. Thurtell was a strong, tall, handsome man, who was a familiar figure in low sporting circles. He belonged to a disreputable gang that infested the turf. He was even better known as a hanger-on of the prize ring. A capable boxer himself, he had acted as the second frequently at the fights of professional pugilists. Although neither his lineage nor his breeding entitled him to a place among the Toms and Jerrys of his day, he had rubbed shoulders with his betters on the racecourse, at prize-fights, and the *esprit de corps* of the world of sport was aroused in his favour. As soon as it was known that he was to be tried for murder, "the fancy" became all agog with excitement, every one of them hoping that the accused man would be acquitted.

Sympathy with Thurtell increased when it became known that Weare, his victim, had been a card-sharper and a cheat, who had swindled him out of a considerable sum of money. Aware of the mean character of the fellow, hundreds of keen sportsmen considered that shooting had been too good for him, and that the subsequent throat-cutting and battering out of brains had been just retribution. Most people were sorry that a fine manly fellow like Thurtell should be tried for his life because he had rid the world of a dishonoured gamester.

> " They cut his throat from ear to ear,
> His brains they battered in.
> His name was Mr. William Weare,
> He lived at Lyon's Inn."

The sanguinary verses were upon everybody's lips, but no one cared a jot for the fate of William Weare while reciting them.

The intrepidity of Thurtell during his trial helped to increase the compassion of the public. In those days counsel was not allowed to address the Court on behalf of a prisoner, so Thurtell had to deliver the speech for the defence himself, making an eloquent oration. As an histrionic effort it was superb, for the accused man had a splendid voice and knew how to use it. In argument it was less effective, because there was no possible answer to the evidence set forth by the prosecution. Nevertheless, everyone in Court, except the Judge, who followed with a most deadly summing-up, was deeply impressed by Thurtell's rhetoric.

The local authorities at Hertford were as much concerned as were the authorities at Bury St. Edmunds when Corder was hanged to secure an experienced executioner. Before the trial was over a message had been dispatched to John Wontner, the Keeper of Newgate, " to send down a proper man," and for some reason Tom Cheshire was chosen. Perhaps Foxen was unwell, or already engaged, but it is strange that he did not make an effort to attend the hanging of such an important criminal. His obituary notice in the *Gentleman's Magazine*, indeed, does credit him with Thurtell's scalp, but on the authority of other documents we are obliged to give the honour to Cheshire.[1]

So before the verdict was pronounced " Old Cheese " travelled down to Hertford on the top of Norris's coach with a complete set of " furniture." Upon his arrival he sought out an appropriate public house, and, having engaged a room, he proceeded to wile away the time in the bar parlour. Being recognized before long, he became the centre of an admiring throng. They plied him with drink and got him to talk freely about his craft, and he opened his bag and exhibited his ropes and his nooses. For a short time he was as drunk as any hangman has a right to be even when his work is finished.

Unfortunately, too, Tom always grew quarrelsome when in his cups. After giving pantomimic displays of the correct way to tie up a " party," he proceeded to wrangle with the other folks in the bar, a quarrel with a coachman leading to a fierce fight. While the hangman and his adversary were pummelling each other the hangman's ropes were stolen by one of the bar-loafers, and finally the landlord interfered, turning Cheshire into the street. Fuming with rage, he went at once to Hertford gaol to complain of his wrongs, whereupon the turnkeys locked him up in an empty cell, so that he could be kept out of mischief and might sleep off the effects of his carousal.

[1] See *Morning Chronicle*, 8th and 9th January, 1824; " Many Coloured Life " (Hugh Cunningham), 1842, p. 14; *The Town*, 25th April, 1840.

And here they made him stay until the day of execution.

His head may have ached on this memorable morning, but he showed no signs of discomfort. Evidently his treatment in prison had been salutary, for no hangman ever acquitted himself with more credit. It was a gala day in the town, and all the countryside seemed to have flocked into the open space around the gaol. A brand-new gallows with drop complete, similar to that used at Newgate, had been built for the occasion. All the sharks and blacklegs who frequented the racecourses in the home counties had journeyed to Hertford to watch the hanging of their notorious comrade. There were scores of young women, of the sort known to their contemporaries as "Cyprians" or "ladybirds," perched up aloft in gigs and cabriolets. Pierce Egan himself, the most popular of sporting editors, had come down especially to write "an account" of the proceedings.

Neither the crowds nor the uproar nor the intemperance of the previous day had any effect upon the nerves of Tom Cheshire. He bound his prisoner and adjusted the noose and knots with perfect nonchalance. While the rope was being tied to the cross-beam Thurtell became anxious about the length of drop that was being given him.

"Have I got enough fall?" he asked, questioning both the keeper of the gaol and the hangman.

Cheshire was not offended in the least, like Foxen at the execution of Corder, assuring the prisoner that the fall he was going to give him was quite sufficient, this opinion being corroborated by the Governor of the prison. And it proved to be correct, for although a fall of only two or three feet had been allowed, the spectators declared that Thurtell's neck broke " with a sound like a pistol shot " when the trap-door tumbled.

Ten years later, on Tuesday, the 25th of November, 1834, Tom Cheshire once more officiated by himself on an important occasion, hanging Joseph Moseley and William Garside at Horsemonger Lane gaol.[1] The two criminals were cotton-spinners at Hyde in Cheshire, and had shot a son of their employer, Mr. Ashton, a well-known factory owner, in consequence of a dispute about wages. Since the Luddite atrocities of 1812 no crime had made greater noise in the north of England, owing to the social position of the murdered youth and because three years elapsed before the assassins were discovered. Then, a companion having " peached " on them, they were apprehended.

When convicted and condemned to death a strange impediment prevented the carrying out of the law. A dispute arose between the Sheriffs of Cheshire and Lancashire as to which of the two was obliged to hang Moseley and Garside. Neither official would undertake the task, so the matter was referred to the Court of King's Bench, which decided that the execution should be done by its own marshal, assisted by the Sheriff of Surrey. Hence it came about that the two murderers met their deaths at Horsemonger Lane gaol and that " Old Cheese " was chosen as " Jack Ketch." Somehow or other they managed to keep him sober for the occasion, since, as in the case of Thurtell, he gave satisfaction to everybody.

[1] *The Town*, 18th April, 1840.

EXECUTION OF THURTELL BY THOMAS CHESHIRE IN 1824

[*To face p.* 202.

III

Hangmen were becoming scarcer all over the country, because of the increased expense of their maintenance. Of the English county towns York alone continued to afford the luxury of keeping a private executioner of its own, John Curry being still alive and competent. In Scotland the chief expert was Thomas Young of Glasgow, who from 1814 until his death in 1840 seems to have done more business than anybody. But even in Scotland local authorities were getting rid of their hangmen. In the same year that Moseley and Garside met their doom the town council of Inverness decided to dispense with the services of Donald Ross, who had been in office for nearly a quarter of a century. During this period he had hanged only three men, and although he had a regular salary, he had broken the world's record in the annexation of perquisites.

"First he had been provided with a house and bedding.

"Second, he was allowed 36 peats for the tacksman of petty customers.

"Third, he had a bushel of coals out of every cargo of English coals imported into the town.

"Fourth, he was allowed a piece of coal, as large as he could carry, out of every cargo of Scotch coals.

"Fifth, he had a peck of oatmeal out of every hundred bolls landed on the shore.

"Sixth, he had a fish out of every creel or basket of fish brought to market.

"Seventh, he had a penny for every sack of oatmeal sold in the market.

> " Eighth, he had a peck of salt out of every cargo.
>
> " Ninth, he was allowed every year a suit of clothes, two shirts, two pairs of stockings, a hat, and two pairs of shoes.
>
> " Finally, he had levied extensive blackmail in the shape of Christmas boxes." [1]

Having drawn up a balance sheet, the Inverness town council made the discovery that it had cost them £400 for every man who had been hanged during the last twenty years. Thomas Young had a wage of a pound a week with free board and lodgings and coal and candles, in addition to sundry articles of clothing and a guinea for every execution. But he was a creature of moderate appetite in comparison with a cormorant like Donald Ross. Unfortunately there is no record of what the hangman of Aberdeen was able to do for himself.

If it were not for the fact that his character and disposition are familiar to historians of the period, Thomas Cheshire would be as elusive a hangman as Richard Arnet or his predecessor Banks. It has been shown already that there are reasons to believe that he was employed occasionally as an assistant in the days of Brunskill and Langley, and it is probable that he co-operated sometimes with Jemmy Botting. Still, as we have seen, nothing definite is known of him until he comes within the ken of history as the assistant of Jim Foxen. He fades away, nevertheless, immediately after the death of his chief to reappear once more as the deputy to the famous William Calcraft a year or two later.

It is not known when he died, but evidently he was

[1] *Sunday Times*, 5th January, 1814.

alive at the accession of Queen Victoria. Somewhere hidden in the files of a chatty newspaper of the late thirties, or perhaps during the forties of the last century, an obituary notice of him must be in existence; or an indication at all events of the date or manner of his death. But whenever such a paragraph comes to light one thing is certain: it can say nothing that is creditable of "Old Cheese," who must remain for all time the most degraded and disreputable of the Hangmen of England.

WILLIAM CALCRAFT
(1829–1874)

XIV

WILLIAM CALCRAFT

(1829–1874)

I

WHEN James Foxen died on the 14th of February, 1829, the Court of Aldermen did not give his place to the assistant hangman as usual in such cases, but cast their eyes around in search of a worthy successor to the dead executioner. They were reluctant to appoint Thomas Cheshire, who was becoming more sottish and disreputable as he advanced in years, always ready to hobnob with any scoundrel in the lowest tap-room if there was a likelihood of being treated to a drink. All possibility of his preferment is said to have vanished irretrievably in little more than a month's time. Deputed to take charge at the execution of three highway robbers on the 24th of March, he made a sad mess of his work in the case of a convict named Thomas Birmingham, for the rope slipped and the man suffered a lingering death. Owing to this blunder " Old Cheese " is supposed to have lost his last chance of promotion.

About this time, moreover, the authorities had sorted out two suitable executioners from amongst the numerous applicants for the vacant position. One, an ex-soldier called Smith, had often been one of the firing-party at a military execution, the other, William Calcraft, by name, had hanged two men already at Lincoln when no one else could be found to operate. Both were young and vigorous men of reputable character. The Committee of the City Gaols, after a lengthy conclave, rejected Smith, whose credentials merely testified that he was a dead shot, and chose Calcraft because of his previous experience of the rope. Accordingly William Calcraft was duly elected, and sworn in as Executioner for the City of London and Middlesex on the 4th of April, 1829.[1]

This famous person was born near Chelmsford in Essex in the year 1800, a village named Baddow being said to be his birthplace, although his name does not appear in the register of baptisms either at Great Baddow or Little Baddow. Forsaking his original trade of cobbler, he drifted to London as a young man, serving for a short time as watchman at Reid's brewery, Clerkenwell. Having become a hawker of meat pies, his occupation led him to attend most of the executions at Newgate and Horsemonger Lane, and in due course he made the acquaintance of Foxen and Cheshire. After moving in hangmen's circles for a short time he took a liking to the hangman's craft, with the result that he volunteered to assist in the hanging at Lincoln, thus graduating for the position of public executioner.

It was not long before he had some work to do. Nine days after his appointment—on the 13th of April—he was called upon the hang Esther Hibner, a female monster of the type of Mrs. Brownrigg and Mrs. Metyard, who had tortured to death one of her girl apprentices. The case had created the greatest indignation throughout the land, the cruelty having been fiendish. The body of the

[1] *Observer*, 5th April, 1829.

dead child was a mass of sores, caused by savage floggings, and aggravated by want of proper food and nourishment, the toes and fingers were mortified and dropping off and the lungs in an advanced state of disease. Everyone cried out for vengeance upon Mrs. Hibner. Everyone was gratified when she was sentenced to death. No woman has ever been more execrated.

The last scene was a horrible one, for the murderess had attempted suicide in her cell and was weak and emaciated. Using her last remaining strength in resistance against the gaolers, she had to be dragged to the gallows. So violent were her struggles that it was only possible to dress her in a black skirt over her night-gown. "With the sallowness of her complexion," says one of the reporters, "this contributed to give her a most unearthly aspect." She was wearing still the strait jacket in which they had been obliged to confine her. The great mob that filled the Old Bailey cheered the hangman when he appeared on the scaffold. They cheered more vociferously when Esther Hibner was carried up the steps, afterwards hooting and hissing until the drop fell. Altogether it was a tempestuous début for William Calcraft.

But he was exceptionally strong, and apparently had no nerves at all in those days, being stolid and unruffled whatever the occasion. He was not in the least bloodthirsty, however, and did not take the ghoulish pride in his trade that Foxen and Cheshire had done. On the contrary, he could be induced to talk about it but rarely, always trying to change the subject, as though ashamed of it, whenever it happened to be mentioned. A simple, silent soul, his chief hobby was the breeding of rabbits and pigeons. He had been married for about four years and was devoted to his wife, who had presented him already with two little hangmen.

On the last day of 1829 he took part in another memorable execution, the victim being Thomas Maynard, a clerk in the Custom House, who was the last person to be hanged for forgery. Although the code in such cases was not altered until seven years later, the public conscience was so averse to the death penalty that the authorities henceforth always found an excuse for a reprieve. The unfortunate Maynard was hanged with three others in the Old Bailey, and his death is significant of what was going to happen during the whole of the Calcraft régime, it being reported that the forger and his fellow sufferers "all struggled very much" after the trap-door had fallen. For the new hangman persisted in using a "short drop," and was allowed to have his way by the authorities.

Besides his work as public executioner Calcraft had other duties as well. Flogging continued to be a punishment still, and it was he who had to administer it. His fee was half a crown for each flagellation, besides an allowance for birch-rods and cat-o'-nine-tails. Two months after his installation he whipped a journeyman silk-weaver for a hundred yards along the Bethnal Green road, administering seventy lashes. It is pleasant to read that "apparently they were lightly inflicted." Accounts differ as to the actual salary that the new hangman received. According to some accounts it was a guinea a week, according to others it was twenty-five shillings. All agree, however, that he had an extra guinea for every person who was hanged.[1] When employed outside London he demanded a special fee, often earning as much as ten pounds.

II

No other executioner had a term of office comparable to that of Calcraft.

We have seen that Dennis reigned for fifteen years, Thrift for seventeen, Turlis for nineteen, and Brunskill—the record breaker hitherto—for as long as twenty-eight years. Calcraft, however, acted as hangman from the 4th of April, 1829, until the 25th of May, 1874, a period of forty-five years! Nevertheless, he was never a skilful craftsman. On the contrary, most of his victims seem to have been "violently convulsed" for several minutes after he had released the trap-door. Many foolish scoffs and jeers are uttered incessantly by smart young people at the expense of mid-Victorian times, but, strange to say, not one of these clever folk has thought it worth while to impeach the Home Office of the forties, fifties and sixties of the nineteenth century for its inhumanity in allowing an ignorant and obstinate old hangman to choke his fellow creatures to death. But Calcraft, until late in life, was such a simple, kindly creature—who, when he visited Newgate for his weekly wages always had a child or grandchild clinging affectionately to his hand—that possibly the authorities were deceived into the belief that his habits as an executioner were as gentle as those of his private life.[2]

1 *Weekly Dispatch*, 7th June, 1829; *Weekly Budget*, 20th December, 1879; "Groans of the Gallows," p. 9.

2 "Chronicles of Newgate," Major Arthur Griffiths, II., 414.

During his long tenure of office he executed many malefactors whose names will remain for ever among the most illustrious in the annals of crime. Of a list of twelve of the most redoubtable, each and all have been the subject of a monograph in one or more recent publications on criminology, and some are mentioned every day whenever there is a discussion upon the *causes célèbres* of the last century. They are familiar in the mouth as household words. In due course no doubt all of them will be allotted a separate volume in the *Notable British Trials* series. A few already have a place there. The list is as follows :—

(1) John Bishop and Thomas Williams, hanged in the Old Bailey on the 5th of December, 1831, for " burking " a poor little Italian boy.

(2) James Greenacre, once a prosperous tradesman in Southwark, hanged in the Old Bailey on the 2nd of May, 1837, for the murder of Hannah Brown.

(3) François Courvoisier, a Swiss butler, hanged in the Old Bailey, on the 6th of July, 1840, for the murder of his master, Lord William Russell, at his residence in Norfolk Street, Park Lane.

(4) James Bloomfield Rush, a tenant farmer, hanged at Norwich on the 21st of April, 1849, for shooting his landlord, Mr. Isaac Jermy, of Stanfield Hall, the Recorder of Norwich.

(5) Frederick George Manning and his wife, Marie Manning, hanged at Horsemonger Lane gaol on the 13th of November, 1849, for the murder of the paramour of the woman, named Patrick O'Connor.

(6) James Mullins, an ex-policeman, hanged in the Old Bailey on the 19th of November, 1860, for the murder of his employer, Mrs. Emsley, at Stepney.

(7) Franz Müller, a German, hanged in the Old Bailey on the 14th of November, 1864, for the murder of Mr. Briggs in a carriage on the North London Railway.

(8) Dr. E. W. Pritchard, hanged in Glasgow on the 28th of July, 1865, for the murder of his wife and mother-in-law.

(9) Allen, Larkin, and O'Brien, hanged at Salford on the 23rd of November, 1867, for the murder of a policeman, named Brett, near Manchester.

(10) Michael Barrett, a Fenian, hanged in the Old Bailey on the 26th of May, 1868, for his complicity in the Clerkenwell Explosion. The last public execution in England.

(11) Walter Millar, hanged in Newgate on 1st of August, 1870, for the murder of the Rev. Elias Huelin and Anne Boss at Chelsea.

(12) John Owen, hanged at Aylesbury on the 8th of August, 1870, for the murder of a family of seven persons at Denham.

Probably most people will be surprised that the greatest name in the criminal calendar of the nineteenth century does not appear in the above category. Calcraft had not the honour of visiting Stafford gaol on the 14th of June, 1856, to hang Dr. William Palmer of Rugeley, the wholesale poisoner, who murdered his wife, his brother, several of his friends and probably all of his five children. In order to save a few pounds the local authorities employed an executioner who charged a lower fee—one Smith of Dudley, the assistant of Calcraft "on great occasions." He is described by a contemporary as "a tall wiry man, with a keen eye, his cheeks and part of his forehead closely shaved, dressed in a velveteen jacket, loose trousers and a billycock hat."[1] It is improbable that Calcraft was disappointed because he had not the distinction of executing the famous poisoner, since he did not worry about such things, taking so little interest in his work that he never could remember whom he had hanged and whom he had not. Nevertheless, the loss of his ten pounds may have vexed him. Palmer, for his part, appeared quite satisfied, making no complaint at the indignity of being attended by a provincial hangman.

III

In looking through the record of Calcraft's twelve chief executions it is difficult to decide which was his *chef d'œuvre*. The case of Bishop and Williams caused a great sensation in England, coming as it did so soon after the similar crimes of Burke and Hare, "the Scottish resurrection men," who had murdered more than a dozen victims in West Port, Edinburgh, by suffocating them with pitch-plasters in order to sell the corpses to the surgeons. Panic reigned for a long time in London, and it was feared that gangs of merciless body-snatchers were infesting the city, like that of Bishop and Williams, on the look-out for unprotected children, so that they

[1] He must not be confused with Smith, the ex-soldier who was Calcraft's competitor in 1829 for the post of executioner for London and Middlesex. Cf. "Heroes of the Guillotine and Gallows," Frederick Farrar, p. 3.

might kill them and take them to the dissecting-rooms.

The crime of James Greenacre became in its turn an equally popular horror, because of the personality of the criminal and the brutality of the murder. The man had been a prominent local politician in the Borough in his palmy days, when proprietor of a large shop in the Kent Road, a radical orator of the robust kind and sanctimonious in his religious opinions. He cut up his victim, whom he killed for the money in her possession, and distributed the pieces in various parts of the suburbs. For weeks nothing was talked of but Greenacre and his murder, while noblemen and members of Parliament visited him in the condemned cell just as in the good old-fashioned days of Jack Sheppard and James Maclean. When the man was hanged—to the great delight of bed-ridden old Jemmy Botting—it was noted by the reporters that Calcraft appeared on the scaffold in a black suit with gold chains hanging from his pocket and " a hat by no means a Townsend."

Three years later another thrill of horror passed through the metropolis when it was known that Lord William Russell, an uncle of the Duke of Bedford, had been found in bed with his throat cut at his home, No. 14 Norfolk Street, Park Lane. A few cynical club-men remarked to one another that it was strange that no one had murdered the cantankerous old fellow long ago, but everybody else pitied the poor old gentleman, who had been done to death in such a cruel manner. Tragedy also had been associated with his birth seventy-three years before, since he had been born five months after his father, Lord Tavistock, had been killed in the hunting-field, and Lady Tavistock, his mother, who was devotedly attached to her husband, had died of a broken heart during the next year. In due course, Courvoisier, the butler of the house, was charged with the murder. After a trial of extraordinary interest, during which the accused man embarrassed his counsel, Charles Phillips, by a secret confession of his guilt, he was condemned to death. The only incident of note in connection with the execution was the presence of Thackeray, the novelist, who described his impressions in one of the most famous of his essays, " On Going to See a Man Hanged."

The execution of James Bloomfield Rush at Norwich was one of the greatest events in Calcraft's life. The peculiar savagery of the murder had aroused the most intense excitement throughout the country, for the ferocious Rush, who had a grievance against Mr. Jermy, his landlord, had come to his home at Stanfield Hall one evening, and after shooting him as well as his son, had seriously wounded the son's wife and one of the maid-servants. Such wholesale brutality had not been known in recent years. Such a bloodthirsty scoundrel as Rush had not appeared since the murders in the Ratcliffe Highway. Other circumstances helped to inflame public interest. For the dead Mr. Jermy was not only Recorder of Norwich, but a country gentleman of considerable estate, while his assassin was well known in West Norfolk, having carried on business for many years as a land agent and auctioneer, besides being a farmer. The trial, too, lasted for no less than six days, the prisoner defending himself with much skill. All over England the greatest excitement prevailed until the result was known, and the local newspapers had a prodigious sale.

On Friday, the 20th of April, 1849, the day before he hanged Rush outside Norwich gaol, Calcraft had carried out another execution at Bristol, which aroused little interest except in the West Country, but affected the hangman himself more than any in which he had been engaged. The criminal was a pretty maid-servant, only seventeen years old, named Sarah Harriett Thomas. She had been very unhappy in her place, having been treated shamefully by a cruel mistress, who beat her and kept her half-starved. Exasperated at length beyond endurance, the girl crept into the woman's bedroom one night while she was asleep and struck her on the head with a stone so that she died. It was impossible to reduce the charge to one of manslaughter, and the unhappy Sarah Thomas was condemned to death.

Although the most uncommunicative of hangmen, Calcraft seems to have confided his thoughts to a reporter on this occasion.

" I never felt so much compunction," he observed on the following afternoon, " as I did yesterday, at Bristol in having to bring that young girl to the scaffold for the murder of her mistress. She was, in my opinion, one of the prettiest and most intellectual girls I have met with in any society."

His task at Bristol indeed must have been the worst ordeal he had ever known. When he entered the girl's cell with the Governor of the gaol she was in an agony of fear, crying pitifully, " I won't be hanged; take me home, oh, take me home! " While being pinioned she resisted frantically, struggling and screaming all the time, and several warders were required to drag her into the yard. Here the chaplain succeeded in pacifying her somewhat by telling her that her last moments should be employed in prayer. Ceasing to weep and to struggle, she allowed herself to be led to the foot of the gallows beyond the prison walls; but at the sight of the scaffold terror overwhelmed her once more, and she was carried shrieking up the ladder. Calcraft declared that he did not "give her time scarcely to appear before the multitude" when he drew the bolt.

Great and famous though Greenacre and Courvoisier and Rush undoubtedly were, and although all England rang with their names, it is probable that the two greatest and most famous criminals to pass through Calcraft's hands were Mr. and Mrs. Manning of Bermondsey. For some reason or other their crime seized hold of the popular imagination more powerfully than any other during his tenure of office, except that of Dr. Palmer. And it occurred during the year of Rush's trial and execution, a vintage year of crime.

Nevertheless it was a commonplace murder and detected speedily. The Mannings shot their victim while he was paying a visit to their home, burying his body afterwards underneath the flagstones of the kitchen. A lover of the wife with the cognizance of her husband, he had been killed for the sake of some railway scrip and money, having secured which, the murderers took to flight. Unfortunately for them, suspicion was aroused almost immediately. The police visited their deserted house, the body was discovered where they had buried it, and a hue and cry was raised after them. Marie was arrested in Edinburgh, her husband in Jersey. At their trial, as was inevitable, both were convicted.

The execution took place on a scaffold constructed

upon the roof of Horsemonger Lane gaol on the 13th of November. Since it was a novelty for the gallows-sated mob to watch the hanging of a husband and wife at the same time, an enormous crowd assembled in front of the prison. Five hundred constables attended to keep order. Marie Manning undoubtedly was the centre of interest, her husband being an object of contempt. A Swiss by birth, handsome and robust, a hard, relentless siren destitute of morals, she was believed by everyone to be the instigator if not the actual perpetrator of the murder.

Husband and wife met in the prison chapel for the first time since their trial just before they were taken to the scaffold. She had been incensed against him bitterly owing to his attempt to cast the guilt upon her, and he was aware of it.

"I hope," he said to her, when they came face to face before the altar, "that you are not going to depart this life with animosity. . . . Will you kiss me?"

She replied that she had no animosity and kissed him. The sacrament was administered, after which they embraced and kissed one another again.

"I think," said Manning, "we shall meet in heaven."

When Calcraft had pinioned Mrs. Manning, he was considerate enough to ask her to resume her cloak—for it was a cold morning—but she refused, and, producing a black silk handkerchief, desired to be blindfolded with it. Thus, with her eyes bandaged, she was led through the long passages and up the steep and narrow staircase to the roof of the gaol. She wore a handsome black satin dress, causing that favourite material to become unfashionable for many years, just as Mrs. Anne

Turner had made starched yellow ruffs unfashionable when hanged for the murder of Sir Thomas Overbury two hundred and thirty years previously. Among the crowd that watched the execution of the Mannings was Charles Dickens, who wrote a scornful letter to the *Times* on the 13th of December from his home in Devonshire Place, complaining of the ill-behaviour of the mob, which suggests that the five hundred constables had no moral influence. Subsequently he depicted Mrs. Manning in "Bleak House" in the character of Hortense, the French maid.

IV

It is unnecessary to give particulars of the next three great events in Calcraft's career—the expiation of Mullins, Müller and Dr. Pritchard. All these criminals were heroes of *causes célèbres* of the greatest interest, especially Franz Müller, the German, who perpetrated the first railway train murder and was the first man to be arrested by means of the Atlantic cable. The two following executions, however, need a few comments, since they were important landmarks in the hangman's life, affecting his health and spirits grievously.

In recent years he had always shrunk from appearing on the scaffold when there was a chance of a hostile demonstration against him, and so during the period of the Fenian outrages he had lived in a continual state of apprehension. Threatening letters arrived at his home, he fancied that he was followed by enemies as he passed to and fro to his work; at every execution there was a party of Irishmen among the mob, who shouted yells of execration. In consequence, when it was his duty to hang the three Manchester Fenians for the murder of a policeman, his nerves were a-jangle and he was sorely afraid. The rebel Irish were furious that Allen, Larkin and O'Brien should have been condemned to death, alleging, and no doubt with truth, that none of the three men had fired the shot that killed the policeman. Nevertheless, they had been members of the party who were attacking the prison van when the murder was committed, being thus in the eyes of the law as culpable as the actual assassin.

The " Three Fenians " were hanged outside the gaol at Salford on the 23rd of November, 1867. Inspired by the idea of martyrdom, they met their fate bravely and with great calm. Calcraft, indeed, was infinitely more terrified than they were. He had received many anonymous letters from the friends of the convicts, threatening him with death, which had driven away all his pluck. He shuffled about the prison yard irresolutely, seeming afraid to mount the steps of the gallows, while the sweat poured in big drops from his brow. It was the same when he had to hang the handsome young Fenian, Michael Barrett, on the 26th of May of the following year in the Old Bailey. More abusive letters had reached him, and he was panic-stricken again. He must have been relieved to know that this would be the last public execution in England, and that hereafter all such exhibitions were to be secrets of the prison house. Old age seemed to have come upon him suddenly. He was no longer the strong, imperturbable hangman of a few years before.

Until recently, however, he had shown little signs of wear and tear. The simple, amiable creature had lived a happy and placid private life without a thought of his profession when not engaged in it. For many years his home was in Devizes Street, near the Rosemary Branch, Hoxton, next door to the " Tiger " ale-house, where he was fond of playing at skittles. Here he used to meet his " brother-snobs," the rabbit-fanciers, he himself being well known in the rabbit world, his breeds winning many first-class prizes. One of his great joys was a pet pony, which used to follow him about like a dog. At this period he has been described as a stout, burly man with grey hair and whiskers and gentle black eyes. Outside his own neighbourhood his only friend was the landlady of a tavern opposite the Sessions House in the Old Bailey, to whom he used to bring flowers from his garden. He was fond of flowers, and we read of him appearing on the scaffold with a rose in his button-hole.

According to Serjeant Ballantine there were occasions periodically when Calcraft was honoured by the recognition of officialdom. At the close of the Sheriffs' dinner on the last day of the Sessions he was allowed to appear in the dining-room, when he was presented with a glass of wine. " This he drank to the health of his patrons," declares the great barrister, who describes him as a decently dressed, quiet-looking man," and expressed with becoming modesty his gratitude for past favours and his hopes for favours to come." [1]

Not long after the abolition of public executions a dark shadow fell upon the old hangman's home. He lost the affectionate wife with whom he had lived for forty-five years, a bereavement that saddened his life for evermore.

[1] " Some Experiences of a Barrister's Life," William Ballantine, 1882, p. 88.

Henceforth he became morose and taciturn, shunning intercourse with his former cronies. He had removed to a house in Poole Street, off the New North Road, close to the Regent's Canal, and no longer visited his favourite tavern for a game of skittles or a chat with his fellow rabbit-fanciers. It is said that some of them ventured to chaff him one day about his occupation, whereupon he left the public-house never to return.[1] With most of his neighbours he was not popular, in spite of the fact that he had attended church with his wife every Sunday morning for many years, and on week-days it was his habit to leave his home either very early or else after dark so that he would not attract attention. He had many sons and daughters, "morally brought up and schooled," of whom he was very proud.

In the early days private executions inside a prison do not appear to have been conducted in a more humane manner than those held formerly in public. Calcraft still persisted in his short drop, aided and abetted by the authorities. At the first private execution in Maidstone gaol on the 13th of August, 1868, when Thomas Wells, a railway porter, was hanged for the murder of Mr. Walsh, the station-master at Dover, "the fall" allowed was only one of two or three feet, and life was not extinct until three or four minutes after the falling of the drop. It was the same in Newgate prison on the 8th of September following, at the execution of Alexander Mackay for the murder of Mrs. Grossmith. According to a reporter "the fall was a very short one, and signs of life were visible for a longer time after the bolt was drawn than we remember to have seen on a similar occasion." Smith

[1] *Daily Telegraph*, 17th December, 1879.

of Dudley, the man in the velveteen jacket, continued to be the assistant.

Calcraft, now in his sixty-ninth year, looked his age. He was still broad and thick-set, but his straggling hair and long beard were snow-white. Always dressed in black, he wore an odd-looking tall hat, and when going about his work carried a small canvas bag containing his "tackle." On such occasions he stared doggedly in front of him, shambling as he walked along.

The late Mr. John Farrell, editor of the *Manchester Courier* about thirty years ago, used to tell a story of an encounter that he had with Calcraft when he was a reporter on the staff of the *Sheffield Daily Telegraph* in the late sixties or early seventies of the last century. It happened on the afternoon before an execution, while Farrell and a fellow pressman were visiting the local gaol in search of copy for their newspapers. Evening was falling, and while standing together before the gallows in the prison yard, one of the young journalists remarked to the other:

"I wonder whether that bloodthirsty scoundrel, Calcraft, has arrived!"

An instant later an old man with a white beard stepped from the gloomy cavern beneath the scaffold.

"The bloodthirsty scoundrel," he growled, "is here."

In spite of his antiquated methods Calcraft was allowed to retain his office until it became apparent that he might break down at any moment. When he officiated for the last time, at the execution of James Godwin in Newgate prison on the 25th of May, 1874, for wife murder, he carried out his task in the usual clumsy fashion. Accord-

CALCRAFT, THE HANGMAN

[*To face p.* 226.

ing to the newspapers, the convict " died hard." His breast heaved convulsively, while his pinioned hands were raised repeatedly to his throat. And the description concludes, as though with a sigh of relief: " It was all over in a few minutes." They did not dislike Calcraft in Newgate, so Major Arthur Griffiths tells us, but nevertheless it is safe to conclude that no one was sorry when he was superannuated at last.

Although the Court of Aldermen granted him a pension equal to his former salary, the old hangman was furious that he had been dismissed. He vowed that he was fit and sound and able to go about his work. Henceforth he grew more snappish and surly than ever, becoming, too, an even greater recluse. Once, so the *Police News* declares, he overcame his reluctance to meet strangers in its favour, granting an interview to two of its reporters, but we have only the editor's word for it. Still, notwithstanding his fuming and frettings, he survived for five years longer, for he did not die until the evening of Saturday, the 13th of December, 1879, in his eightieth year.[1]

[1] *Morning Advertiser*, 16th December; *Illustrated London News*, 20th December; *Weekly Dispatch*, 21st December; *Police News*, 27th December, 1879; " Dictionary of National Biography " under " William Calcraft "; " Life and Recollections of Calcraft, the Hangman."

WILLIAM MARWOOD
(1874-1883)

XV

WILLIAM MARWOOD

(1874–1883)

I

" If Pa killed Ma who'd kill Pa ? "

" Marwood."

To anyone born as long ago as fifty years this must have been a familiar riddle in childhood. In those days Mr. William Marwood, the public executioner, was a popular celebrity. His exploits were chronicled at full length in the newspapers, where his habits and customs also were discussed in innumerable paragraphs. He was as well known to everybody as Fred Archer or W. G. Grace or John Roberts.

" If Pa killed Ma who'd kill Pa ? "

" Marwood."

People were not ashamed of taking an interest in their executioner. In those days it seemed right and natural so to do. William Marwood was a decent and well-conducted member of society, a good husband and a God-fearing man, and everyone believed, moreover, that he was the greatest master of his trade that England had ever seen. Like Fred Archer and W. G. Grace and John Roberts, he was a champion in his own particular line. And that, as few people were ashamed to acknowledge, was one of extraordinary fascination. Almost everyone, in his heart of hearts, loved " a good hanging."

Marwood, like Calcraft before him, was bred a shoemaker. He, too, was a native of East Anglia, having been born at Horncastle in Lincolnshire, in 1820. But, unlike Calcraft, he did not desert his home in early youth. Instead he remained in the town of his birth, sedulously plying his trade as cobbler in a little two-storied cottage close to the churchyard until he was past middle age. He was very poor all the time, but was encouraged by dreams of better days in store and by the ambition to achieve fame in another calling. For many years he had taken an interest in public executions, although he had never witnessed one of them, coming to the conclusion that the present method was unsatisfactory. By experiment and careful calculation he was convinced at last that he could effect an improvement. So he began to write to the authorities to protest against the inhumanity of strangling men and women slowly to death, pointing out that by adjusting the length of the rope to the weight of the body the neck would be dislocated and death become instantaneous. It was a long time before he had a chance of proving the truth of his belief; but at length, in 1871—when he was past fifty years of age—the Governor of Lincoln prison engaged him to perform an execution. One commission led to another, and it was soon manifest that the Marwood system was the right one. After the dismissal of Calcraft it was inevitable that the Horncastle cobbler should be chosen to fill the vacant place.

No previous executioner had ever taken such an intense pride in his craft. He regarded himself very properly as an important public official. He declared that he was a real benefactor to the human race, since owing to his reforms the mode of execution had become a swift and merciful one. Indeed, he assured Major Griffiths, the Inspector of Prisons, that he took up the work in order to be useful to his generation. Naturally this self-respect earned for him the respect of his contemporaries. Alone among the men of his trade, he was never reviled in the public street. No obscene little boys dared to pursue him with cries of " Jack Ketch." Usually he was received with deferential salutations. Certainly Marwood is entitled to be called " the Gentleman Hangman."

Naturally he had the utmost contempt for Calcraft, expressing withering scorn whenever his name was mentioned. " The short-drop man," he used to style him, adding disdainfully, " He choked his prisoners to death ! " He was fond of saying of his predecessor, " He *hanged* them, I *execute* them." A bitter piece of sarcasm indeed, since the verb to hang was a most malodorous word in the Marwood vocabulary. He would never allow himself to be spoken of as the hangman. He was always the executioner.[1]

His new occupation did not cause him to desert his old. Even after his appointment as successor to Calcraft he continued to carry on his trade as shoemaker at his home in Church Lane, but he stuck up the sign " Crown Office " outside the door to announce that he was now a Government official. The advertisement was a shrewd one, resulting in much increase of business. As soon as the townsfolk of Horncastle and its vicinity were aware that their old friend and neighbour had obtained the coveted and fascinating position of public executioner,

[1] *Law Journal*, 8th November, 1883.

they began to flock to his shop—which had been neglected by them hitherto—and became customers. Aware that he was a cheerful, chatty soul, they were sure that it would be worth their while to let him have their patronage. And they were not disappointed.

As time went on the little cobbler's shop in Church Lane became a museum of criminal relics, those of which he was most proud being the coils of rope that were dangling from the ceiling. One of them was his special treasure, that which had hanged Charles Peace and Lefroy, Dr. Lamson and Kate Webster, his great quartette of most eminent criminals. The Marwood rope, moreover, was a fearsome object which made one's blood run cold, a contraption of his own invention with a running noose fitted with a ring of metal, fashioned to his order at a Government workshop. Beside it he used to display one of Calcraft's ropes, of which somehow he had obtained possession, a rope that terminated in a clumsy slip-knot of most unworkmanlike appearance. And while he requested his visitors to compare the two he would murmur, cynically :

" He *hanged* them, I *execute* them ! "

Nevertheless, there was nothing morbid or repulsive in his talk about his trade. He spoke of an execution just as a clever surgeon speaks of an operation in the lecture-room, dwelling upon the details with professional pride if his auditors were intelligent or appeared to be interested, reiterating without any false modesty that he was the most humane and merciful operator that the world had ever seen. Weigh carefully and give as long a drop as possible, such was the text from which he preached eternally. He found tongues in trees, books in

Wm MARWOOD
EXECUTIONER
CHURCH LANE, HORNCASTLE
LINCOLNSHIRE, ENGLAND.

June 4th – 1879

Sir in Replie To your Letter of this Day i Will give you a Compleat Staitment for Executing a Prisoner — 1-Place Pinion the Prisoner Round the Boadey and Arms Tight — 2 Place Bair the Neck — 3 Place Take the Prisoner to the Drop 4-Place-Place the Prisoner Beneath the Beam to Stand Direct under the Rope from the Top of the Beam 5-Place Strap the Prisoners Leggs Tight 6 Place Putt on the Cap 7—Place Putt on the Rope Round the Neck thite. Let the Cap be Free from the Rope to hide the Face angine Dow in Freunt 8-Place Executioner To go Direct Quick to the Leaver Let Down the Trap Doores Quick

No-Greas to be Putt on the Rope all Rops to be Well Tested before Execution and all Rops to be Kept Dry in good Order

Sir the araingements of the Place of Execution you Can git at H.M. Prison Newgate London it Wanting 2 Feet Deeper in the Pitt beneath then it is Perfect say 10 Feet beneath

Sir Pleas i thaught it would be the Best Way to give you a Clear understanding in the Araingements of a Execution of a Prisoner To Prevent aney Mistake in the Araingement in the Matter in Question

Sir i Shall be glad to asist you in all improvements

Sir i Remain your Humble Servant
Wm Marwood
Church: Lane Horncastle Lincolnshire.

LETTER WRITTEN BY MARWOOD, THE HANGMAN

[*To face p.* 234.

the running noose, sermons in ropes, and good in everything that concerned his own handicraft.[1]

In appearance he was the usual type of the Lincolnshire farmer, a sturdy person of middle height, with handsome, clear-cut features and a bluff, good-humoured manner. He wore the ordinary coat of the countryside, with tails and side-pockets, and was fond of a high black stock and a low felt hat, which helped to emphasize his individuality. With his fellow townfolk he was popular, more so, indeed, after he became " Crown Officer " than hitherto, owing to the greater interest of his conversation and because the people of Horncastle were proud of his celebrity. Although supposed to be a man of some piety, he was not a communicant, neither did he attend church, although he lived so close to it. Perhaps it was thought that the presence of the public executioner would divert the attention of the congregation, especially after events of such national importance as the hanging of Charles Peace or Lefroy or Kate Webster.

The first criminal of the front rank with whom Marwood had dealings was Henry Wainwright, who was executed in Newgate prison on the 21st of December, 1875, for the murder of a mistress. It was a crime not unlike that of James Greenacre, with some resemblance to the murder in the Red Barn. Wainwright had been a respectable tradesman in the Whitechapel Road, a local politician of some note, a talented reciter at Penny Readings and one of the most zealous churchmen of his neighbourhood. In secret he had led an immoral life, veiling his debauchery, like Greenacre, under the cloak of religion. In imitation of Corder he had buried his

[1] *Police News*, 15th September, 1883.

paramour in a grave in his workshop, and probably never would have been detected had not the police caught him by chance in the act of removing the dismembered body to another place. In spite of overwhelming evidence he persisted in denying his guilt, maintaining also his *sang froid* to the end. He chose the hymns for the service in chapel on his last Sunday; and on the evening before he died he strolled up and down the yard in the company of the Governor of the prison, smoking a cigar—allowed as a special privilege—while he recounted some of his amorous adventures. On the fatal morning he stepped briskly from his cell, nodded cheerily to the Governor and strode firmly to the execution-shed with a smile on his lips. The smile, however, died away when he beheld the crowd of spectators in front of the gallows, for the Sheriffs had given permission to almost a hundred persons to watch the exhibition.

"You curs!" cried Wainwright, pausing before he took his place beneath the beam, "so you have come to see a man die!"

III

It has been shown that the English hangman effected a peaceful penetration into Scotland on the occasion of Dr. Pritchard's execution—and possibly the innovation may have come earlier—but it was not until eleven years later that Marwood succeeded in obtaining employment at York. Until then the patriotic Tykes had persisted in maintaining a "Jack Ketch" of their own. Two capable functionaries had succeeded John Curry. The former, Nathaniel Howard by name, officiated between the years 1839 and 1853; the latter, who was the famous Thomas Askern, held office from 1853 until 1874. At last, on the 15th of May, 1878, the Newgate executioner was summoned to York Castle to hang Vincent Knowles Walker for a murder at Hull. On this occasion, unluckily, Marwood was in his worst form. Calcraft himself could not have mismanaged things more disgracefully, and the officials must have wished that old Tom Askern was back again. "The convict," we are told, "died very hard, so much as *seven minutes* elapsing before life was fully extinct."

Towards the end of the same year Marwood had an unusual experience, when he went down to Wales to hang Joseph Garcia, a Spanish sailor, who had butchered a poor labourer, named William Watkins, along with his wife and three children in their cottage home at Llangibby. The murder had been so wanton and unprovoked and cowardly that every man, woman and child in the West Country loathed the infamous Garcia—probably a homicidal maniac—with the most deadly hatred. After the execution a great multitude awaited Marwood outside Usk gaol and greeted his appearance with frantic applause, escorting him amidst cheers to the railway station, where he was compelled to hold a sort of levée. Everyone was proud of him, they all declared, nearly wringing his hand off. Called upon for a speech, he replied that he had never had such a magnificent reception before, adding amidst great laughter that he hoped that he would soon come that way again. Later, when another speech was demanded as he was coming out of his hotel at Newport, it is related that he told the people that he had " never hanged a man with greater satisfaction." [1]

Marwood, however, was not a good speaker. A few days before Christmas in the year 1879 he gave a lecture in one of the public halls in Sheffield. The place was crowded, at least six hundred people being present. Marwood, the executioner, was as " big a draw " as the great Vance or the great Macdermott. He commenced his address with various commentaries on the Bible, then rambled off into a disquisition about the Irish question, made several references to the Queen and the General Election, and harked back again to religious matters.

" The wheel of Time," he declared, " is constantly casting people into Eternity."

" So's the rope," interpolated a wag in the audience.

The people became restive and there were more interruptions. This was not the sort of thing at all that they had come to hear. Everyone had expected to listen to some of Marwood's professional experiences. The disappointed Yorkshirebites, as is their wont, began to express their disapproval in no uncertain manner. It was in vain that the Chairman appealed for order, explaining that the public executioner was not allowed to reveal official secrets. The audience refused to be appeased and demanded their money back. Finally the meeting broke up in disorder.[2]

Marwood's great quartette of criminals passed through his hands during the space of three years. Of these the first is the most illustrious by far, for it was Charles

[1] *Daily Telegraph*, 19th November, 1878.

[2] *Police News*, 27th December, 1879.

Peace, who occupies one of the topmost niches in the temple of crime, taking equal rank among homicides with Eugene Aram and William Palmer. For a murderer to achieve the highest renown two things are necessary: there must be romance of some sort in his environment and a particular atrocity about his crime. Certainly both these requirements are fulfilled in the case of Peace.

For several years before his arrest and the revelation of his villainies he was living in turn at Lambeth, Greenwich, and at Peckham, occupying a decent villa, posing as Mr. Johnson, a man of independent means. Owing to his talent as a musician, he became popular with his neighbours wherever he resided, and no one had a notion that he earned his living as a thief and a house-breaker. A small man with mobile features, he was clever in inventing all sorts of disguise, while his audacity as a burglar was unparalleled. Frequently he pillaged the house of a friend for whom he had played the fiddle a few days before at a musical party.

It was a great shock to everyone who knew him when he was arrested at Blackheath for breaking into a house and attempting to shoot a constable. The general public also became interested when it was discovered that Mr. Johnson of Peckham was a notorious crook named Charles Peace, who formerly had carried on his depredations in Yorkshire and the Midlands. This interest was increased enormously as soon as it was realised that the man was wanted by the police for the murder of Arthur Dyson at Banner Cross, near Sheffield, two years before. There was a piquancy about the crime, for it was suggested that there had been a liaison between the murderer and Mrs. Dyson. In spite of being as ugly as a monkey, Peace was a lion among the ladies. At his respectable home at Peckham he had been living with a mistress.

Other incidents helped to surround the criminal with a romantic atmosphere. He made a valiant endeavour to escape by leaping from the railway carriage while being taken in custody from London to Leeds to stand his trial, almost killing himself in the attempt. In the condemned cell he confessed to having shot a policeman in Manchester four years previously, for which crime another had been condemned to penal servitude. Although only two murders lay at his door, he had done his best to kill the Blackheath constable, while it was beyond doubt that he always went about his robberies with a loaded revolver, ready to shoot anyone who interfered with him. It was not long before the public was satisfied that few more desperate scoundrels had appeared on the criminal stage, and it appraised him accordingly. In addition to his eminence in crime and the strange vicissitudes of his career, his reputation was enhanced by the fact that he was more sanctimonious and hypocrital than either James Greenacre or Henry Wainwright.

The conduct of this amazing little man at his execution in Armley gaol, Leeds, on the 25th of February, 1879, was as hectic and typical as the rest of his career. While awaiting his doom he was fond of addressing religious homilies to the friends and relatives who visited him and to the warders who guarded him, and even to high officials who came to see him out of curiosity. When Marwood entered his cell on the last morning Peace submitted tranquilly—although it was obvious that his nerves were on edge—while the executioner fastened around his waist the usual leather belt to which his arms were secured by straps. He walked bravely to the scaffold, which was eighty yards away across the prison yard—a platform six feet high reached by steps with a pit underneath. When Marwood was about to put on the white cap Peace checked him, wishing to listen to the chaplain who was reading the service.

"Stop a minute," he cried. "I must hear this."

A moment later Marwood advanced again.

"No, no!" exclaimed Peace, "I want to speak," and then, turning to the reporters, the nervous excited little man began to address them.

"You gentlemen reporters, I wish you to notice the few words I am going to say to you. I know that my life has been base and bad. I wish you to ask the world after you have seen my death what man could die as I die if I did not die in the fear of the Lord. Tell all my friends that I feel sure they have sincerely forgiven me, and that I am going into the Kingdom of Heaven, or else to that place prepared for us to rest in until the great Judgment Day. I have no enemies that I feel to have on this earth. I wish all my enemies, or those would-be enemies—I wish them well, and I wish them to come to the Kingdom of Heaven at last. And now to one and all I say good-bye. Good-bye, Heaven bless you, and may you come to the Kingdom of Heaven at last. Amen. Say that my last wishes and my last respects are to my dear children and to their dear mother. I hope no person will disgrace them by taunting them or jeering at them on my account, but will have mercy on them. God bless you, my children! My children each good-bye. Heaven bless you! Oh, my Lord God, have mercy upon me."

Marwood, always considerate to a convict, waited until the speech had ended before adjusting the white cap.

"Almighty God," groaned Peace, "have mercy upon me," adding abruptly, "I should like to have a drink."

The chaplain continued:

"In the midst of life we are in death. . . ."

Peace was beginning to tremble.

"Can't I have a drink?" he implored. "Oh, it's too tight, it's too tight!"

"Keep still," remarked Marwood, soothingly. "I won't hurt you a bit."

The chaplain had come to the words, "I am the Resurrection and the Life," whereupon Peace ejaculated, "God bless you . . . good-bye." Marwood stepped back and pulled a string, which released the bolt, and the trap-door fell. Those standing around declare that the murderer died without a struggle.[1] The *Times* devoted three whole columns to a description of the execution, besides a leading article.

The scene on the scaffold may be gruesome, but few incidents in a life affords an equivalent revelation of psychology.

[1] *Times*, 26th February; *Daily Telegraph*, 26th February, 1879. Strange to say, Peace has not been given a place in the "Dictionary of National Biography." A whole volume, however, written ably by Mr. W. Teignmouth Shore, is devoted to him in the *Notable British Trials* series.

WILLIAM MARWOOD, HANGMAN

[*To face p.* 242.

III

Kate Webster, the Richmond murderess, was hanged on the 29th of July of the same year in Wandsworth prison. She was a savage and malicious Irishwoman, who had cut up her mistress into small parts, which she threw into the Thames. Every criminal who tries to conceal his guilt by dismembering his victim and scattering the débris over the countryside always achieves an immense celebrity—as is shown in the case of Catherine Hayes and James Greenacre—and no sooner were the bits and pieces of the unfortunate Mrs. Thomas retrieved from the river than the public realized that another epoch-making crime had been committed. The murderess disappeared when her work was done, and it was some time before she was tracked down—a circumstance which always excites popular interest. After her arrest, too, she tried to inculpate an innocent person, another sure way to win notoriety. Kate Webster's name was on everybody's lips during her lifetime. Posterity regards her as equal in rank even to Sarah Malcolm.

The Lefroy murder was committed on the London and Brighton Railway. The criminal was a decadent youth of inordinate vanity and some manifestations of talent, who had been a failure hitherto as an actor and a journalist and was miserably poor. Reduced to his last penny, he jumped into a first-class carriage in a fit of desperation, as a train was leaving Victoria Station, with the intention of robbing the sole occupant of the compartment, a retired merchant, named Frederick Gold. Mr. Gold, however, who was a sturdy old gentleman, made a vigorous resistance, and in the struggle that followed he was thrown out on to the line and killed by the fall. Being covered with blood and exhausted by his fight, the murderer was detained on suspicion by the police at Preston Park. Although the dead body had not yet been discovered in Merstham tunnel, detectives accompanied Lefroy to his alleged home at Croydon, but here he eluded them by the old expedient of entering the house by the front door, where he left his captors to await his return, and making his escape at the back. For some weeks there was a frantic search for him all over the country, while the whole of England rang with his crime.

At his execution in Lewes gaol on the 29th of November, 1881, the miserable Lefroy—according to the reports in the Press—was in a state of collapse. It is said that he had to be assisted by the warders on his journey to the scaffold, " a mere limp rag," scarcely able to move. Marwood, nevertheless, denied that the young man was almost fainting.

" All my eye," he protested. " The newspapers were wrong. Lefroy meant mischief. If I had not had him by the belt he would have given me a run round the yard." And he added, significantly, " When I tap a prisoner on the shoulder he nearly always comes to me."

Yet he seems to have been kind and gentle invariably in his manner, a contrast to James Botting and Thomas Cheshire. He always behaved like a gentleman.

Dr. Lamson was just as popular a murderer as Kate Webster or Percy Lefroy. He poisoned his brother-in-law, who was at school at Wimbledon, and his methods were both novel and audacious, since he administered a dose of aconitine to the boy in the presence of his schoolmaster either in a gelatine capsule or in a piece of plum cake while paying a casual visit. Although he had held a good position in life, he was in financial difficulties at the time, which would have been relieved by the legacy that he inherited on the death of his young relative. In spite of the doctor's craftiness and effrontery, the evidence brought against him at his trial gave him no chance of escape, and in spite of a speech of great eloquence for the defence by Montagu Williams—who had been counsel for Lefroy also—the jury returned a verdict of guilty. Marwood always spoke with admiration of the bravery of Dr. Lamson at his execution in Wandsworth prison on the 28th of April, 1882.

"The doctor," he used to say, "died like a gentleman."

In the following year Marwood had much work to do in Ireland. The secret societies were carrying on a murderous campaign, outrages of every kind were taking place all over the country. Many a Larry in consequence had to be "stretched," and the English executioner was called upon to officiate on every occasion. Unlike Calcraft under similar circumstances, Marwood did not show the least timidity. A couple of detectives always accompanied him on his journeys across St. George's Channel, and he seemed to consider their presence a sufficient protection. His confidence was justified. No attempt was made against his life. No one tried to interfere with his movements. At various dates during May and June he had the satisfaction of hanging Joseph Brady and his four accomplices for the brutal murder of Lord Frederick Cavendish and Mr. Burke in Phœnix Park.

Two months later, however, when the hangman was

taken ill suddenly at his home at Horncastle, it was rumoured that the Irish Invincibles in some way were responsible. It was a false impression entirely, Marwood's complaint being inflammation of the lungs, the result of a chill while on active duty, and complicated with jaundice. From the first there was no hope for him. After lingering a few days he died at his little house in Church Street on the 4th of September, 1883.

His death made no little noise throughout the British Isles. It was felt that a distinguished public character had passed away. Obituary notices appeared in most of the newspapers, while the sinister rumours with regard to the cause of his fatal illness were repeated everywhere. To put an end to these false reports, Dr. Sharpley, the local coroner, decided to hold an inquest, at which a physician and a surgeon both testified that death was due to pneumonia, complicated with disease of the liver. Scandal having been thus appeased, the body of the executioner was buried in Trinity churchyard, hard by his home.[1] According to the newspapers he left considerable property.

[1] "Dictionary of National Biography," under "William Marwood." The only other hangmen to be included in this work are Calcraft, Richard Brandon and Jack Ketch.

LATER HANGMEN

LATER HANGMEN

I

THE prestige of the executioner, which had been raised by Marwood to the highest level that it had ever reached, declined speedily and immeasurably when he was dead. Without question he is the last of the great hangmen. Those who came after him, good citizens though they may have been, did not possess character enough to sustain the Marwood tradition. Apparently they never realized that their predecessor had extinguished most of the ignominy that was attached to their profession.

The next in order was BARTHOLOMEW BINNS, who, according to the *St. Stephen's Review*, performed his first execution at Wandsworth prison on the 6th of November, 1883, when he hanged Henry Powell for the murder of the son of his employer. Binns also executed Patrick O'Donnell, the Irish Invincible, for shooting James Carey, the informer—whose evidence had secured the conviction of the Phœnix Park murderers—on the high seas between Cape Town and Natal. It is believed that Binns was the hero of a popular music-hall song during the 'eighties.

> "I'm the ghost of John James Christopher Benjamin Binns,
> I was cut off right in the midst of my sins."

It is immaterial to the purpose of this volume to record the date of this man's death or retirement, but he cannot have held office for much longer than a couple of years, since on the 8th of February, 1886, BERRY of Bradford, with the assistance of a sporting baronet, executed Rudge, Martin and Baker for the murder that followed the burglary at Netherby Hall. On the whole Berry appears to have been the most eminent of Marwood's successors. It was he who hanged Lipski, a commonplace murderer, whose case was made famous for all time because seventy Liberal members of Parliament signed a petition on behalf of the criminal. It was Berry also who hanged Dr. Cross, a South of Ireland wife poisoner, whom he praised—just as Marwood had praised Lamson—for being a " very brave old man." And it was Berry who would have had to hang Mrs. Maybrick had she not been reprieved, although it was whispered that he was going to lay down his tools and strike at the last minute, being convinced of her innocence. It was stated, however, that the hangman had denied the rumour, declaring that he would do his duty whatever his own feelings.

The successor to Berry of Bradford was BILLINGTON of Bolton, with regard to whose career the present writer must plead complete ignorance. It is noteworthy, nevertheless, that in recent times the provincial executioner seems to have been called in to redress the balance of the metropolitan. From the days of Billington onwards all of them appear to have been obscure persons, unknown to the general public.

II

The modern hangman is not wholly to blame because he has failed to live up to the reputation of William

Marwood. In the Victorian era, as far down at least as the late 'eighties, the bright light of publicity continued to shine upon him continuously. Calcraft and Marwood especially had an excellent Press, which referred to them invariably as though they had held honourable positions in the police administration. Naturally the attitude of the newspapers helped to influence the attitude of the public, with the result, as we have seen, that the social position of the Finisher of the Law advanced appreciably. The uplift did not continue. Within a few years after the death of Marwood the journalists had ceased to take an interest in the executioner, mentioning his name as rarely as possible, treating him as though he were an outcast. No more successful means could have been taken to effect the degradation of an individual.

The reason of the change is not far to seek. During the last decade of the nineteenth century some busybody at the Home Office took it into his head that a newspaper account of an execution was harmful to the morals of the people. The word was passed around to the Sheriffs that reporters should be excluded on these occasions, and the staffs of the various prisons were warned that the Official Secrets Act debarred them from giving information to outsiders. Now and then, it is true, the pressman was permitted to attend on the understanding that his description should be as meagre as possible, practically being blue-pencilled by the authorities. Henceforth, to all intents and purposes, officialdom carried out its executions in secret, like a mediæval Inquisition, while the great public in whose name such deeds were done were kept in ignorance of what was happening.

Had our newspaper descriptions been as lurid and

melodramatic as those in France or the United States there would have been justification for the attitude of our mandarins. But such was not the case. Nothing can have been more solemn or decorous, or has conveyed a more useful warning to everyone who read it, than the customary account in the British Press of a scene on the scaffold at the period in question. No schoolboy of the time with any imagination can have glanced through a report of the execution of Lefroy or Lamson or Lipski without believing that a terrible object-lesson had been displayed for his special benefit. " There but for the grace of God goes William Hicks," he must have murmured, and would decide on the spot that when he grew up to be a man he would never do anything to get himself hanged.

Not only did publicity act as a deterrent—which surely is the aim and object of every punishment—but no supervision of officialdom can have been more efficacious or disciplinary. In order to keep a Government department sweet and clean the fierce rays of popular opinion must be allowed to beat upon it periodically. Since the capital penalty can only be allowed to exist with the approval of democracy, it follows that democracy must be allowed to know what occurs when a murderer is hanged. No melodramatic details need be published. All that is necessary is a grave and solemn description, such as appeared in the newspapers forty years ago. The " Aberdare Report upon Capital Punishment " in 1888, with its many instances of mishaps and bunglings, proves how unwise it is to allow the prison authorities to preserve a dead secrecy.

Still the present system prevents the Home Office

at all events from being pestered by feminist propaganda. If the common hangman had continued to receive as much attention from the newspapers as William Marwood it is certain that the sex equality folk would have clamoured for the appointment of a hangwoman. We can even imagine Jill Ketch's picturesque uniform, designed specially by the authoress of "Hypatia"—a brown Homburg hat and a brown velveteen jacket, like Mr. Smith of Dudley, a white silk shirt and a crimson bow tie, with brown corduroy breeches and leather gaiters—such a costume, if worn by a bright young thing, might have robbed hanging of half its terrors. Under the present circumstances, however, there will be no feminist agitation. In these days the hangman is neither seen nor heard. His place, therefore, is no place for women.

No doubt had the feminists succeeded in setting up a female executioner they would have congratulated themselves upon having brought about an innovation. Nevertheless, they would have been mistaken, which is proved by the following extract from the *Dublin University Magazine* of January 1850:—

> "Who think you, gentle reader, officiated upon this gallows high? A female! a middle-aged, stout-made, dark-eyed, swarthy complexioned, but by no means forbidding woman!—The celebrated Lady Betty, the finisheress of the law, the unflinching priestess of the executive for the Connaught circuit and Roscommon in particular. Few children born or reared in that county thirty or even twenty-five years ago who were not occasionally frightened into being good by the cry of 'Here's Lady Betty!'

> This woman (who had been previously convicted of a horrible murder) officiated, unmasked or undisguised, under the name of Lady Betty, as the hangwoman for a great number of years, and she used also often to flog publicly in and through the streets as part of her trade or profession, being always extremely severe, particularly on her own sex."

Perhaps the hangman is not destined to remain a pariah for ever. Some time, no doubt, Mr. Bernard Shaw will make a play of him, and he will be rehabilitated.

BIBLIOGRAPHY

I BEGAN what I hoped was going to be a comprehensive bibliography, but soon desisted. It became obvious that if it was adequate it would occupy fifty pages or more, robbing my book of all proportion. A glance at a list of authorities in any of the best-edited volumes in the *Notable British Trials* series, where an attempt is being made to compile a complete bibliography of crime, will prove the truth of my assertion.

I have contented myself, therefore, with a few reference notes in order to show that my facts are not imaginary, and to assist the reader in ascertaining the various dates. These I believe will be sufficient for the purpose, besides indicating to the intelligent student that my labours in research have not been inconsiderable.

APPENDIX I

THE KEEPER OF NEWGATE

JAMES FELL, who is mentioned in Major Arthur Griffiths' "Chronicles of Newgate" (I., 163), was in office at the beginning of the eighteenth century, retaining his post until 1707. He lived for many years in retirement, surviving until the 5th of November, 1728.

WILLIAM PITT, "citizen and grocer, was admitted Keeper of the gaol of Newgate to have, hold and exercise and enjoy the same place with all fees, profits, commodities thereunto," on the 16th of December, 1707. Besides a yearly rent of £40 for a lease of the Press yard, the incomer had to pay a sum of £315 to the Lord Mayor and Sheriffs, as well as a premium of £4500 to his predecessor, James Fell. The office was a valuable one, the rents charged to well-to-do prisoners for apartments in the Press yard yielding a considerable revenue. On the 10th of April, 1716, Pitt was arrested on a charge of high treason for being concerned in the escape of Thomas Forster, one of the Jacobite prisoners, but he was acquitted eventually and restored to office. Some years later (in 1724) this same Keeper was the victim of Jack Sheppard's two famous escapades. Pitt died on the 16th of May, 1732, "in the little house near the news cells" (*i.e.* the condemned cells) in Newgate Street, after a reign of nearly twenty-five years. The place was not filled until several months later, the Court of Aldermen having agreed meanwhile that "the office in future shall not be sold, but that the Sheriffs shall nominate such person . . ."

For a while JOHN REED acted as *locum tenens*, until the appointment of ROWLAND INGRAM "citizen and merchant taylor," on the 28th of November, 1732. Ingram died in January, 1738.

THOMAS BOLD, Esq., "bailiff of Southwark," became keeper on the 10th of January, 1738, holding the office until his death on the 13th of February, 1744.

Bold was succeeded by RICHARD AKERMAN, the elder, who was "admitted keeper" on the 1st of May, 1744. He had been a turnkey in the prison as early as 1727, and on the 20th of August, 1736, had succeeded Mr. Alston as Head Turnkey (*Gentleman's Magazine*, VI., 488). Evidently he was a man of character and ability, since it was unusual for "a ranker" to hold such an important post. The elder Akerman retained the position until the 12th of March, 1754, when he resigned owing to ill-health.

RICHARD AKERMAN, the younger, was the next Keeper, being sworn into office on the 15th of October, 1754. This is the Mr. Akerman to whom Boswell refers in the "Life of Johnson" as "my esteemed friend Mr. Akerman, the Keeper of Newgate, who long discharged a very important trust with an uniform intrepid firmness, and at the same time a liberal charity, which entitles him to be recorded with distinguished honour." His kindness and consideration to the prisoners under his charge are often mentioned in the memoirs and newspapers of the period. Edmund Burke spoke of him with praise, and Johnson himself declared, "He who has long had constantly in view the worst of mankind and is yet eminent for the humanity of his disposition, must have had it originally in a great degree and continued to cultivate it very carefully." During the Gordon Riots, when Newgate was burnt, Richard Akerman behaved with splendid courage, and it was believed afterwards that if proper assistance had been sent to him by the magistrates the prison would have been saved. He held office until his death at the age of seventy on the 19th of November, 1792—a period of thirty-eight years—and is unquestionably the greatest of all the governors of Newgate. That the place was a valuable one is proved by the fact that he left £20,000 ," accumulated not parsimoniously," declares one of his obituary notices, " but during a very long possession of a lucrative office."

After Akerman came JOHN KIRBY, formerly Keeper successively of the Compter in Wood Street and Giltspur Street, who ruled over the prison from 1792 until his death on the 30th of August, 1804, in his seventy-sixth year. Like his predecessor, he was celebrated for his humanity (*Gentleman's Magazine*, 1804, Pt. II., 887).

JOHN A. NEWMAN, who had been Keeper of Ludgate prison, succeeded Kirby in 1804. On the 4th of February, 1817, he surrendered his office, since, " owing to additional labour thrown on the Keeper of Newgate, he found himself unable, from infirmity and other reasons, to execute his duties."

The name of the next Keeper was BROWN, who held the position from 1817 till 1822.

Brown was succeeded by JOHN WONTNER, a former City Marshal, who lost his leg in consequence of a fall from his horse on the 16th of November, 1821, and received the appointment in consequence. This excellent official was

Governor of the gaol for eleven years. He died on the 7th of November, 1833, at the age of fifty.

William Cope followed him and was Keeper in 1840 at the time of the execution of Courvoisier. Major Griffiths declares that he was careless and incompetent.

[The names of the subsequent Governors of the prison until the time of its demolition are to be found in the Index to the Repertories at the Guildhall Record Office.]

APPENDIX II

THE ORDINARY OF NEWGATE

THE Ordinary or Chaplain of the prison from September, 1698, until October, 1719, was the REV. PAUL LORRAIN, the author of innumerable Dying Speeches and Confessions of criminals, the profits of which publications were his perquisite. It was an ill-paid post, the salary even as late as 1777 being only £35 a year with a house in Newgate Street, rent free, and "clear of Land Tax." Although, in addition, the City of London made a present of two Freedoms annually, which sold for £25 each, and the Ordinary received also the income from two legacies of £6 and £10 respectively, the stipend did not exceed £100 a year.

The REV. THOMAS PURNEY, a minor poet, who wrote "Pastorals in the Simple Manner of Theocritus" and was a protégé of White Kennet, Bishop of Peterborough, was Ordinary from the 17th of November, 1719, until the 14th of November, 1727. During his term of office Jack Sheppard accomplished his famous achievements, but Purney only visited the young thief once or twice during his imprisonment, being detained in the country by illness, so he had to leave the shriving of Sheppard to a parson named Wagstaff, who was acting as his deputy.

The REV. JAMES GUTHRIE, the next Ordinary, was the author of as many Dying Speeches and Confessions as the prolific Lorrain, guarding the prerogative even more zealously. In February, 1745, he presented a petition to the Court of Aldermen representing that John Applebee, the printer, was infringing his copyright by printing his own versions of Dying Speeches and Confessions, but the petition was ignored. Guthrie was " removed " and pensioned on the 14th of May, 1746, after having been Ordinary for nineteen years, " being rendered incapable of performing his office by age and other infirmities."

The Rev. Samuel Rossell, who had been curate of St. Giles, Cripplegate, for nearly twenty years, succeeded Guthrie, but he died a few months later, on the 12th of March, 1747.

The Rev. John Taylor, who was appointed on the 12th of May following, was as voluminous an author of Dying Speeches as either Lorrain or Guthrie, which is shown by the collections " on manners and morals " in the eighteenth century by Francis Place in the British Museum. Taylor held the post until at least the end of 1755.

The Rev. Stephen Roe came next. He appears to have been a person of truculent humour and was a hearty *bon-vivant*. He was Ordinary till his death on the 22nd of October, 1764.

The Rev. John Moore followed Roe, remaining Ordinary until the 20th of June, 1769, when he died.

The Rev. John Wood, appointed on the 19th of July, 1769, retired on the 20th of October, 1773. An unsuccessful attempt was then made by James Townsend, the Lord Mayor, to secure the election of Silas Told to the vacant place. Told, who was a Methodist, had become notorious owing to his habit of accompanying criminals in the cart to Tyburn to pray with them.

The Rev. John Villette was elected on the 8th of

February, 1774. He is perhaps the most famous of all the Ordinaries, and officiated for twenty-five years. His apparent hardness of heart at the execution of Dr. Dodd was commented upon adversely, but probably he had become inured to his unpleasant duties. Both Boswell and John Wesley speak of him with approval. Apparently he was a worthy man. He died in office on the 26th of April, 1799.

The REV. BROWNLOW FORD—described so graphically by J. T. Smith in " A Book for a Rainy Day "—occupied the post from 1799 until 1814, when he resigned because a committee of the House of Commons did not approve of the manner in which he discharged his duties.

Another very famous Ordinary followed, viz. the REV. HORACE SALUSBURY COTTON, who, like Villette, reigned for twenty-five years. He was a robust, rosy, well-fed, unctuous individual, whose picture may be seen in Cruikshank's plate of the Press yard in Pierce Egan's " Life in London." His condemned sermons were more terrific than those of any of his predecessors, and he was censured by the authorities for "harrowing the prisoner's feelings unnecessarily " in the case of Henry Fauntleroy, the banker. Cotton held office until 1839.

Of the succeeding Ordinaries a clergyman named CARVER came after Cotton, and was followed by the REV. JOHN DAVIS from 1843 until 1865. The REV. F. E. JONES succeeded Davis.

NEWGATE

PLAN SHEWING RECENT DISCOVERIES of ROMAN WALL Etc

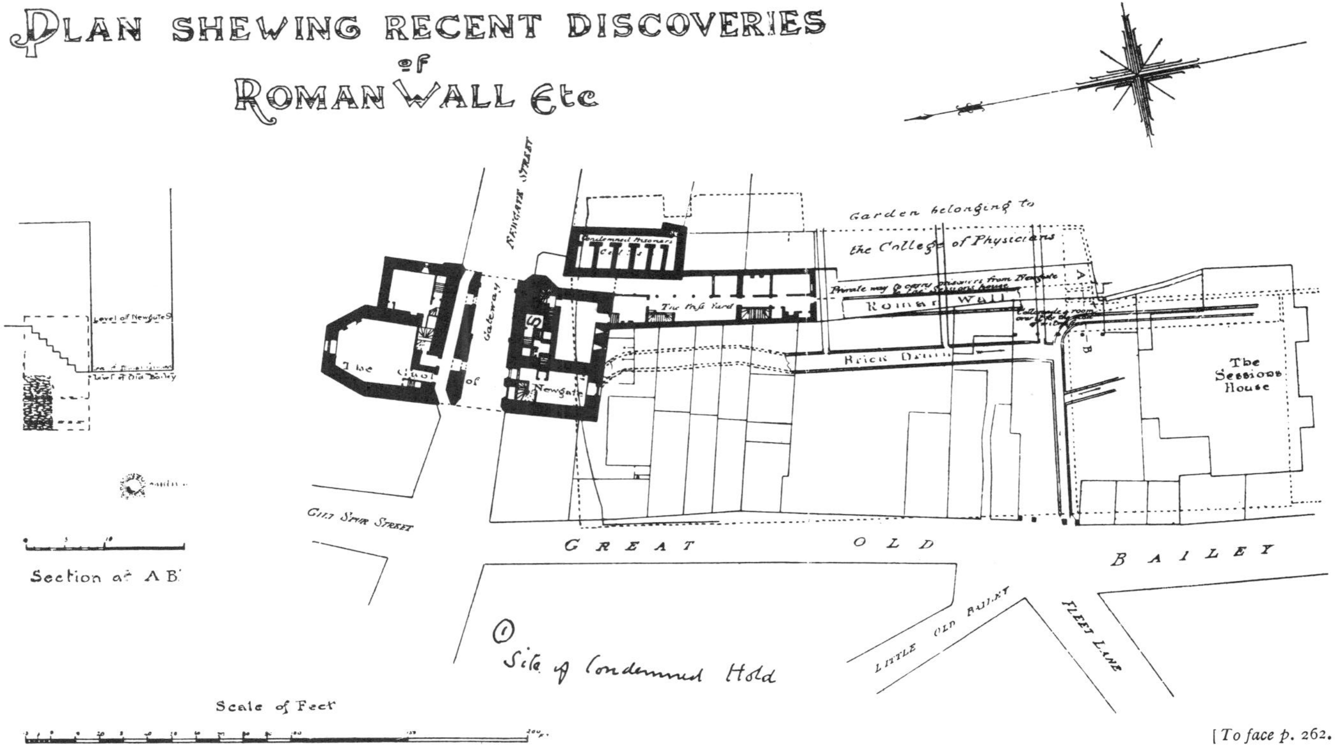

[To face p. 262.

INDEX

INDEX

INDEX

INDEX

INDEX

INDEX

INDEX

INDEX

INDEX

INDEX

THE DRAMATURGY OF STATE EXECUTIONS

By John Lofland

Acknowledgement: I am indebted to Katherine Buckles for library research assistance, and to Lyn H. Lofland for support, suggestions, and editing.—J.L.

THE DRAMATURGY OF STATE EXECUTIONS

By John Lofland

IN SHARING this new edition of Horace Bleackley's classic study with its author, I attempt through applying the sociological perspective to give meaning to its substance—the hangmen of England—by conceiving it within broader principles of social organization. The more than two hundred years covered by Bleackley produced some truly remarkable transformations in social arrangements that require explicit analysis for their proper appreciation. My elucidation of the "dramaturgy" of state executions strives to provide a framework for such an analysis. After treating of dramaturgics, I discuss the aristocratic and dynamic Mr. Bleackley, so many years headquartered in Regent's Park, London.

HARD FACTS AND DRAMATURGIC OVERLAY

Societies may be distinguished in terms of the degree to which they honestly, forcefully, and openly face the nature and import of the basic acts and arrangements of life and death in which they engage, as opposed to the degree to which they mask, deny, and conceal such acts. By "basic acts and arrangements of life and death" I mean, among others, giving birth, acquiring food and shelter, distributing resources, doing sex, establishing and maintaining hierarchy and authority, performing punishment, dying. As fundamental aspects of existence, each of these is laden with anxiety, each engages our basic, our deepest "gut" feelings. Each admits of no easy solution or stance or coping device. But existence is flexible enough to permit a range of ways in which humans collectively cope with them. Among the large varieties of ways in all these areas, I want here to explicate and contrast the dimension of openness versus concealment, of brutalness, even, versus genteel and "hypocritical" covering. I assume that the existential facts of a basic aspect of life may be identical in two societies, but seem quite different at the public level because of contrasts in their "dramaturgic overlay," as it were. Thus, contemporary Americans tend to think of their society as being relatively free of "social classes" even when, structurally, one can demonstrate their society to be virtually as stratified as any other ever known. What is different is the degree to which social class is *openly signaled* by dress and speech differentials, class-specific laws, and the like. What is different is the degree to which social class is openly accepted and acted on and toward as a social fact. Among the Americans, facts of class are remarkably disattended and even concealed at the public level; a kind of out of sight, out of mind maneuver is accomplished.

Openness versus concealment are varying dramaturgic or stylistic *strategies* for dealing with problematic existential matters where the substantive arrangements are identical. Leaving aside the moral merits of either, it is useful to explore at a logical and theoretical level the abstract features of each as "pure" strategies for coping with the uncomfortable. Believing, however, that pure theoretical analyses are mostly useless in social matters, I want to tie this exploration to a specific body of empirical materials, namely, *state-conducted executions.*

Consider the features of this basic life and death situation: A court sentences a person to die in payment for a crime. The person now there in court must by some means, at some place, by someone be killed. The person's *death* is the basic, *invariant,* existential fact—the situation. What can vary is the manner in which the death is accomplished, the relevant dimension of manner here being the degree to which the actions of execution are socially open or concealed with regard to the fact that a human being is about to die, is dying, and is dead.

A person is going to be killed, is being killed, and has been killed.

What might be some general features of a strategy that deals openly, honestly and unashamedly with these brute facts? And, what might be the general features of a strategy that deals in a concealing, denying, and ashamed way with the brute facts of killing a person?

An embarrassed, *concealing* strategy would seem, logically, to have features such as these:

1. Death Wait. The time between sentencing and actual execution would need to be kept as short as possible. The longer the condemned is left alive after sentencing, the more the act of execution can be thought about, and can be an embarrassment. Ideally, the condemned is executed immediately.

2. Death Confinement. If there is to be much time between sentencing and execution, the condemned must be kept some place. In order to minimize the presence of the now "living dead," he needs to be kept sequestered in a concealed place, visitor access to which is either prohibited or minimized under stringent regulations. Obviously, the more people who interact with the condemned, the more that can be reported, thought, and perhaps even done about him. The condemned cannot be allowed to initiate contacts with citizens of his own choosing, most especially agents of print or electronic media.

Concealment may include insulation of the death-cell's occupant from knowledge of the execution place, especially from noises of death preparation, as in the thud of sand bags testing ropes, the crackle of electricity testing circuits, and inspection of the condemned's body to determine the proper drop for his hanging or his fit in the electric chair.

3. Death Time. The execution itself is most auspiciously scheduled on a day of the week and at a time of the day that is socially inconspicuous. The day ought not to coincide with the society's holidays, be these religious or frivolous. An inconspicuous hour of the chosen day likewise deemphasizes the event.

4. Death Trip. The distance between the condemned cell and the actual place of execution is best kept short and the route unencumbered. To escort the condemned over a course that involves walking him hundreds of yards, mounting stairs, or leading him in and out of vehicles is to increase time during which the condemned and his executioners can become distraught over the prospect of the condemned's death. The longer the distance, the greater the condemned's opportunity to refuse to walk or to lose consciousness and have to be carried. Since the condemned will often be stupefied or otherwise distressed, an up-and-down course might cause stumbling, and stumbling would communicate the condemned's distressed state. Any faltering during the death trip would impress too openly upon participants that they are about to be party to killing someone. The trip itself would also best be physically shielded from witnesses by physical structures.

5. Death Place. The place of execution ought to be concealed within a building that looks like a normal building, one that is emotionally neutral, suggesting neither pleasure nor pain. The building is best placed away from heavy pedestrian or vehicular traffic in order to inhibit establishing its reputation as a place of death through public view. A single society ought probably have only *one* such place. The more there are, the greater the number of people who will have some proximity to them and the greater the likelihood of thinking about what happens in them. The scheme of internal decoration is best bland and neutral in character and color, rather than either cheerful (which suggests hypocrisy or inappropriate frivolity) or drab (which directly suggests death). The interior blandness of public schools, government offices, and modern prisons seems most fitting.

6. Death Witnesses. Mere witnesses to the execution (as distinct from "instrumental" personnel) ought to be kept to a minimum or prohibited altogether. Agents of print and electronic media need especially to be excluded, for they can all too vividly, explicitly, and widely convey the fact and the details of the death. If witnesses are permitted, career officials of the police or penal system had best decide whom to admit, to assure a cooperating, circumspect, and close-mouthed ("respectable") audience who will not say or do much about what they see. To allow "anyone" to attend can only allow the possibility of unsolemn, perhaps disorderly, behavior or even protest against the imminent death.

7. Executioners. Likewise, the executioner and his supporting personnel, such as clergy and doctors, contribute best to the dramaturgy of concealment:

(a) If they are heavily trained and drilled in performing executions swiftly and efficiently, and can be counted on so to conduct themselves. A minimum of words and acts by the executioner serves to conceal, not only by moving events along more quickly, but also by inhibiting any thoughts that each additional utterance or gesture might stimulate.

(b) If they treat the condemned in a highly ritualized and impersonal manner, engaging in no verbal interaction with him and refraining from physical exchanges, such as receiving money or selling his clothes after the execution. Such personal acts would constitute a direct, personalized recognition of the person who is about to die.

(c) If they remain unknown to the general public, the better to inhibit public consciousness of and thought about executioners *per se*. This requires a bland and perhaps "bureaucratic" personal style. Colorful, troublesome, robust executioners are likely to be in the public eye too much, betokening a brutally open vision of state executions. Further, executioners who perform executions only part time and at piece-rate and who pursue some undistinguished career for their main living are preferable to executioners who make a living at executions. Professional executioners are more easily identifiable in the public eye, and are likely to form an interest in being so identified and in earning fees for interviews and the like. They are public embodiments of death, devoutly to be avoided in any strategy of concealment.

8. The Condemned. The regulation and concealment of the condemned in a death cell should be continued in practices that maintain the blandness of his perceptibility throughout his last days. (a) Colorful, self-chosen clothes endow the condemned with the capacity for personal taste and preference. This personalizes the scene, as does allowing him to provide any of the death equipment, such as the rope that hangs him or binds his hands. Bland, state-controlled or state-provided clothes and state-standardized death equipment serve better to depersonalize and conceal. (b) To allow the condemned to speak in the moments before his death is to acknowledge his individual existence, to confer a unique, personal identity upon him that prompts others more clearly to perceive that a person is in fact dying. Such perceptions can be inhibited by prohibiting speech, especially *a speech.* If "final words" are permitted, the executioner can through intimidating the condemned, limit their number by means of a brisk, quick, machine-like manner when approaching him in the death cell, marching him through a short death trip, and positioning him in the death machine.

9. Death Technique. The perfectly concealed technique of death is one in which the condemned's body instantly disappears, never again to be seen. Short of this, the act of dying can be diminished in several ways. First, the technique of death should be speedy. The quicker it is over, the less there is to see, and the less death need be thought about. Second, a death in which the condemned dies immediately and therefore without pain is somehow less openly a "death" than one in which the condemned dies slowly and painfully, with attendant struggles, facial contortions, and screams. Third, a death without mutilation of the body appears to be less a death than one which does involve clear mutilation. Fourth, to conceal lingering, painful, and mutilating deaths which might occur despite all precautions, the body can be shielded from view during dying. Fifth, the machinery of death had best not only work with unfailing effectiveness and swiftness, but also *quietly.* Banging gallows trapdoors, thuds of dropped bodies, sizzling flesh, and the like, all communicate too clearly the presence of death.

10. Corpse Disposal. Since the condemned does not simply disappear upon death—since there is now a corpse—he needs somehow to be disposed of. Greatest concealment would be achieved in not moving the corpse very far if at all, transporting it in a highly shielded manner, if transport is required, and burying it (if burial is the social practice) in an unmarked grave. Similar principles apply to cremation. Certainly, to transport the corpse openly through the public streets and publicly to display it for viewing can only communicate the fact of the death more clearly.

11. Death Announcement. Last, the government should not signal the death through prominently publicized announcements, as opposed to highly circumspect and minor acknowledgment. To shut down the schools, ring church bells, and fly black flags has an open quality much in contrast to the mere posting of a small sheet of paper by a prison gate.

I have tried abstractly and logically to elucidate basic elements of a concealed as opposed to an open dramaturgic strategy of state executions, emphasizing features of a concealed strategy, of a strategy that seems virtually to make death not death.

If one has little acquaintance with the history of state executions, this strategy and its implied contrast may seem far-fetched and even silly. In fact, I have with only slight exaggeration characterized the historical state executions in England and the United States (and to some extent all of

Europe and the world) in the twentieth century. To contrast English and American state executions circa 1950 with those circa 1700 is virtually to contrast pure strategies of dramaturgical concealment and openness. There is a sense in which agrarian England and America, with all their rawness, indifference, brutality, and cruelty were also more open and even honest about how they dealt with the basic, life-and-death aspects of social existence. There was a sense in which communication was more straight-out and direct, in which conflicts were perhaps not so much more intense as more openly acknowledged and acted out rather than covered over and muted. Perhaps many of the practices of those vanished societies can be seen as experiments in how far any society might with ease proceed toward dramaturgic openness in its basic arrangements and dealings. It is at minimum clear that regardless of political and economic organization, societies have in only a few centuries retreated *en masse* from an open dramaturgy of state executions (and even from state executions themselves, but that is another matter).

The historical record suggests, indeed, a *generalized* retreat from dramaturgic openness and directness which is one thing we imply when we speak of the "rationalization" and bureaucratization of the world in the sense that Max Weber employed those terms.[1] Consider other basic aspects of living and dying and how the directness of our relation to them—their dramaturgy—has changed. Consider modern scenes of birth, mating, and dying, both of humans and of other animals. Their dramaturgic structure is rather like the modern state execution. Consider conflicts between individuals that easily became direct fights or duels in former times but become highly elaborate, convoluted and conspiratorial

[1] Max Weber, *From Max Weber: Essays in Sociology* (New York, 1958), chap. 8.

affairs in modern times. Consider defication, urination, fornication and their residues, ubiquitous and open in former times, dramaturgically shielded and contained in modern times. Consider disease, hunger, gross impairment, and deformity of the human body—formerly open, now concealed, using many of the same devices used to shield state executions—and so on through other aspects of living.

There are, perhaps, some profound psycho-social constraints on the directness with which we can deal with basic matters of life and death. We may as humans (or maybe only as modern humans) require (or merely desire) to take our medicine sugar-coated, to avoid as much as possible direct encounter with the brutal truths of much we do. Such, at any rate, is suggested by the very striking contrasts between the open and concealed dramaturgy of state executions.

This, then, is the contrast I seek to draw and the "theory" of the contrast I desire to advance.

THE DRAMATURGY OF HISTORIC AND MODERN STATE EXECUTIONS

Let me now try to make more plain, concrete and therefore plausible this still abstract and perhaps implausible distinction between open and concealed dramaturgic strategies of state executions (and of social actions generally). I will do so by detailing variations I have alleged to obtain in practices between agrarian (as opposed to industrial) England and the United States (and many parts of Europe and the world). For simplicity's sake, I will refer to the periods which broadly exemplify these variations as "historic" versus "modern."

1. Death Wait. It is fittingly ironic that on the initial point of contrast, waiting time until death, the results are exactly opposite to expectations generated by a model of open versus concealed dramaturgy. However open historic executions were in other regards, they failed in this regard by (especially in the 1600s and earlier) often taking the condemned directly from trial to execution. English law of 1752 required that murderers be hanged on the day after sentencing; by the 1820s many capital offenders were "tried on a Friday and executed in rows of from three to six the following Monday."[2] Such dispatch obviously limits the degree to which the reality of the death can be communicated, a deficiency for which, as we shall see, historic executions more than compensated.

Modern executions have tended toward enormously longer death waits, averaging a year or two at various periods in England and the United States.[3] In some cases, death waits have gone on for a decade. It is the stern reminders that such waits offer that seem, indeed, to generate so much strong feeling about state executions, for example among those who argue that long waits (caused, proximately, by the availability and use of appellate and executive remedies) constitute "cruel and unusual punishment."

2. Death Confinement. Historic places of confinement until death—prisons—were much more bustling, lively, and emotionally polymorphic places than their austere and solemn modern counterparts. Before middle-class prissiness and universalistic bureaucrats took over the management of prisons, the more colorful and wealthy of condemned persons, at least, could enjoy the companionship of virtually any visitors they desired. Popular criminals were visited by

[2] John Laurence, *A History of Capital Punishment* (New York, 1960), p. 102.

[3] United Nations, *Capital Punishment: Part I, Report, 1960; Part II, Developments, 1961 to 1965* (New York, 1968).

"men and women of the highest position." Perhaps the most famous, Jack Sheppard, executed in 1724, received "no fewer than three thousand persons" in his death cell at Newgate Prison.[4] In 1744, another had "seven girls to dine with him on the evening before he was hanged," a party at which the condemned was reported "not less cheerful than those who hoped to live longer."[5] A condemned called the "monster of London" held a "Monster's Ball" for about 40 people at Newgate Prison in 1790. "Tea was served at 4 P.M. to the music of violins and flutes, after which the company danced until 8 P.M. when a cold supper was produced. The party broke up at 9 o'clock, the usual hour for closing the prison."[6] Alcohol and other amenities were available, prompting some contemporaries to complain that their effects detracted from an appropriate pall of death.

It was, indeed, against these kinds of easy and open death confinements that such champions of austerity as Henry Fielding and Charles Dickens railed. In 1849 Dickens plotted out the concealed strategy of state executions that was to become the reigning reality of virtually the entire world within a hundred years:

> From the moment of a murderer's being sentenced to death, I would dismiss him to . . . dread obscurity. . . . I would allow no curious visitors to hold any communications with him; I would place every obstacle in the way of his sayings and doings being served up in print on Sunday mornings for the perusal of families. . . .
>
> We should not return to the days when ladies paid visits to

[4] Horace Bleackley, *The Hangmen of England: How They Hanged and Whom They Hanged, supra,* p. 79.

[5] Justin Atholl, *Shadow of the Gallows* (London, 1954), p. 66.

[6] *Ibid.*

> highwaymen, drinking their punch in the condemned cells of Newgate.[7]

Modern dramaturgy is, nonetheless, a bit less strict: "the prevailing [world-wide] practice is to keep condemned prisoners in solitary confinement and under heavy surveillance, but to allow them special privileges."[8] Among these privileges is, in some jurisdictions, access to sedative drugs for inhibiting disconcerting breakdowns.

To be open about death is, in part, to talk about it, to impress upon the condemned the imminence of his own demise. Historic executions had *death-talk specialists,* people whose duty it was forcefully to impress the condemned with their state. By forcefully, I mean that the condemned was required to listen to them and that their actions were vigorously performed. The sexton of St. Sepulchre's church filled such a role on the eve of executions in London. He came tolling a handbell under the windows of Newgate Prison, chanting verses recommending repentance. Given the high frequency of executions, he was a familiar sight and sound. Prison clergymen were more ubiquitous and formidable figures. At Newgate, the condemned sat in the black Condemned Pew of the prison's chapel and suffered admonitions during the compulsory and daily religious service attended by all prisoners. The condemned were also often subjected to a special, religious service close to the time of execution. In one version, all condemend sat round a coffin listening to a sermon, perhaps hearing the ceremony for the burial of the dead. In another version, the last service and

[7] Charles Dickens, "Letters to the Editor of the London Times" (13 November 1849, 17 November 1849), vol. 22, collected works (New York, 1892), pp. 242, 243.

[8] United Nations, *Report,* p. 99.

the sermon on the torments which the condemned could expect to suffer after death were so harrowing and upsetting to the prisoner that they became a popular entertainment for the aristocratic ladies and gentlemen of London. Sheriffs sometimes had to control attendance by ticket. The clergy of Newgate, especially, seemed to enjoy their work, for complaints of over-zealousness were sometimes lodged and authorities on one occasion censured an Ordinary for "harrowing a prisoner's feelings unnecessarily."[9] The contrast with the modern concealed strategy is striking; such specialists today are mild-mannered and their employment is optional.[10]

Death has its physical preparations and historic folk were not squeamish about the condemned seeing them if he were within range, as was the case when executions took place near to or inside prison walls. Gallows were noisily tested, graves openly dug, the condemned assessed face-to-face for the drop appropriate to his weight, build, and neck defects, and his coffin brought casually into view. Modern folk go thoroughly out of their way to shield all these sorts of preparations from the eyes of the condemned and virtually everyone else. This modern shielding of sight and sound is all the more remarkable because the condemned is often brought within a few feet of the death place during the period of final preparations. Among the English, the last "dummy rehearsal" for the hanging occurs while the condemned is "exercising" in a remote part of the prison. Hangman Pierrepont and his assistants took care to work in total silence in the final hours, even when the door adjoining

[9] Bleackley, *Hangmen,* p. 262.

[10] See e. g., Truman Capote, *In Cold Blood: A True Account of a Multiple Murder and Its Consequences* (New York, 1965), pp. 330–343; Robert G. Elliott with Albert R. Beatty, *Agent of Death: The Memoirs of an Executioner* (New York, 1940).

the execution room and the condemned cell was soundproof. The American electrocutioner Robert Elliott always tested the chair "as quietly as possible. I would not want any sound of the preparations to reach the person or persons who must die that night."[11]

3. Execution Time. Historic British executions occurred (in public) in the early afternoon, insuring the largest number of possible witnesses. Despite the shield of a physically enclosed place, modern executions tend even to concealed times: early morning (such as 7 or 8 o'clock) or late at night (such as 11 o'clock).[12] The prison context has frequently prompted officials to choose times when prisoners are locked in their cells or fully at their work. A prison population at milling leisure is a population thought to be too easily preoccupied with the execution; hence the off-hour execution times.[13]

4. The Death Trip. The condemned must in some manner be removed from the death cell and taken to the death place. A dramaturgic policy of openness, of bluntly proclaiming the condemned's ordained death, requires that the trip itself be long, accomplished by elaborate transport devices, employ a complicated cortege, involve dramatic events along the way, traverse a complex and public route, and promote long and complex talk along the route and at the execution. Such was the dramaturgy of historic death trips.

(a) In early years, executions were often held on the spot of the condemned's crime, a feature making for long death trips. In London, as in other cities, particular spots came to be places of public execution. Tyburn, a site more than two miles through crowded streets from Newgate prison—the

[11]Elliott, *Agent,* p. 137.
[12]*Ibid.,* p. 129.
[13]Atholl, *Shadow,* p. 41.

place of the condemned—provides the ideal type of dramaturgic routing, sometimes requiring up to three hours to move the condemned the length of the route. The modern concealed strategy brings the condemned within a few steps of the death place beforehand (while not letting him perceive it). The British have even devoted considerable study to shortening the distance and timing the interval between calling upon the condemned in his cell and actually killing him. In some places, it was reduced to "eight steps" and nine to fifteen seconds.[14] Pinioning devices of lightning application and drills in cap and rope placement insure that the walk and the hanging happen so fast that one need watch closely in order to have seen it—to know that it in fact happened. (British gallows redesign of 1876 provided a scaffold-top lever for releasing the drop, thus eliminating the delay between adjusting the noose, descending the steps, and going under the scaffold to draw the bolt.)[15] Electrocution death trips are reported to be a bit slower, requiring somewhat more than a minute fully to accomplish.[16]

(b) Eight steps and fifteen seconds contrast with the dramatic, historic flair of earlier times when the condemned were transported on hurdles or in horse-drawn carts along with their coffins. The more wealthy or popular condemned were allowed to ride in mourning coaches. Thus elevated, these condemned were more visible to crowds of spectators who lined the route or merely happened to observe while conducting their routine pursuits in the action-filled streets of pre-industrial cities.[17]

[14] George Ryley Scott, *The History of Capital Punishment: Including an Examination of the Case For and Against the Death Penalty* (London, 1950), pp. 209–210; Atholl, *Shadow,* p. 110, 129–130.

[15] Atholl, *Shadow,* p. 103.

[16] Elliott, *Agent,* p. 144.

[17] Lyn H. Lofland, *A World of Strangers: Order and Action in Urban Public Space* (New York, 1973), chap. 2.

(c) The condemned were taken quite seriously in the sense that they were stars of a cortege of several hundred people which was typically "headed by the city marshal on horseback, followed by the under-sheriff with a cavalcade of peace officers, and a body of constables armed with staves. Then came the cart or carts with the condemned, more constables, and finally a company of javelin men. Sometimes a party of javelin men headed the procession."[18] When the condemned were markedly popular or unpopular, there might be more armed strength to protect against the mob's rescuing or killing them. Cutting the trip to a few steps and seconds drastically reduces the possibilities of forming a cortege, which in modern times amounts to a mere four or five career officials, or even less when the trip is very short.

(d) Historic London corteges passed through narrow, people-glutted streets in which spectators pressed upon the procession. Popular condemned were cheered and kisses were blown at them; despised condemned were jeered, hissed, groaned at, and pelted with garbage and mud. The scene was frequently one of confusion and borderline chaos, a scene in sharp contrast to the modern de-peopled, streamlined death trip.

(e) As befits a social event, the cortege made stops; its course was punctuated by *events,* which more clearly indicated the kind of procession afoot. At the *church stop,* a clergyman tolled a bell, admonished the condemned, and perhaps presented each with flowers, wine, or a nosegay.[19] Depending upon the popularity of the condemned, there might be five or more *pub stops* and *friend stops,* all involving alcoholic drinks and farewells. Not infrequently the condemned got quite drunk, making possible jovial partings with flippant comments, such as telling an inn-keeper one

[18] Laurence, *Capital Punishment,* p. 187.

[19] *Ibid.,* pp. 186–188.

would pay for the wine on the way back.[20] *Running conversations* took place between the condemned in the cart and his friends who walked or rode part of the distance with him.[21] Fifteen seconds and eight steps provide for none of this.

(f) The jiggling of the cart, its various stops and starts, mountings and dismountings, and objects flung at it made for an obstacle-ridden course. Upon arriving at the death place, the condemned perhaps had even to climb a ladder or mount steps, depending upon the hanging technique of the time. The condemned, that is, very much *interacted with his situation,* thereby expressing himself in calmness, clumsiness, or whatever. Modern executions prevent such expression by abbreviating the death walk, the ultimate abbreviation being the construction of the death cell and chamber on the identical level so that the condemned will not encounter grades.[22]

(g) Last, throughout the death trip there was a torrent of words: from the mob in the street, between the condemned and their friends and others, between officials and the crowd, from the clergy who orated at various points, and from the condemned in his death speech. Church bells tolled. Modern death trips are virtually wordless and no bells toll.

In sum, historic death trips were dramaturgically open in the sense that they were rather long in time and distance, complex in transport, large and heterogeneous in cortege and spectators, complex and diverse in events and routing, and long and complicated in verbal interaction.

[20] August Mencken, ed., *By the Neck: A Book of Hangings* (New York, 1942), p. 250; Laurence, *Capital Punishment,* p. 66.

[21] Horace Bleackley, *Jack Sheppard* (London, 1933), p. 50; Laurence, *Capital Punishment,* p. 66.

[22] Scott, *History,* p. 209. In one innovation, the rope is held daintily off the scaffold floor by a silk cord to insure the condemned will not trip.

5. *Death Place.* Social places vary in the degree to which they are dramaturgically open or concealed. Dramaturgically open places provide unobstructed views of contained activities, of "front" and "back" regions.[23] Dramaturgically concealed places obstruct viewing by 1) erecting physical barriers and 2) guiding and controlling what the viewer sees despite physical barriers.

Historic state executions were open. They took place *outdoors,* in early periods in open fields and later in city streets. Even when closed to the public, they remained outdoors for a time, in prison yards. Their "roof" was the sky, their "walls" the horizon or exteriors of buildings. Death was in this sense "integrated" with much else in social life. Modern executions, in contrast, are extremely concealed within doors, often even in windowless rooms.

Earlier historic executions were highly integrated in the additional sense that they took place at the scene of the condemned's crime; that is, in multiple and unspecialized places. Over time, places specialized in executions, as the famous Tyburn, but there were many such *local* places.[24] Modern societies have moved decisively to concealment by having only *one* place of execution for large regions or for the entire society. These are called execution "chambers" or "sheds," terms which tellingly reveal their concealed character. The movement is, in one sense, from a highly personalized to a highly impersonalized place; from an open definition of the condemend's personal identity at the place of his particular crime to an obscured and generalized treatment of him at a centralized place where everybody and anybody and hence nobody is executed. Even the exteriors of modern

[23] On this and other concepts of the dramaturgic perspective see Erving Goffman, *The Presentation of Self in Everyday Life* (Garden City, Anchor Books, 1959).

[24] L. H. Lofland, *Strangers,* p. 35.

death places are highly inacessible to view in that they are always inside prison walls.

Outdoor historic executions had little specialized "furniture" or decor save objects that enhanced openness, primarily bleachers, benches, scaffoldings or "open galleries like a racecourse stand."[25] Entrepreneurs erected and charged for sitting on them. Nearby windows and housetops were observation points for which the public also paid.[26] And "public houses in the neighborhood often kept open the whole of the preceding night" for the "refreshment and enjoyment" of the gathering crowd.[27]

Modern sheds and chambers are tiny cubes compared to the space accommodating thousands upon thousands of witnesses at historic executions. Barriers of various kinds effectively shield much of the execution process: the condemned is held backstage until the last moment (historically he approached openly and slowly), witnesses are carefully confined to certain areas (historically they had great leeway), the body disappears in the execution (through the drop) or immediately after death (compared to practices discussed below). The chamber itself is decorated in the institutional drab of its prison context

6. Death Witnesses. Historic executions attracted many by-standing witnesses and were indeed held in the public outdoors partly for that reason. Hundreds and even thousands of person appeared. The most famous or infamous condemned could draw enormous crowds (fifty- to one hundred-thousand, according to some estimates). A hanging on New York's Bedloe's Island in 1860 had "steamboats, barges, oyster sloops, yachts and rowboats swarm[ing]

[25] Scott, *History,* p. 50.

[26] Laurence, *Capital Punishment,* pp. 209–211; Scott, *History,* pp. 48–52.

[27] Laurence, *Capital Punishment,* p. 184.

everywhere in view of the gallows. Large steamers such as carry hundreds of people . . . on pleasure excursions were there, so laden with a living freight of curious people that it seemed almost a wonder that they did not sink. There were barges . . . with awnings spread, under which those who were thirsty imbibed lager beer."[28] Sometimes people packed city streets so tightly that fear and panic ensued, killing a few and injuring dozens.[29]

These many witnesses were extremely *diverse* in social standing and types of social identity. First, most infamous and most numerous were what is called variously the *rabble,* the mob, and the dregs. This was itself a heterogeneous assortment of pickpockets, harlots, unemployed, highwaymen, rogues, dandies, floaters, trollops, ruffians, thieves, vagabonds, and criminals, to use a few terms of contemporary observers. Dickens described them as the "lowest, the most depraved, the most abandoned of mankind."[30] The streets of pre- and early industrial cities were (and still are) home to this *floating population,*[31] the poorest segment of the society. They were a ready-made audience for any public event, and a constant precipitator of public disorder.[32] Second, *hawkers* circulated selling broadsides detailing the life, crimes, and words of the condemned and food such as sweetmeats, tarts, meatpies, and oranges.[33] Third, *children* were brought by schoolmasters and mothers to be morally instructed and edified. To warn a child he might come to a

[28] Eyewitness account reprinted in Mencken, *By the Neck,* p. 175.

[29] Bleackley, *Hangmen,* pp. 142–143; Mencken, *By the Neck,* pp. 218–221; Atholl, *Shadow,* pp. 79–80.

[30] Dickens, *Letters,* p. 240.

[31] L. H. Lofland, *Strangers,* p. 42.

[32] *Ibid.,* chap. 2 and 3.

[33] Laurence, *Capital Punishment,* pp. 177–178.

bad end had literal meaning in the rope he saw directly.[34] Fourth, in favored places arranged by the sheriff and in discreetly rented windows, various *aristocrats* watched. Dickens described some as people "from the fashionable clubs of the West End," including "fashionably dressed women who levelled their lorgnettes towards the scaffold."[35] Fifth, there were sometimes people with *physical blemishes* and wens who came to be touched by the hand of the hanged man in the belief they would be so cured.[36] Sixth, many businesses closed to enable their owners, *craftsmen and tradesmen,* and their *families,* to enjoy the "hanging day." Seventh, soldiers, constables, and other *agents of state force* strove to prevent the crowd from pressing too close upon the gallows and to keep order generally. Larger executions employed several hundred agents of state force. Eighth and last, *intellectuals and reporters* were present, some to enjoy and some to deplore the execution horrors in their subsequent writings. Boswell is among the most famous of the enthusiastic "regulars" at hangings, while Thackeray and Dickens were repulsed by them. The writings of such observers were widely read and influential.

If these are some of the main classes of witnesses, what were they *doing* before, during, and after the execution? First and most striking, many were engaged in a complex of acts best labeled *holiday-making,* consisting of sporadic group singing, laughing, food munching, joking, shouting, beverage sipping, and the like. Such activities frequently began on the eve of the hanging. Observers described this behavior in many ways: "Vying with each other in low and

[34] Atholl, *Shadow,* pp. 72–75.

[35] Dickens, *Letters,* p. 243.

[36] Mencken, *By the Neck,* p. xii.

coarse jests," "Carnival-like spirits," "festive behavior," "screeching and laughing and yelling in strong chorus," "cat calls, comic choruses, dances and even mock hymns," "cries, howls and screechings," "a ceaseless din of sounds and war of tongues—voices in every note, shrill whistles and slang calls," "the roar of voices occasionally swelled into a chorus of vulgar doggerel," "scenes of drunkenness, . . . the street crowded with young boys and girls full of play and frolic . . . public houses just by were crowded, and noises of tipsy mirth and jollity proceeded from them all." The mood was one of a "sporting occasion" or fair. *Rough play and fights* punctuated time in encounters of pushing, tripping, "kicking dirt about," wrestling and straight fighting over imagined or real offenses. One form of rough play involved

> the dead Carcasses of Dogs and Cats or, for want of them, Rags, and all Trompery that is capable of imbibing Dirt. These, well trempled in Filth, and, if possible, of the worst sort, are by the Ringleaders, flung as high and as far as a strong Arm can carry them, and commonly directed where the Throng is the thickest: Whilst these ill-boding Meteors are shooting Thro' the air, the Joy and Satisfaction of the Beholders is visible in every Countenance and Gesture; and more audibly express'd by the great Shouts that accompany them in their Course; and, as the Projectiles come nearer the Earth, are turn'd into loud Laughter, which is more or less violent in Proportion to the Mischief promis'd by the Fall. And to see a good Suit of Cloaths spoiled by this Piece of Gallantry, is the tip-top of their diversion, which they seldom go home without enjoying.[37]

The press of the crowd and excitement caused *faintings* among the "gentler sex" who were often "indecently exposed" in the course of being taken away. *Pickpocketing* and

[37] Eyewitness account of B. Mandeville, 1725, quoted in Scott, *History*, p. 47.

pickups were rampant. Occasionally, large, compressed crowds *panicked,* trampling and killing many of their number. Agents of state force—constables, soldiers, police, or gaolers—worked at *order keeping,* arresting thieves, striking spectators to keep them back from the procession or the gallows or fighting off attacks on the condemned, the executioner or both. However, a large proportion of the witnesses simply engaged in *quiet socializing* while waiting, perhaps discussing other executions within their knowledge or other matters of the day.[38] When the scaffold or the condemned arrived at the appointed time, *crowd acknowledgements* went up. There might be "great cheers," as in greeting the hangman with "Good Old Calcraft! Three Cheers for the Hangman!" or hisses and boos. To Thackeray's ear it had a nightmarish quality:

> As the clock began to strike, an immense sway and movement swept over the whole of that vast, dense crowd. They were all uncovered directly, and a great murmur arose, more awful, bizarre and indescribable than any sound I had ever before heard. Women and children began to shriek horribly. I don't know whether it was the bell I heard; but a dreadful quick feverish kind of jangling noise mingled with the noise of the people, and lasted for about two minutes."[39]

Witnesses continued to *yell comments* during the execution itself. If the condemned were faced away from the crowd, or people could not see, shouts of "turn him around," and "stand out of the way" were forthcoming. Despised criminals were likely to hang to the accompaniment of yelling and shouting. For one, "several tremendous cheers" went up "the moment the drop fell." For another, there was a "shout of

[38] William Makepeace Thackeray, "Going to See a Man Hanged," in *Miscellanies,* vol. 26, collected works (London, 1910–1911), pp. 417–431.
[39] *Ibid.,* p. 427.

exultation that was prolonged for some minutes."[40] During the convulsion of strangling, witnesses might provide "loud huzzas" and even a final cheer when the corpses were cut down. If the executioner were clumsy—which was reportedly frequent—commentary ensued. When it was the custom to cut off the heads of traitors and hold them up following hanging, the executioner on one occasion dropped the fourth head so displayed and was met thereupon with the clamor, "Ah, Butter-fingers."[41] Witnesses were sometimes *direct participants,* as when they rescued the condemned, or carried him off for resuscitation after hanging. Friends of the condemned were sometimes allowed to pull his legs after he was suspended in order to shorten the agony of strangulation. Last, but far from least, businessmen and intellectuals of the bourgeoisie were *deploring* it all. Their deploring was invisible at the scene, but highly visible in print media and legislative enclaves, where public hangings were called "inconceivably awful," "wicked," "offensive and foul behavior," gatherings of "unruly and vicious mobs," "scene[s] of horror and demoralisation," "vast moral desert[s]," "callous and bad."[42]

The dramaturgic openness of (a) large numbers of witnesses wearing (b) diverse social identities and (c) carrying on heterogeneous activities in the historic era contrasts sharply with the concealed character of (a) a small number of witnesses, (b) wearing a narrow range of social identities and (c) engaging in a homogeneous set of activities in the modern era.

Virtually throughout the world, executions are, as reported in a United Nations survey, "not held in public view

[40] Scott, *History,* pp. 57–58.

[41] Atholl, *Shadow,* p. 75.

[42] These phrases are used by Dickens, *Letters.*

and attendance is carefully limited and controlled."[43] Execution "chambers" themselves limit the possible number—holding 50 to 75 people if they are packed in—and statutes often specify maximum attendence, as in the United States, where the maximums varied from three to twenty in the nineteen sixties.[44]

Mere witnesses are sometimes excluded altogether, allowing only execution personnel *per se.* When permitted, witnesses are defined as "symbolic representatives" of the public at large and typically include newspaper reporters, representatives of the prosecution or defense and perhaps members of the condemned's family.[45] The presence of others may be left to the discretion of the prison wardens, who, it seems, have tended to prefer politicians, other government officials, and professionals such as doctors from among the thousands who make application to be witnesses.[46] Following the British, "the trend in most countries now is increasingly to exclude [journalists] from attendance," or to set strict limits and rules on what and how they report.[47]

Witnesses and executioners alike hardly say or do anything, owing in part to the short period of time available to them. A large sign reading "SILENCE" hanging over the door into the Sing Sing death chamber epitomizes the modern stance and reduces witnesses to conversing in "low voices" while waiting, if they talk at all.[48] Photography is specifically forbidden.

Overall, then, the dramaturgy of concealment—of virtual denial—is impressive: at most, a handful of silent, carefully

[43] United Nations, *Report,* p. 103.
[44] *Ibid.*
[45] *Ibid.*
[46] Elliott, *Agent,* pp. 230–233.
[47] United Nations, *Report,* pp. 103–104.
[48] Elliott, *Agent,* p. 142.

selected and constrained people witness the modern execution.

7. Executioners. Like the witnesses before whom they performed, historic executioners were a colorful, robust, and rule-breaking lot—in their personal lives as well as their roles as executioners. They comported themselves in ways that endowed them with distinctive public and personal identities, they performed their duties along lines of their personal choosing, and they related to the condemned in a personal manner. Modern executioners, in contrast, are virtually anonymous, bland and colorless men who carry out bureaucratically generated and well practiced "drills" upon condemned who are treated in a severely impersonal manner. The historic executioner dealt honestly and directly with death; the modern one bounds flinchingly by it.

(a) Historic, public executions rendered executioners public figures. As the ultimate and personally known agents of state force, they attracted much interest, both supportive and threatening. They were ostracized or lionized depending upon whom they had most recently executed and the social group he was a member of. Either way, they were "celebrities" about whom stories circulated and upon whom comment was made. As is inherent in being *somebody,* there was imputed to them stereotyped personal characters. Horace Bleackley has chronicled this nicely for historic London hangmen, as in brutal Price (1714–1715), grim Marvell (1715–1717), laughing Hooper (1728–1735), morose Botting (1817–1820), indifferent Calcraft (1829–1874), gentleman Marwood (1874–1883).[49] Each was endowed with a unique, distinctive and public personality; each had a *personal style.* Flattered or insulted, each *existed.*

They existed, in part, because executioner was a full-time

[49] Bleackley, *Hangmen.*

job. Business was heavy and social ostracism was strong; hangmen were barred from other modes of employment even when they wanted to quit. Moreover, their "deviances" did not get them fired. When executions moved indoors and into private, executioners gradually ceased to be publicly known figures and, moreover, the volume of executions decreased. Executioner is a part-time job in the modern era. As a consequence, executioners have become virtual non-entities.[50]

This social fading is seen sharply in the areas of their deviance and misfortune and their "personalities." The earliest executioners were themselves often recruited from among the condemned. They executed others in order to save themselves. Throughout the seventeenth and eighteenth centuries in England, significant numbers of hangmen were "unable to officiate because they were in gaol, on charges ranging from bigamy to rioting or ended their lives under the gallows."[51] Bleackley's history reports frequent drinking, wenching, debt, and theft among London hangmen, who also seem to have had many misfortunes of health.[52] Perhaps it is but the exaggeration of historical reporting, but historic executioners thus seem a more diverse and *strong* set of personalities, some with ghoulish attachments to the job, some of sullen, angry and violent disposition, and some talkative, boastful and proud. Even such transitional and quasi-modern British hangmen as Marwood (1874–1883) and Berry (1884–1892) were far more colorful than any of their twentieth-century descendants. Marwood, for exam-

[50] Cf. Finn Hornum, "The Executioner: His Role and Status in Scandinavian Society," in Marcello Truzzi, ed., *Sociology and Everyday Life* (Englewood Cliffs, N.J., 1968), pp. 125–137.

[51] Atholl, *Shadow,* p. 144.

[52] Gerald Robin, "The Executioner: His Place in English Society," *British Journal of Sociology* 14 (1904): 243-253.

ple, enjoyed lecturing reporters on his techniques immediately before executions; Berry collected testimonials from wardens and others to the excellence of his work in order to obtain additional employment.[53] Fully modern executioners have been, as summed up by one student of them, "quiet men and well-behaved."[54] As executions have themselves "faded," so have executioners.

(b) Such personal diversity seemed prompted, in part, by the less routinized and specified character of historic executions. The greater the leeway afforded by a role, the greater the leeway its occupants are likely to exercise. At an execution in 1760 "the sheriffs fell to eating and drinking on the scaffold and helped up one of their friends to drink with them as [the condemned] was still hanging."[55] London's hangman of 45 years, William Calcraft, joked and swore at executions, wearing, indeed, a rose in his button-hole. Thomas Cheshire, who practiced between 1808 and 1840, openly relished his work, pouncing upon the condemned with a "basilisk gleam" in his eye and a "stealthy cat-like clutch" as described by one eyewitness.[56] Many liked their duties less and performed them drunk; one was so intoxicated he had to be restrained from hanging the clergyman by mistake.[57]

Detailed, technical aspects of executions were left to the executioner, thus allowing for "mistakes." Some bought cheap rope that broke; others were "incompetent even in the tying of knots."[58] Occasionally, the executioner and other officials fell to arguing upon the scaffold over the adjustment

[53] Laurence, *Capital Punishment,* pp. 116–117; Atholl, *Shadow,* pp. 152–153.

[54] Laurence, *ibid.,* p. 137.

[55] Eyewitness account reprinted in Mencken, *By the Neck,* p. 240.

[56] Bleackley, *Hangmen,* pp. 196-197.

[57] Atholl, *Shadow,* p. 143.

[58] *Ibid.*

of the rope, the length of the drop, or the division of the condemned's property.[59]

The incredible quickness of the modern execution by itself largely robs executioners of opportunities for self-expression. Like much of modern work, individual variation and craftsmanship (or lack thereof) have been engineered out. Those involved in the modern British execution even called it "the drill" and practiced hangings with a dummy. The "engineering out" occurred historically among the British through a set of Parliamentary commissions that studied the subject "scientifically" and produced a collective binding set of procedures. Individual craft was thus transformed into bureaucratic procedure. While historic executioners supplied some equipment (e.g., rope, pinioning harness), modern ones have everything carefully supplied and controlled by the state.

Procedural rationalization requires, of course, methodical and objective recruitment of personnel (including technical testing and character assessment) and formal tranining. Both procedures have been undertaken for modern British and other executioners.[60] This is a far cry from the historic practice of haphazard recruiting and "training" among the condemned and the kinsmen and friends of executioners.

(c) Modern executions severely restrict and impersonalize the duration and amount of contact between executioner and condemned. Hardly any words need pass between them. There is virtually no bodily contact, or other vehicle of personalism such as the passing of goods or money. The executioner need not ever even see the condemned except

[59] E.g., Bleackley, *Hangmen*, pp. 128, 181.

[60] Atholl, *Shadow*, pp. 156–57. These developments are interestingly satirized by Charles Duff, *A Handbook on Hanging: Finally Revised Edition* (London, 1955).

during the few seconds of the execution.[61] Accompanying prison officers may purposively be strangers to the condemned, the better to inhibit the emotional arousal of all parties.[62] All these narrowings of the relation serve the purpose of death concealment. Historic executions had much more *talking and viewing* between executioner and condemned. Executioners might visit the condemned in order to console or admonish (in addition to size up for the drop). Hangmen customarily requested and received the condemned's pardon for executing him. Sheriffs took formal leave of and shook hands with him. Clergy delivered religious exhortations, hymns, and prayers, hoping, sometimes successfully, to enable him to experience salvation. The crimes of the prisoner might be read aloud and in detail. In England, the condemned gave the executioner *cash, presents and his clothes.* Because execution techniques were uncertain in their effect, the executioner was tipped in cash or expensive objects, such as a watch, in the hope of improved service. Such gifts might be openly awarded upon the gallows. Additional money was realized from the sale of the condemned's clothes, which the executioner was likely to strip from the corpse at the scene, just before placing it in the coffin. The hanging rope was often cut up into short lengths and sold. Some clergymen sold pamphlets of what purported to be dying speeches, confessions, and prayers of condemned they had seen hanged. The stripping of clothes involved, of course, the personalism and intimacy of *physical contact,* as did the standard practice of pulling the condemned's legs as he hung, the quicker to bring death.[63]

[61] Elliott, *Agent,* p. 139.

[62] Atholl, *Shadow,* p. 133.

[63] Atholl, *ibid.,* pp. 158–159; Mencken, *By the Neck,* pp. 118–119.

In such ways as these, the historic executioner and his condemned experienced a more direct and personal relation to each other. In all these ways, executioners dealt openly with the fact that someone was dying.

8. Condemned. We have seen that historic death cells and trips, especially, provided the condemned with a margin of freedom to express their personal uniqueness. They were visited and went visiting; they were talked to and talked. This leeway to behave in diverse and personal ways facilitated others perceiving them as particular and unique humans. Death was thus personalized and, in this sense, dramaturgically open, as opposed to the dramaturgic concealment and impersonalization of masking and supressing diverse personal expressions. Historic executions continued this leeway through the execution itself in permitted accouterments, actions, and words.

(a) Condemned of substance and flair were allowed to express these qualities. Aristocrats and dandy highwaymen decked themselves in formal finery, perhaps in the manner of the Earl of Essex who in 1600 wore "a gown of wrought velvet, a satin suit, and a felt hat, all of black, and with a small ruff about his neck."[64] Peculiarities of taste, such as wearing a wedding suit or a shroud, were permitted. One wealthy condemned rode to Tyburn in his own mourning carriage drawn by six horses. More modest bits of executional equipment might be supplied by the condemned: cushions or handkerchiefs on which to kneel and pray upon the scaffold; a pliable silken rather than stiff hemp rope in order to hasten strangulation; black handkerchiefs with which to be blindfolded, bound at the wrists, or drop as a signal to execute; presents for the executioners.

[64] Laurence, *Capital Punishment,* p. 125.

Accouterments were not only personal; they were pointed. No meanings were minced in the practice of the condemned wearing the noose around his neck and the rope around his body on the trip from London's Newgate prison to the Tyburn execution site.

(b) The final moments of the execution scene were not hurried through in wordless, rushed fashion as is the modern penchant. Their public character seemed, indeed, to have encouraged the condemned to give vent to an array of rather histrionic actions and words. Friends and acquaintances might be acknowledged and *greeted.* A condemned's infant child or others might be kissed or otherwise given farewell *gestures.* Deep formal *bows* might be directed to the crowd. An orange might be sucked upon, a pinch of snuff taken or other *minor comforts* indulged in. Possessions and money might be presented as *gifts* to officials or nearby friends. Those who disliked the clergy's readings, prayers, and demands for repentance might counter with *pithy putdowns* as in shouting, "There is no God, or if there is, I hold him in defiance."[65] *Contempt* might be expressed by kicking one's shoes into the crowd (thus depriving the executioner of one of his perquisites) or by doing a dance. Ineffective pinioning methods made *struggling defiance* possible through wrestling, striking, or kicking the executioner. (In one hanging the condemned three times hauled himself up and straddled the trap door, finally requiring three men to hold him at rope's end.) The more compliant condemned gave *help* to their executioner, perhaps by kissing the rope, positioning the noose, shaking hands and formally forgiving him; or dropping or waving a handkerchief when ready. Most spectacularly, the condemned might deliver a long and elaborately

[65] Atholl, *Shadow,* p. 62.

prepared *scaffold speech.* Last minute reprieves were not uncommon in the historic era, a fact that encouraged "long discourses and prayers," perhaps "lamenting misdeeds," expounding "pious sentiments" and exhorting the crowd to avoid crime. One condemned is reported to have been denied reprieve in order not to deprive him of the opportunity to read in public his long and brilliant scaffold speech![66]

Taken together, the condemned had abundant opportunities to establish for himself a *public character,* be that character heroic, villainous, courageous, cowardly, or whatever. The loose, uncodified, and public nature of the historic crime control apparatus in many of its aspects *other than executions* made possible, moreover, a more general personalization and high intensity of feeling about individual criminals. Historic England appears to have loved, hated, and generally focused upon individual criminals much more intensely than is true in modern times. Highwayman Jack Sheppard, for example, was a "national hero," and other criminals were national villains on a public, emotional scale seemingly not attained in present day societies (although numerous people have been candidates: Richard Speck, Sirhan Sirhan, and Charles Manson, to mention only a few.) A likely explanation for the publicly "bland" criminals of modern times and the low level of the public's emotional response to them is the restriction on the possibilities for criminals and public serving as audience to one another. Modern sequestering prevents criminals from doing or saying much of interest and the public's knowing and therefore feeling much about it. In modern executions, the array of character-endowing possibilities—visiting, pub-stopping, speech making, resistance, and the like—is carefully prohibited. Not least of blandness-producing strategies is the

[66] *Ibid.,* p. 56.

engineering of *swiftness.* It is obviously hard to *be* anybody in but nine, fifteen, or sixty seconds. Even if time and opportunity are permitted for a few "last words," the process moves in a manner so mechanized that it doubtless serves to inhibit speaking by many condemned. As hangman Berry would say to condemned upon entering the death hold: "If you have anything to say, now is the time, because once I get you on the scaffold you won't have time."[67] Robert Elliott describes the 387 condemned that he electrocuted as virtually without exception "meek as lambs."[68] That is a way to go, of course, but it is only *one* of many historic ways. As one commentator has put it about England, "The old legends of courage on the scaffold . . . would not have sprung from executions as practiced . . . [there]" in modern times.[69] Nor are they now likely to generate legends with other character styles, such as that of the sniveling coward, the defiant sociopath, the eloquent revolutionary, the indifferent retardate, or the dazed ordinary bloke.

9. Death Technique. The condemned must by some technique be killed. How, dramaturgically, is this to be accomplished? Nine aspects are relevent: the *reliability* of the technique; the temporal *duration* of lethal application; the amount and kind of *noise* it makes; the amount of pain it inflicts; the amount and kind of *sound* it elicits from the condemned; the amount and kind of bodily *mutilation* the technique causes; the amount of *movement* by the condemned it produces; the *visibility* of the condemned during and after application, and the amount and kind of odors associated with the technique.

A strategy of dramaturgic openness is a strategy that

[67] *Ibid.,* p. 139.

[68] Elliott, *Agent,* pp. 66–67.

[69] John Maddox, "An Indecent Ritual," in Louis Blom-Cooper, ed., *The Hanging Question: Essays on the Death Penalty* (London, 1969), p. 87.

modern people are likely to define as "inhumane" and "brutal" in that it makes inescapably clear the existential fact that a human being is being killed. How are these facts made most clear and dealt with most openly? Employing the nine dramaturgic principles, the technique should be highly unreliable and ineffective, take a long time to work, make a great deal of noise, mutilate the body, and inflict terrible pain, causing the condemned to cry out in anguish and struggle strongly to resist—all of which actions are highly visible to witnesses and accompanied by noxious and abundant odors. Not all historic executions could claim to display all these features of openness, but on the whole they were rather well approximated. The modern concealed strategy of killing while looking the other way, so to speak, strives to achieve the opposite: unfailing, lightning fast, noiseless technique that is painless and non-mutilating, involves no struggle, dying sounds, or odors, and is carried out in a way that shields the condemned's body in case something "goes wrong" despite all precautions. Modern people call this "humane." Dramaturgically, it is concealed. Below we will consider it as possibly "inauthentic," "hypocritical," "dishonest," or "squeamish."

(a) A technique is reliable if it works *every* time one tries it. Reliability had little value in historic executions. The more pain, time consumed, and mutilation the better, it seems. Reliability is a virtual fetish for moderns, though, who have discarded some techniques, such as beheading by sword, on this ground. As societies became squeamish, they disliked seeing the executioner require five or more swings completely to decapitate. On occasion in England, even the *condemned* complained of the executioner's ineptitude after the first or even the second blow. The guillotine was designed to increase reliability, although even it has been known to fail. Hanging was notoriously unreliable for hundreds of years: some condemned had to be hanged again after the rope broke; the drop might be too short; the drop doors might fail to open; some condemned revived hours after being hung. In a hanging of 1819, the condemned's toes rested on a platform that was not fully released, leaving him "half-standing, half-suspended, and struggling in the most dreadful manner."[70] Firing squads sometimes merely wounded the condemned. Even electrocution, promoted by legislators who had witnessed bungled hangings, almost failed of acceptance because of initial mishaps, including the collapse of the chair during an execution in 1893, which required that the condemned be held in a semi-conscious state awaiting its repair.[71]

(b) Early historic executions were calculated to maximize the condemned's period of dying and his consciousness during it. Pressing to death by a progressively heavy weight placed upon the chest, breaking upon the wheel, crucifixion, strangling, burning at the stake, cutting off strips of flesh, stabbing non-vital parts of the body, drawing and quartering, and other techniques all consumed rather prolonged periods of time. Even hanging was a slow-working technique for most of its history. When the cart was merely driven from beneath the condemned or the trapdoor merely opened, the condemned slowly strangled, writhing for many minutes before succumbing. (It was to shorten this struggle, as noted previously, that the executioner sometimes went beneath the scaffold to pull the condemned's legs.) The

[70] Eyewitness report quoted in Laurence, *Capital Punishment,* p. 95. See also, Franz Schmidt, *A Hangman's Diary: Being the Journal of Master Franz Schmidt, Public Executioner of Nuremberg, 1573–1617* (1928; reprinted Montclair, N.J., 1973). Atholl, *Shadow,* chap. 8, is devoted entirely to survivors of historic hangings!

[71] Laurence, *Capital Punishment,* p. 65; Elliott, *Agent,* p. 27ff.

modern English practice of dropping the condemned some six to nine feet (varied according to weight and other body features) through a trap is calculated to effect instantaneous death, or at least the outward appearance of it. It is so quick and shows so little dying that some observers doubt that people would turn out to watch it even if it were performed in public. The so-called gas chamber and the electric chair have apparently not yet achieved the instantaneousness of the modern English hanging. Many seconds and perhaps minutes ("slightly more than two," Robert Elliott reports of electrocutions) are required before both unconsciousness *and* lack of movement is achieved.[72]

(c) Historic executions were noisy: pounding to bend bodies onto the wheel; hammering to attach bodies in crucifixion; fire crackling and wood tumbling to prepare pots for human boiling; hooves clattering, whipping, and shouting to force horses in drawing and quartering; chopping in beheading; rifle reports in execution by firing squad. The modern desire is for silent techniques. Virtually no effort has been spared to make the English hanging quiet. At the beginning of the modern period, hanging drop doors were baffled with bales of cotton, and, when the technology became available, rubber cushions and spring catches were installed. Trap hinges get careful oiling. In America, air-tight gas chambers constructed of metal and glass are almost soundproof. Electrocutions have, however, never fully solved what is seen as the problem of electricity crackling between electrodes and flesh. A difficult-to-judge amount of water is required to achieve silence while avoiding sparks (too wet) and burning (too dry).

(d) Physical mutilation draws blood and disfigures. It

[72] Elliott, *Agent,* p. 148; Maddox, "Ritual," p. 89.

inescapably signals violation of bodily integrity, which alone threatens incapacity or death. Consequently, executions with mutilation proclaim openly their purpose, the infliction of death. Historic techniques illustrate the point: burning, beheading, drawing and quartering, breaking on the wheel, stoning, cutting off strips of flesh, crucifying, garroting, guillotining, throat slitting, impaling, shooting. The dramatic case of John Hooper, burned at the stake before 7,000 witnesses in 1555, stands for others. "Hooper's face turned black, his tongue swelled so that his very cries were silenced, one of his arms fell off, his bowels fell out—for three quarters of an hour the ghastly affair dragged on."[73]

Modern techniques strive assiduously to avoid mutilation and hence such open communication of their purpose which it would imply. The most widely used technique, hanging, is designed to drop the condemned just far enough to dislocate the neck and sever the spinal cord but not far enough even to rupture blood vessels, much less to pull off the head, as happened in the early years of working out proper drops. The rope itself is likewise carefully selected: not so thick that it is clumsy, not so thin that it cuts and ruptures.[74] This delicate combination of instant unconsciousness, quick death, non-mutilation, and other dramaturgic achievements, could, of course, only have been accomplished through many years of careful record-keeping and experimentation in actual hangings. Such procedures have not rendered the electric chair entirely satisfactory on this score. It has always been difficult fully to avoid burning. Non-mutilation is *the* signal virtue of the gas chamber. Other methods of execution, such as various sorts of orally or intravenously admin-

[73] Scott, *History,* pp. 30–31. See also Alice Morse Earle, *Curious Punishments of Bygone Days* (1896; reprinted Montclair, N.J., 1969).
[74] Scott, *ibid.,* p. 208.

istered poison, might logically be employed, but they pose other dramaturgic problems.

(e) Modern death techniques try to avoid all sounds, movements, odors and their presumptive cause, pain. Modern hanging, shooting, and guillotining are extremely effective in these terms, if carried out skillfully. Electrocution involves some difficulty in that the condemned lurches and becomes taut, emits a "loud gurgling noise" if his lungs are full of air when the current strikes, and gives off a noxious smell from the electrodes that is not immediately exhausted by the fans blowing for that purpose. In Robert Elliott's words:

> The figure in the chair pitches forward, straining against the straps. There is the whirring cry of the current, and a crackling, sizzling sound. The body turns a vivid red. Sparks often shoot from the electrodes. A wisp of white or dull gray smoke may rise from the top of the head or the leg on which the electrode is attached. This is produced by the drying out of the sponge, singed hair, and, despite every effort to prevent it, sometimes burning flesh. An offensive odor is generally present. . . .
>
> Five seconds after the initial shock of 2,000 volts, I decrease the current to 1,000 volts or somewhat under. The purpose of this is to avoid sparking and needless burning. At the end of half a minute, I increase it to 1,800 or 2,000 volts, and after another few seconds, cut it down again. This is repeated at half-minute intervals. As the current is increased and lowered, the body in the chair rises and sinks. Finally, after the fifth shock, I reduce the current gradually.[75]

The lethal chamber is reported sometimes to produce untoward and contorted movements by the condemned as the gas spreads. Electrocutions and gassings are in this respect reminiscent of historic hangings wherein the condemned

[75] Elliott, *Agent,* pp. 67, 146-147.

customarily convulsed as he strangled. However, the *modern* hanging is dramaturgically most concealed. The "long drop" eliminates all sound, movement, odor or evidence of pain.

(f) A truly concealed dramaturgic strategy shields the actual death from *anyone's* view. Again, the modern English hanging is the leading dramaturgic example. The condemned—especially if his light weight requires a greater fall—drops almost totally from view. In many designs, the body comes to rest in a shielded pit below the scaffold. Even if the head pulls off, the knot slips from the instantly lethal position on the neck, or the body writhes, it does not matter, for no one can see. None of the other modern techniques have quite this dramaturgic advantage. There is a certain irony in this because hanging was promoted over other techniques in historic times precisely because it made the condemned *more* visible than other death techniques. It was necessary to specify "hanged by the neck until dead" because the condemned were also hung up in other ways and after death, frequently in a suit of chains. Hanging as the most open and purposefully ignominious technique thus became in modern times the exact opposite: the most concealed of techniques.

In sum, historic and modern death techniques are premised on opposed dramaturgic principles. It is obvious, however, that the modern principles of concealment have not been fully realized in practice, save perhaps in the case of English hangings. Electrocutions, lethal chambers, firing squads, and guillotines—the other four principal modern techniques—have the serious (and perhaps dramaturgically fatal) flaws enumerated. As long as there continue to be executions and modern people strive for increased dramaturgic concealment, there is likely to be a search for techniques that realized these principles more fully. One major candidate is the lethal injection or tranquilizer, which has been studied intensively by the British, but which, given the dramaturgic perfection of their hangings, they, not suprisingly, eschewed. The Royal Commission on the matter held, indeed, that the English hanging was less painful than an injection![76] In this light, one should not be surprised to hear an American governor suggest the possible advantage of lethal injections and tranquilizers. It is simply the next logical step in a long and consistent historical progression. Those who oppose this progression find themselves placed in the position of advancing dramaturgic openness in all the implicit and concrete meanings I have elucidated.[77]

10. Corpse Disposal. A policy of open dramaturgy disposes of the corpse in a public manner that is reasonably prolonged and that brings the corpse to rest in some obvious and marked place. A closed dramaturgy disposes of the corpse in a private manner that is carried out in a brief period of time and that brings it to rest in an obscure and unmarked place.

Historic folk had some ingenious devices for actualizing these principles. The common British and European practice of *gibbeting* expresses them best, by far. However killed, the corpse was treated by boiling or tarring and hung up in a chain or wicker suit at the scene of the crime, along heavily traveled roads and rivers, or at a special gibbet place. The preservative retarded decay and the chain or wicker suit prevented large parts of the corpse from detaching. By such

[76] Atholl, *Shadow,* p. 216.

[77] Left-liberal criminologists who unthinkingly attacked everything said by California's right-wing Governor Ronald Reagan trapped themselves into the hard-hearted stance of promoting painful state executions! See "Reagan's Humane Death Penalty Raises Serious Questions of Ethics" *Sacramento Bee,* 29 September 1973, p. 1.

means, the corpse's public display was prolonged until carrion birds eventually picked the bones clean. Less public, prolonged, and marked was the historic English practice of *anatomization* or dissection. In its most extreme form, the corpse was conveyed through the crowded streets of London to the barber-surgeons for public display and dissection before an auditorium packed with spectators (who were sometimes charged admission).

The *opposite* principles are likewise well actualized in the modern British practice of holding an inquest in the prison right after the execution and thereupon burying the body in an unmarked, quicklimed grave within the prison walls. Execution and complete disposal are thus accomplished in but a few hours and within a small, protected space. Only a minimum number of officially required personnel attend.

11. Death Announcement. A state execution is "announced" to the degree that members of the society *not* present at it are aware of its occurence and of its social and physical details. An open dramaturgic policy strives to maximize and a concealed policy to minimize the number of "absentees" who are informed and the amount of detail they are given. Today the ideally open announcement would presumably involve something on the order of worldwide, live television, repeated often on video tape and embroidered by the observations of experts and moralists (such as the Pope and Norman Mailer). Unrestrained print media would provide more permanent and weighty words and pictures. Announcements of historic executions were as open as technology then allowed. Newspaper, broadside, and pamphlet accounts were produced in profusion. (Before the age of printing, the condemned's corpse was left as its own announcement.) Historic folk employed, moreover, *symbolic acts* from which a modern dramaturgy of openness could well borrow: church bells were tolled, black flags were run up, public notices were posted. Many shops and schools were closed by their masters' absence on a hanging day. In modern society the closing of government, educational, and other establishments would have a similar announcing effect upon the citizenry.

The dramaturgics of "concealed" announcements is obvious. All publicizing media are barred: witnesses, who might talk, are few and controlled: government notice is zero. This is virtually the modern British practice, among whom executions are classified as official state secrets.

ON THE NATURE OF DRAMATURGIC ANALYSIS

The above is an application of the dramaturgic perspective on social life. A central tenet of the dramatism is that *how* people do things, the *style* in which they do things, is virtually as important as *what* they do, the *substance* of their actions. The world is ruled perhaps as much by the dramaturgic encasement of actions as by the actions encased. Public figures, especially, rise and fall as much on the manner they display as on the actions they perform. Of late, realization of this principle has led to the development of operating procedures of enormous efficiency, particularly in the creation and promotion of political figures. Applied to state executions, the principle suggests that their frequency rises and falls as a function of how they are done and not merely of why they are done. To the degree they persist, they do so by means of the concealment strategy explicated.

Dramaturgic analysis takes many forms, only one of which is employed here. Its formal and methodological features might usefully be indicated. Sharply contrasting styles of dealing with substantively identical situations are located and exhaustive descriptive materials collected on them. These materials are decomposed into their major abstract components. In the present case, these are the eleven phases or aspects of state executions. Each component is in turn decomposed into its internal dramaturgic variations, as summarized in Chart 1. The result is an ideal-typical portrayal of, in effect, logical extremes. Although actual, concrete examples only approximate the ideal-typical depiction,[78] the exaggerated abstraction from, and summary of, concrete reality provides an articulate, clear guide to "seeing" and *ordering* what is otherwise an incoherent, raw, and indiscrete collection of social events. Its purpose is to foster new perception through providing *concepts*—in this instance, open and closed dramaturgic strategies and their elements. By such means, the range of ordered experience is widened and our understanding of it enhanced.

THE THEORY OF DEATH DENIAL

Modern executions are only one front on which death is hidden in modern society. Modern people in general die in physical settings and personal surroundings whose features are remarkably like those of the modern execution: stark, impersonal, solemn, unemotional, privatized. That is, they tend to die in hospitals and nursing homes.[79] Combined with the life-imitating aspects of modern funerals, the above features suggest to some theorists that modern people are death-denying. Opponents of this theory claim that death segregation and concealment are merely products of modern

[78] Joseph Lopreato and Letitia Alston, "Ideal Types and the Idealization Strategy" *American Sociological Review* 35 (February 1970): 88–96.

[79] Monroe Lerner, "When, Why and Where People Die," in O. Brim, H. Freeman, S. Levine and N. Scotch, eds., *The Dying Patient* (New York, 1970), p. 21.

CHART 1

OPEN AND CONCEALED DRAMATURGY OF STATE EXECUTIONS

	OPEN	CONCEALED
DEATH WAIT	Long	Short
DEATH CONFINEMENT	Many, self-chosen visitors Diverse activities allowed Exhorted about death Exposed to death preparations	Few, regulated visitors Few activities allowed Left alone about death Insulated from death preparations
EXECUTION TIME	Socially conspicuous day and hour	Socially inconspicuous day and hour
DEATH TRIP	Long Elaborate and specialized transport devices Large cortege Dramatic events en route Complicated, public route	Short No transport devices Tiny cortege, if any No events en route Simple, private route
DEATH PLACE	Public, outdoors Large, open, visible Multiple and dispersed locations Specialized decoration	Private, indoors Small, enclosed, buffered Centralized location Neutral decoration
DEATH WITNESSES	Unlimited number Socially diverse Perform personal and diverse activities	Small, controlled number Socially homogeneous Perform impersonal and restricted activities
EXECUTIONER	Professional Publicly known Performance discretionary Strong, colorful, deviant personal style Personal contact with with condemned	Part-time Publicly anonymous Performance drilled Bland, conformist, quiet personal style Impersonal, limited contact with condemned
CONDEMNED	Self-chosen, diverse accouterments Diverse acts and speech	Narrowly restricted accouterments Narrow range of acts and speech
DEATH TECHNIQUE	Unreliable, long-acting, noisy, painful, scream-provoking, mutilating, struggle-inducing, odor-causing, highly visible	Reliable, fast-acting, quiet, painless, non-scream-provoking non-mutilating, non-struggle-inducing, odorless, concealed
CORPSE DISPOSAL	Public display Prolonged Marked grave	No display Quick Anonymous grave
DEATH ANNOUNCEMENT	Unrestricted media Suspension of institutional activities and other symbols	Restricted media No suspension of institutional activities or other symbols

medical technology. Maximum medical aid at lowest cost requires assembling the ill and the old in specally equipped places. Their segregation, therefore, need not be explained in terms of death-denying sentiments. Until further evidence develops in this debate, it seems logical that people might feel differently about normal dying than about state-conducted executions. In my opinion, the concealed dramaturgics of state executions have a definite death-denying quality, but this attitude could well be confined to state killing. It is not in itself evidence of a more general death denial among modern people.

THE PURSUIT OF HUMANENESS

Some readers might feel the present analysis confuses concealment with humaneness. Modern executions are designed to be kind to the condemned rather than to conceal their fate, one might argue. I would not deny that humane sentiments have importantly motivated—have been a cause of—features of the modern execution. We need, however, to distinguish causes of features of social arrangements from their functions and their consequences, which are often unanticipated. There is some irony in the fact that humanely inspired concealment features of state executions have the consequence of making executions more acceptable because of their concealment. Moreover, some humanely inspired features have unanticipated *inhumane* consequences. However raucous or crude historic executions may have been, they did provide the condemned with opportunity for dying with a display of courage and dignity utterly denied in modern executions. In achieving humaneness in some respects, we have lost it in others. It seem, indeed, a basic rule of human life that in achieving one set of goals, we find ourselves forced to sacrifice others.

HORACE BLEACKLEY

Born in 1868 in the house of his father and grandfather, Horace Bleackley lived the 63 years of his life in privilege. His family was classic industrial elite, British variety, the sort portrayed in Galsworthy's *The Forsyte Saga.* Its cotton bleaching and other business pursuits gave it a prominent place in the affairs of Manchester. Horace's father was highly cultured, a connoisseur of fine wines, possessed of literary sensibilities, and staunchly conservative, all of which traits the son acquired along with the family business and fortune.[80]

Horace Bleackley's career began with an education appropriate to one determined upon a literary career. From birth to mid twenties it centered upon educational institutions: Cheltenham College, Repton School and, as befits a gentleman, University College, Oxford, where he earned an M.A. degree and a second class in History. He published his first novel at age 24. The death of his father required that he assume management of the family business in Manchester, a role he played for seven years in his late twenties and early thirties (1894–1901). Despite this involvement he published four more novels during these years. A large inheritance and a reorganization of the family's industry permitted his retirement from commerce in 1901. He moved to Hersham in Surrey (a few miles south of London), remaining there eleven years (1901–1912, ages 33 to 44) researching and publishing three historical books and a novel. Presumably attracted by urban amenities, he acquired a Regency-period

[80] S. M. Ellis, "In Memoriam: Horace Bleackley," in Bleackley, *Jack Sheppard,* pp. 243–255.

house in Cornwall Terrace, Regent's Park, London, where he resided almost the rest of his life, writing during this period five more historical books (including *The Hangmen of England,* published at age 61), six novels, and an account of his travels in Southern Asia. Severe asthma compelled him, at the end, to live in southern France, where he died in 1931.

Bleackley's memorialists describe him as possessing a "bearing ever calm and courteous," friendly but reserved, a bit distant and almost "a figure strayed from the eighteenth century,"[81] the focus of his scholarship. He belonged to many elite clubs, entertained "largely and elegantly," "liking the company of his kind,"[82] played cricket well into middle age, and maintained a satisfying family life with his wife, one daughter, and two sons. As is fitting for a person accustomed to living in named houses (successively, Myrtle Grove, Homleigh, and Fox Oak), his London residence contained "fine Georgian furniture," "fine prints and engravings," "a charming, tranquil library, a big room at the back of the house,"[83] and a large collection of eighteenth-century memoirs, tracts, and the like. His social views were predictably those of his social location. *Who Was Who, 1929–1940* lists his recreation as "baiting Bolshies," that is, communists. His highly conservative ideas about social order cropped up throughout his books, such as this comment from the present work: "A passion for destruction is latent in the hearts of all uneducated folks."[84] *A Tour in Southern Asia* (1928) closes with the italicized declaration: "No measure can be

[81] *Ibid.,* p. 244.

[82] W. H. Maxwell, "Mr. H. W. Bleackley" in *Times* (London), 7 August 1931, p. 12.

[83] *Ibid.*

[84] Bleackley, *Hangmen,* p. 125.

too drastic that will prevent the contamination of our race by the infusion of black blood."

Bleackley wrote 21 books in the 40 years between his early twenties and his death at age 63. Alternating between fiction and history throughout his life, he produced twelve novels and the eight historical biographies for which he is primarily noted. In addition, he published a travel account and wrote some plays and a musical comedy (which were never produced). The nature of Bleackley's biographies is apparent from their titles:

1905. *Some Distinguished Victims of the Scaffold.*
1907. *The Story of a Beautiful Duchess: Being an Account of the Life and Times of Elizabeth Gunning, Duchess of Hamilton and Argyll*
1909. *Ladies Fair and Frail: Sketches of the Demi-Monde during the Eighteenth Century*
1917. *Life of John Wilkes*
1924. *Casanova in England: Being the Account of the Visit to London in 1763–4 of Giacomo Casanova Chevalier De Seingalt, His Schemes, Enterprises & Amorous Adventures, with a Description of the Nobility Gentry & Fashionable Courtesans Whom he Encountered, as Told by himself*
1924. *Trial of Henry Fauntleroy: And Other Famous Trials for Forgery*
1929. *The Hangmen of England: How They Hanged and Whom They Hanged. The Life Story of "Jack Ketch" through Two Centuries*
1933. *Jack Sheppard*

Commentators have characterized the series in such terms as: dealing with "the seamy side of the eighteenth century," "the less frequented bypaths of the eighteenth century," and "picturesque, historical biography."

Memorialist S. M. Ellis and others have emphasized Bleackley's devotion to basing his historical works on "original research and new documentary material." "He . . . loathed the production of books by what he called 'The Scissors and Paste School'—books compiled from the works of earlier students of the subject.[85] What is considered his most thorough work, *Life of John Wilkes,* resulted from four years of unearthing new and obscure material. "An infinitude of trouble" would be taken "to verify a date or detail" in his "passion for accuracy and first-hand evidence."[86] (The apparatus of scholarship presented in the volume reprinted here is considerably reduced from that of his earlier works, although still founded upon original sources. This relative neglect stems, I suspect, from the severe health problems of his last years.)

Bleackley was, it seems, an established, minor, but respected figure in the British world of letters. He apparently had no trouble publishing either his novels or historical biographies, although they seem not to have sold widely. W. B. Maxwell characterized them as always receiving "'a good Press,' but the praise of the critics lacked enthusiasm."[87] Being wealthy, Bleackley was under no pressure to write on fashionable topics or in haste. And, he was reported not personally disposed to promote himself or his books. Secure in his class and culture, he lived and worked at his own pace on matters of his personal satisfaction.

Bleackley was, in sum, an instance of that endearing British type, the wealthy private scholar. He followed a life pattern virtually unknown among wealthy Americans, a class more given to political and industrial world-moving.

[85] Ellis, "In Memoriam," p. 244.

[86] *Ibid.*

[87] Maxwell, "Bleackley."